SCHOOL ADMINISTRATION

SCHOOL ADMINISTRATION

Persistent Dilemmas in Preparation and Practice

Edited by
Stephen L. Jacobson
Edward S. Hickcox
Robert B. Stevenson

PRAEGER

Westport, Connecticut
London

Library of Congress Cataloging-in-Publication Data

School administration : persistent dilemmas in preparation and
    practice / edited by Stephen L. Jacobson, Edward S. Hickcox,
    Robert B. Stevenson.
        p.   cm.
    Includes bibliographical references and index.
    ISBN 0–275–95247–9 (alk. paper)
    1. School management and organization—United States.
    2. Educational leadership—United States. I. Jacobson, Stephen L.
    II. Hickcox, Edward S. III. Stevenson, Robert B., 1948–   .
    LB2805.S394   1996
    371.2'00973—dc20   96–15328

British Library Cataloguing in Publication Data is available.

Library of Congress Catalog Card Number: 96–15328
ISBN: 0–275–95247–9

First published in 1996

Praeger Publishers, 88 Post Road West, Westport, CT 06881
An imprint of Greenwood Publishing Group, Inc.

Printed in the United States of America

The paper used in this book complies with the
Permanent Paper Standard issued by the National
Information Standards Organization (Z39.48–1984).

10 9 8 7 6 5 4 3 2 1

Copyright Acknowledgments

The authors and publisher gratefully acknowledge permission to reprint the
following material.

Jacobson, S. L. (1995). Monetary incentives and the reform of teacher compensa-
tion: A persistent organizational dilemma. *International Journal of Educational
Reform*, 4(1): 29–35. Reprinted with permission of the *International Journal of
Educational Reform*.

Contents

VI
Dilemmas of Shared Leadership in
Decentralized Schools

Preface

Much of administrative preparation and practice is concerned with the process of problem solving, that is, identifying and framing problems, developing alternative solutions, and selecting among competing alternatives for the most feasible solutions. Common administrative problems, such as enrollment and workforce projections, course and transportation scheduling, and facility construction and maintainence are amenable to solution by scientific principles that produce contingencies that have well-defined rules and procedures. Other problems, however, seem to be more difficult to resolve. They defy a neat overlay of scientific rationality because they represent ongoing struggles between competing values. Attempting to use the "template of technical rationality" to address such situations may simply hide the inherent values in conflict, thus causing the problem to persist (Cuban, 1992). In other words, when we have problems, we seek solutions. Yet these potential solutions may perpetuate the problems if they do not make explicit the underlying competing values.

Larry Cuban, in his presidential address to the American Educational Research Association in 1991, "Managing Dilemmas While Building Professional Communities," contended that dilemmas are conflict-filled and persist because they require choices between "competing, highly prized values (that) cannot be fully satisfied." Unlike problems that can be solved, dilemmas can only be managed, and the key to managing these persistent dilemmas is to recognize the values in conflict.

In this book, developed from papers first presented at the 1994 International Intervisitation Program in Educational Administration held in Toronto, Ontario, and Buffalo, New York, May 15–27, 1994, persistent dilemmas in administrative preparation and practice are examined by scholars and practitioners of educational administration from around the world. The book is divided into six sections. The three chapters in the first section develop Cuban's notion of dilemmas within the broad context of school administration, in both developed and developing nations. Chapters in the next four sections are clustered by category, specifically societal and ethical dilemmas, organizational dilemmas, role dilemmas, and professional development dilemmas confronted by school administrators. The final section focuses on emerging dilemmas of leadership in decentralized schools, which have resulted from recent reform initiatives in many Western industrialized countries.

PART I: UNDERSTANDING EDUCATIONAL DILEMMAS

In the first chapter, "Reforming the Practice of Educational Administration through Managing Dilemmas," Cuban offers examples of the types of enduring dilemmas that are at the core of administrative work, specifically dilemmas over the purposes of schooling and over strategies in making improvements and ascertaining results. He argues that without a practical understanding of these deeply rooted value conflicts, and the varied ways administrators have learned to deal with them, schools will continue to be administered as they are and face dim prospects for meaningful reform.

In "Managing Dilemmas in Education: The Tightrope Walk of Strategic Choice in Autonomous Institutions," Ron Glatter builds on Cuban's discussion by employing the terminology of balance and reconciliation to help avoid the indecisiveness associated with dilemmas. He suggests that we must pay heed to the degrees of severity of different situations and that it is important not to be beguiled by notions of the reconciliation of opposites or to allow them to foster "the mirage of simple solutions."

In the final chapter of this section, "Persistent Dilemmas in Administrative Preparation and Practices in Underdeveloped and Developing Countries," Earle H. Newton examines dilemmas in developing small states. He argues that traditional approaches to training are unsuited to the needs of these states. Instead, what is needed is collaboration of colleagues across cultures to develop more suitable, practice-oriented theories, texts, and materials for developing states. Higher education institutions in developing societies must develop curricula that reflect histories, traditions, and cultural values appropriate to their societies.

PART II: SOCIETAL AND ETHICAL
DILEMMAS IN SCHOOL ADMINISTRATION

In "Administering for Diversity: Dilemmas in Multiethnic Schools," James Ryan and Rouleen Wignall describe the experiences of administrators encountering cultural beliefs that differ from their own. Although many basic tasks, such as communicating with parents, community members, and students, require at least a rudimentary understanding of other ethno-cultural perspectives, principals must recognize the limitations of "understanding" in administering schools with diverse populations.

Elizabeth Campbell has two objectives in her chapter, "Suspended Morality and the Denial of Ethics: How Value Relativism Muddles the Distinction between Right and Wrong in Administrative Decisions." The first is to explore the conceptual and philosophical question of defining right and wrong, specifically dilemmas of suspended morality, false necessity, and compromise. The second objective is to relate this discussion to the responsibilities of an administrator in modern educational organizations.

In "Imagination and Character in Educational Administration," Susan Sydor contends that the work of school administrators is literary. They are writers of texts called educational communities, which, similar to all other literary works, are products of the writer's imagination. In creating artistic educational texts, administrators must have a particular bent of the imagination and a habit of value and care. This idea is illustrated by a case study of a reform program at a federal penitentiary.

PART III: ORGANIZATIONAL
DILEMMAS IN SCHOOL ADMINISTRATION

In "Monetary Incentives and the Reform of Teacher Compensation: A Persistent Organizational Dilemma," Stephen L. Jacobson examines conflicting values that underlie the reform of teacher compensation. Two key issues are normative expectations of teacher behavior by the public and teachers' differential responses to income/leisure substitution. The way society views teachers and the way teachers view themselves are often at odds. School systems use monetary incentives to motivate teachers, but do not want teachers who are primarily motivated by money. Teachers want respect for their dedication to children but often demand extra compensation for activities the public perceives as part of their professional responsibilities. In other words, teachers and their employers exhibit behaviors that seemingly conflict with their beliefs and values.

In "Performance Related Pay and Professional Development," Harry Tomlinson argues that a systemic approach to educational reform requires that all policies be aligned to produce the desired effect, and pay policies are no exception. There has been no attempt in Britain to consider thoroughly, how the national, or even locally determined, pay systems might be developed to complement and reinforce the educational reforms. It would seem rational to at least consider the advantages and disadvantages of the various alternative approaches to performance-related pay.

In "Equity and Efficiency: Tensions in School-based Management in England and Wales," Tim Simkins notes that while the primary purpose of reform is to raise the quality of education, it is important to recognize that reform also has equity implications. This chapter explores reform from an equity perspective, with particular reference to resource distribution. Simkins argues that such an approach raises major issues that have received little attention because of government's emphasis on the objectives of effectiveness, efficiency, and choice.

PART IV: ROLE DILEMMAS OF SCHOOL LEADERS

In "Principals' Dilemmas: Intraorganizational Demands and Environmental Boundary Spanning Activities," Jack Y. L. Lam contends that schools are embroiled in a controversy, that is, declining resources clash with rising expectations of what schools should achieve academically in light of international comparison and competition. He explores principals' internal needs for greater coordination and environmental demands for more assertive leadership.

Robert B. MacMillan investigates the "chasm" separating administrators and teachers in "New Principals' Experiences with Leadership: Crossing the Cultural Boundary." He finds that the nature of schools and the nature of their role require exclusion of principals from participating equally in the life of their institutions. Context, culture, and personalities seem to be influential to some extent and need to be investigated further.

A persistent puzzle in the study of administration is how to account for significant policy changes, given the pervasive bias toward incremental decision making in most educational systems. In "The Dilemmas of Exercising Political Leadership in Educational Policy Change," Hanne B. Mawhinney analyzes the dilemmas in adopting an ideological policy change and discusses their theoretical, political, and ethical implications for political leadership.

PART V: DILEMMAS IN THE PROFESSIONAL DEVELOPMENT OF SCHOOL ADMINISTRATORS

This part begins with a chapter by Brigid Limerick and Frank Crowther, "Problem-based Learning as an Approach to the Professional Development of School Leaders: A Case Study," that self-critically examines the authors' efforts in an innovative professional development project to assist principals to reconceptualize some of the problems they identified as dilemmas in their schools. They reveal the dilemma they in turn faced by addressing the question of whose reality was being constructed in conceptualizing the principals' problems in this way.

Angela Thody and Lee Crystal, in "Boundary Mentoring: A Solution to the Persistent Dilemma of How to Educate School Administrators," contrast two different approaches to mentoring: an intraprofessional program in which experienced principals mentored new principals, and an extraprofessional program in which business executives were partnered with education faculty. The purpose of their research was to compare the socialization effects of these different approaches with respect to reinforcing the cultural norms and ideas of the profession or to destabilizing that culture by introducing new ideas.

In developing countries, where principals tend to function in relative isolation, the professional development of beginning principals is often neglected. In their chapter, "The Need for Mentoring in a Developing Country," Morkel Erasmus and Philip C. Van der Westhuizen examine the potential role of mentoring in these countries. They note that when experienced principals mentor less-experienced colleagues, the relationship is often seen by both as the most important aspect of their development.

PART VI: DILEMMAS OF SHARED LEADERSHIP IN DECENTRALIZED SCHOOLS

In "Reframing Educational Leadership in the Perspective of Dilemmas," Jorunn Møller offers a carefully crafted analysis of the contradictory orientations experienced by principals and superintendents in the decentralization of school management in Norway. She argues that the central dilemma of legality (the formal steering of schools) versus legitimacy (the informal control mechanism embedded in traditions and culture) provides a helpful lens for viewing a range of dilemmas confronting school administrators.

This theme is continued by Robert D. Connors and Fenton G. Sharpe in "Devolution and the Changing Role of the Principal: Dilemmas and a Research Agenda." They discuss principals' perceptions of their role in the Australian context of school-based management, which they argue is creating a tension between principals' desires to be instructional leaders and demands to be managers. They also outline a conceptual framework for conducting research to determine the linkages between school-based management and improved student learning.

In the final chapter, "Knowledge-in-use: Reconceptualizing the Use of Knowledge in School Decision Making," after emphasizing the importance of studying the kinds of information that informs school decision

making, especially given the current press of distributing further authority to individual schools, Robert B. Stevenson argues for an alternative
conceptualization to the traditional scientific and craft views of how
knowledge is used by school leaders to make decisions. He discusses
knowledge use as part of a larger process of informal inquiry in which
decontextualized theoretical knowledge is integrated with contextualized
or local practical knowledge to make sense of a situation and to inform
actions that school leaders take.

I

UNDERSTANDING
EDUCATIONAL DILEMMAS

1

Reforming the Practice of Educational Administration through Managing Dilemmas
Larry Cuban

I begin by outlining my argument. Without a practical understanding of the value conflicts deeply rooted in educational administration and the varied ways practitioners have learned to tame these perpetual struggles, schools and districts will continue to be administered as they are and face dim prospects for engaging in either meaningful or substantial reform. Such a practical understanding constitutes knowledge and survival skills for those principals and superintendents who hope to continue in their posts and, of equal importance, to improve their schools and districts.

To extract that essential knowledge and apply those survival skills requires disentangling value conflicts that are deeply embedded in the practice of educational administration, reforming schools, and reconciling their competing claims. Hence, I will first distinguish among the common types of dilemmas facing administrators over the purposes of schooling, over strategies in making improvements, and in ascertaining results. Then I will analyze the fundamental dilemma of conflicting role expectations that generates these more obvious and visible struggles. By concentrating on the tight coupling between surface and underlying dilemmas, I will argue that attention to both in preparation programs and for practicing administrators will help principals and superintendents figure out more clearly what they can and cannot do as administrators and why. In analyzing the dilemmas that administrators face, I hope to provide a more realistic platform for reshaping the practice of educational administration and coping with school reform.

THE LANGUAGE OF DILEMMAS

In turning to the concept of dilemmas, words like "conflict," "constrained choices," and "satisficing" get used often.[1] Rather than present abstract definitions of these terms, let me apply them to an elementary school principal I know. She is deeply committed to being an instructional leader who works closely with teachers in spurring curricular and pedagogical improvements. She is also deeply committed to maintaining the school's effectiveness by attending to the scores of details that need her personal touch. However, she lacks the time and energy to fully satisfy both highly prized values. She constructs compromises.

On a typical day she listens to two parents angry with different teachers, sympathizes with a crying student whose money was snatched on the way to school, negotiates with the custodian who has to take three days off because of a family illness, supervises morning recess, calls her superintendent who is demanding a report that is already a week late to say that it will be on his desk at five o'clock that afternoon, and returns the call of an unpaid vendor whose check went astray. In between listening, problem solving, report writing, and calming loud voices, our principal slips into two classrooms for brief visits with teachers who wanted her help in adapting the new state math curriculum to their lessons on fractions. Here in the jangled world of the elementary school principal, value conflict, constrained choices, and satisficing take on concrete meaning.

Such individually constructed, adequate compromises are normal. They vary from person to person. From time to time, they must be reconstructed. That is, the compromises that are built by principals, superintendents, and even professors are good enough for one time change simply because of life events (for example, marriage, children, divorce, illness, deaths) and shifting organizational conditions (for example, new school board, superintendent exits, influx of students from other backgrounds).

Struggles over competing values do not go away. Unattractive options still present themselves and choices must be made. The satisficing compromises that were made at one time are rebuilt to meet new conditions. Hence, dilemmas, unlike problems, are continually managed, not solved. This is the vocabulary of dilemmas that I will use (Ben-Peretz & Kremer-Hayon, 1990; Berlak & Berlak, 1981; Burroughs, 1986; Elbow, 1983; Fenstermacher & Amarel, 1983; Getzels, 1982; Miles & Huberman, 1984; Sarason, 1982).

Before describing and analyzing the fundamental dilemma facing practitioners, I need to draw a further distinction. Dilemmas can be distinguished between those embedded in the purposes for education — those that deal with strategies of change — and those that deal with outcomes of schooling. An example of each should make clear what I mean.[2]

Dilemmas of Purpose

Parents, employers, and taxpayers want their schools to accomplish inherently competing purposes. They want teachers, for example, to socialize children into the habits of mind and behavior essential for becoming a wise citizen, an able employee, and a person of solid character, while, at the same time, encouraging questioning, problem solving, and independence. They want graduates to be responsive to authority but not docile, to be fair-minded in treating others whose beliefs and behaviors are different but also committed to a common core of beliefs, to be loyal to community values but willing to go it alone, and to follow the rules but be flexible in responding to new situations.

Administrators who have considered these contending purposes often note the tension between them, especially when there is a six-hour school day, competition for students' attention in and out of school, and short supplies of money and energy. When the teacher sponsor of the high school newspaper, for example, brings to the principal a student's article sharply criticizing the principal's decision to ban a survey of sexual activities, the teacher asks her whether he should include the piece in this month's issue. The principal has to make a choice among competing values in schooling. This is a dilemma of purpose.

Dilemmas of Strategies over Change

This refers to how administrators wrestle with implementing highly desired changes. For example, an ordinary, run-of-the-mill superintendent appointed to his first post is intent upon leaving his mark on the district that has just hired him on a three-year contract. The school board made it clear in his interview that, were he appointed superintendent, he would be expected to reverse the decline in district scores on state tests, reduce a swollen budget that his predecessor had pumped up, and ensure the implementation of a new policy of evaluating teachers (highly popular with a cadre of vocal parents), while avoiding a threatened teachers' strike over lagging salaries.

Charged by the school board to make changes, the superintendent faces a crescendo of strategic dilemmas: What do I focus on first? Teacher evaluation? Declining test scores? Cutting the budget? A little of each? Should the superintendent figure out a compromise on this strategic question, he faces additional conflicts: Where in the system do I focus my initial attention? Of course, I will work on many things simultaneously, but I need to concentrate my energies. Should I focus on the district headquarters? School site? Classroom? Then I need to consider how much change I can undertake in my initial years. Should I be ambitious or practical? How much change can a district tolerate in a few years? After all, negotiations for renewal of my contract would begin in just two years. If I concentrate on raising test scores through a teacher improvement program, where does the board's mandate on the new evaluation policy fit in, especially because activist parents have identified that policy as crucial for district improvement? How much should be done by my district administrators and how much by principals and teachers who actually put the policies into practice?

These questions reveal the strategic dilemmas that face our young, new superintendent. Whether he consciously can lay out the issues or even is prepared to do so is important. However, open or hidden, these dilemmas lie in wait for our ambitious school chief.

Dilemmas over Results

Results are what taxpayers, policymakers, practitioners, and researchers view as desirable outcomes of achieving the goals of schooling. These results are related to definitions of success and failure. What gets labeled as a successful school or district (or the opposite — a failing school or district) has enormous consequences for those who send their children to school, the people who work there, and the graduates themselves. Thus, to identify dilemmas over results is to focus on administrators facing conflicts over what constitutes success or failure in reaching different goals.

For those parents, taxpayers, and educators who prize high academic performance, such measures as performance on state and national standardized tests, promotion rates, grade-point averages, and college attendance matter a great deal. For others who prize graduates who work in local businesses, dropout rates and corporate-school partnerships count heavily. For those who prize independent thinking, the quantity and quality of student questioning in class and, in the larger school, volunteering in the school and community and voicing of dissent matter. These quantitative measures, and others like them, become the basis for determining success and failure in achieving competing district goals. Surely, if there are value conflicts embedded in the purposes of schooling (for example, socialization and independent thinking) there will be similar controversies over what constitutes success and failure in schooling.[3]

Consider the high school principal who has seen his student enrollment shift from predominantly white, middle- and upper-middle class teens to one heavily populated by working class and poor Latino and black youth. His school board and superintendent have been pressed by activist parents to raise eleventh-grade test scores that have fallen from the 70th percentile in math and reading to the 25th and 30th percentiles, respectively. He does not believe that these standardized achievement test scores reflect the hard work, creativity, and imagination that his students have demonstrated in drama, music, art, varsity athletics, and jobs in local businesses through the school's vocational education program. The scores do not capture the increasing numbers (albeit small) of minority students entering community college and earning scholarships to the nearby university. The teachers in these departments are proud of their accomplishments, but, aside from occasional articles in the local newspaper and trophies in the glass case outside the principal's office, the state and national awards that students have won in art, sports, and vocational education do not seem to count much with his superintendent or vocal parents.

His assistant principals have come to him with a plan for raising test scores: buy a commercial package from a national consultant to train all the math, English, and social studies teachers to prepare students for standardized achievement tests. Launch a campaign two months before the tests, complete with pep rallies, before- and after-school coaching sessions, and visits from local celebrities, to urge students to do their best. Finally, give cash awards to those classes that improve their scores by five percentile points over last year.

The principal has sufficient money to buy the package, but he worries about using cash awards and setting aside so much time for test preparation and pep rallies. He asks himself: suppose we do improve our scores from, say, the 25th percentile to the 30th, will that change the view that some parents, the school board, and superintendent have of an academically failing school? He knows that the school is succeeding with students in nonacademic areas, but those arenas are less prized by the people putting pressure on him and his teachers. What should he do? This, then, is one example of a dilemma over results and determining what constitutes success.

Thus far, I have introduced the vocabulary of dilemmas and distinguished between dilemmas of purpose, strategies of change, and outcomes. I will argue, however, that these dilemmas derive from a deeper, more fundamental tension that exists within the occupation of administrator and accounts for these more visible conflicts that I have just presented. I now turn to the basic struggle that all administrators face at different points in their careers: the dilemma of identity (Am I a manager, politician, or instructional leader?). Each role contains desirable values that compete with one another. Reconciling the conflicting demands of these roles is the perpetual task that superintendents and principals face openly or wrestle with silently (Blumberg, 1985; Cuban, 1988). Because these are familiar, I will describe them briefly and move on to why they persist and how they affect attempts at school reform.[4]

THE IDENTITY DILEMMA

I will elaborate on the roles of instructional leader, manager, and politician briefly by focusing on the superintendent[5] and refer to the professional standards set forth by the American Association of School Administrators (AASA) for those preparing for and those already serving as superintendents. I use these standards because they are the result of almost a decade of work combining research findings and the best thinking of acknowledged leaders in the occupation. They encapsulate current thinking of practitioners, researchers, and policy makers in charge of the professional association for administrators (American Association of School Administrators [hereafter AASA], 1993).

Instructional Role

Historically, superintendents have been expected to be well-versed in the curriculum and instructional program. Among the earliest superintendents were teachers and scholars who prided themselves on being able to teach teachers and design curriculum. William Harris, Aaron Gove, and John Philbrick were late–nineteenth-century urban school chiefs who, among their many duties, designed curriculum, examined students to determine what they had learned, and evaluated teachers. The expectation of the superintendent as an instructor continues. Two of the eight AASA standards deal directly with curriculum planning and instructional management, presenting 23 performance indicators to determine if the administrator is meeting these standards (AASA, 1993: 9–10; Cuban, 1976).

Exactly what kind of instructional role, however, is left unclear. Just in the past decade, for example, mainstream thinking about superintendents leading the instructional team — a spin-off from the Effective Schools movement — has shifted markedly with the strong focus on school-site decision making. Prodded by the rhetoric of school-based management and radical decentralization moves in Chicago, the notion of the central office as a service agency for school sites has emerged strongly. The center of gravity of instructional leadership has seemingly moved from the superintendent's office to the coffee plate in the teacher's room. Hence, one of the AASA's standards is labeled instructional *management*, not leadership (AASA, 1993: 8; David, 1990).

According to most superintendents and the official position of the AASA a high premium is placed on administrators performing an instructional role, but, beyond drawing up plans, managing information systems, and issuing accountability report cards, exactly what that instructional role is remains unclear. This is much less so for the superintendent's managerial function.

Managerial Role

Superintendents have always been hired to administer the system of schooling. For the AASA, four of the eight standards call for the superintendent to manage some aspect of district affairs. Half of the standards call for superintendents to develop procedures for working with the school board and state and federal agencies, set priorities, use data for decision making, plan and schedule the work of the organization, establish procedures to regulate flow of work, allocate personnel and fiscal resources, and oversee the budget. Even instruction is considered a management function and is listed as a separate standard (AASA, 1993: 7–8, 10–11).

Managing is a central role according to the AASA and most working superintendents. Leading is also a central role. The very first AASA standard calls for superintendents to demonstrate leadership by developing a collective vision, providing purpose and direction for individuals and groups, and shaping an educational culture for the district (AASA, 1993. 6).

In these standards, managing and leading are highly valued, but separate, functions. Both are expected in superintendents even though they produce friction. Managing, on the one hand, means keeping the organization working efficiently toward its goals. Stability is the password. Reducing conflict is highly prized. Taking organizational risks threatens continuity. Leading, on the other hand, means seeking changes, accepting conflict as a natural state of the organization, and taking risks by introducing novel policies and programs. Within these AASA standards, tension between managing and leading is hidden (Kotter, 1990; Rost, 1991; Selznick, 1957; Zaleznick, 1977).

Political Role

Historically, turn-of-the-century reformers successfully divorced partisan politics from the conduct of schooling. The absence of involvement in machine politics and campaigning for election left the superintendent largely voiceless in the public arena about the role of schools in society. The norm of political neutrality held that professional educators not reveal their political preferences and serve lay boards who set the direction for policy. Democratic politics, where candidates and voters negotiate over what policy goals should prevail, was considered outside the pale of professionalism (Peterson, 1985; Tyack & Hansot, 1982).[6]

The power of that norm remains strong today. It should come as no great surprise that debates over curriculum content (from AIDS to the Holocaust), national goals for education, and national tests have involved private-interest groups representing educators (National Educational

Association, American Federation of Teachers, American Association of School Administrators, Association of Supervision and Curriculum Development, and so forth) who react to initiatives taken by public officials campaigning for office. Superintendents are expected to exercise their technical and organizational skills in implementing what others — school boards, governors, state legislatures, and presidents — decide the purposes should be (Cuban, 1976; Tyack & Hansot, 1982).

None of this means that superintendents do not engage in politics. They do — within the organization. This is what I mean by their political role. To advance their agendas, superintendents negotiate with school board members, principals, parent groups, and city officials. They figure out ways to build political coalitions for their schools at budget time or to put a positive spin on bad news during crises. Such organizational politics aim to improve a school's image, implement a desired program, or secure new resources rather than the often partisan politics of determining overall direction for a school.[7]

This circumscribed political role is recognized in the AASA professional standards. The AASA expects superintendents to know the district as a political system and use that knowledge to "align constituencies in support of district priorities; build coalitions to gain financial and programmatic support, [and] formulate . . . strategies for referenda." Furthermore, as an indicator of such political behavior, the AASA lists an example of superintendents acting to "persuade the community to adopt an initiative for the welfare of students." Such phrases as "align constituencies," "build coalitions," and "persuade the community" speak to both the political role within the boundaries of school organizations and the necessity for the superintendent to lead, rather than manage (AASA, 1993: 7).

The Dilemma of Identity

Here, then, are three overlapping roles that others expect of superintendents and superintendents expect of themselves. Superintendents value each of these roles. The roles are clearly connected, but, in many instances, they conflict. Some superintendents carve out a dominant role among the three and become characterized as political (Bob Alioto of San Francisco between 1975–85), managerial (Dick Wallace in Pittsburgh in the 1980s), or instructional (Ella Flagg Young in Chicago before World War I). Yet they still had to perform the other roles and endure the continuing tensions of juggling the conflicting expectations (Feilders, 1981; Tyack & Hansot, 1982; Wallace, 1985).

Implementing the entangled instructional, managerial, and political roles while finessing the struggle between leading and managing is the DNA of superintending. The conflict of identity is embedded in the genetic code of the occupation. Hence, the dilemmas that I described earlier deriving from conflicting purposes stem from the political role and the expectation that the superintendent leads. Dilemmas of strategy are linked to both the managerial and political roles; the dilemmas of results connect to all three roles. What gives an edge to these surface and underlying dilemmas, what makes these tensions nail-biters, is the constant impulse to reform schools (Cuban, 1988).

Superintendents are expected to improve schools while retaining the status quo, implement innovations while minimizing conflict, and solve community problems while enhancing harmony within the district. Superintendents are expected to juggle these paradoxes with elegance and poise.[8] This distinctly American impulse for improvement perpetually fuels the dilemma of identity that superintendents face. This dilemma encoded in the DNA of the superintendency and linked to other, more obvious, clusters of value conflicts comes together in the current and pressing question of shrinking superintendent tenure in big cities. How, for example, can urban superintendents who must struggle continually with competing roles turn around a deteriorating education when their terms in office get increasingly shorter?

CAN SUPERINTENDENTS REFORM CITY SCHOOL SYSTEMS AS TERMS SHRINK?

Behind this question is a complicated argument founded on implicit assumptions. The argument goes like this: Public officials, academics, and social critics say repeatedly that revitalizing cities is crucial to the social and political survival of the nation. Center cities continue to die as the United States becomes a collection of suburbs on the outskirts of decaying metropolises. Because schools are assumed essential in a democratic society, the mandate to reform urban schools is self-evident. The quality of schooling, it is assumed, is linked to the effectiveness of the superintendent. Superintendents are hired to be instructional leaders, astute managers, and wily politicians to carry out these mandates and ensure that reforms occur. Yet, according to popular wisdom and recent research, superintendent turnover has increased and tenure in big city posts is now down to less than three years. Researchers report that it takes at least five to seven years for reforms to take hold and begin to show results. The superintendent's job, therefore, has become impossible. There are too many conflicts and too many traps for any superintendent to survive for more than a few years. Reforming schools over the long haul is out of the question (Bradley, 1990; Fullan, 1982; Ornstein, 1990).

Is it simply too much to expect that superintendents perform all three roles? Is it too much to expect that superintendents finesse the enduring tensions between competing values? Is it too much to expect that superintendents leave behind a clearly-marked trail of reform in a big city district? These questions, however, are off the mark. The argument that superintendents need longer terms in office to provide the continuity for the adoption and implementation of reforms is certainly plausible, but the facts and questions upon which the argument is built are distorted.[9]

First, media reports of "turnstile" superintendencies and research findings on tenure in big city posts have turned an already difficult job into one that offers little hope for reform ever taking place. For example, newspaper and magazine reports point out that, since 1990, school districts serving 24 of the country's 25 major cities have appointed at least one new superintendent. The Council of Great City Schools reported that, of the 47 districts in the Council, 42 have hired new superintendents since 1990 (Wintrip, 1993). Such figures produce the image of a revolving door superintendency and an impossible job, raising the obvious question: If tenures are so short, how can school reform ever occur and continue in an urban district?

Those figures, however, come from calculating how many superintendents leave office in any given year. That number produces a turnover rate. Such figures say nothing about how long that superintendent actually served in office. By using a data set covering big city superintendent tenure since 1900, we can calculate how long each superintendent served. The "completed tenure" rate is very different from the turnover rate in a given year. The turnover figure has contributed to the widespread belief that big city superintendents serve about two and one-half years.

Popular belief in short tenures for urban superintendents feeds the public perception of instability, low morale, a loss of organizational vitality and, for staff after the departure of a superintendent, a sense of "here we go again." The fact is that superintendents do not exit every two and one-half years. In 1990, for example, urban superintendents who completed their terms served an average of almost six years in office — double the time reported in both professional and popular articles. "Almost six years" is in the range of what researchers and academic entrepreneurs engaged in school reform claim is necessary to institutionalize changes and begin to see results (Fullan, 1982; Louis & Miles, 1990; Yee & Cuban, 1994).

The figures that Gary Yee has compiled offer a completely different picture of tenure of urban superintendents and of possibilities for reform that is missed when tenure is calculated only by turnover rate. Will this alter the grim pessimism embedded in the notion of a revolving-door superintendency? I doubt it. However, these figures do point to longer tenure for superintendents and a stronger potential for implementation of reform agendas.

There is, however, another question that must be answered. Even if the current tenure of superintendents is longer than thought, has tenure remained the same, declined, or risen in this century? We have found that cycles of increasing and declining in superintendent tenure have occurred in the past 90 years, but the average number of years served has declined. In 1900, the average completed tenure of big city superintendents was just under 15 years; in 1990 it was almost 6 years (Yee & Cuban, 1994).

There are many possible explanations for why cycles in tenure appear amid an overall shrinking of time in office for superintendents. Surely, the conflicts facing superintendents have increased and spread. Most assuredly, the constraints superintendents experience have become tighter. Surely, public expectations for big city schools have escalated. And, just as surely, the dilemma of identity may be a possible explanation because of the personal cost such a struggle exacts upon superintendents when conflicts, constraints, and expectations press unrelentingly upon them.

Whatever the explanations are for big city superintendents' tenure over this century, the grim picture painted by popular media and professional journals of current brief tenures is much less bleak than portrayed. It is true that superintendents' terms in office have been decreasing in this century, but this varies substantially in the periodic cycles of longer and shorter terms that mark this trend. It varies by city. Of far more importance, however, is that the completed tenures of big city superintendents are almost twice as long as most insiders and outsiders have thought. Superintendents determined to adopt and pursue reform agendas, at the very least, have facts on their side that the job, while intimidating, is possible. Yet, even such superintendents will still have to cope with these persistent dilemmas. Why exactly have these dilemmas of purpose, strategy, and roles been around so long?

WHY DO THESE DILEMMAS PERSIST?

I have already suggested that these dilemmas are in the genetic code of the job and nature of public schooling in the United States. The metaphor of a genetic code helps me to understand the durable conflicts that superintendents and principals face again and again. The image of an occupational DNA partially explains the continuing struggle that grips principals and superintendents when they consider what ought to continue as is and what ought to change in their schools and districts.

This DNA is also written in the diverse and conflicting aims of schooling in a democracy where citizens are policy makers and professionals work in bureaucracies. The purposes of preparing children to become contributing citizens, skilled workers, and individuals of sterling character conflict with institutions constrained by the limited human and financial resources allotted to achieving them. Administrators make choices and satisfice. Further, public schools are tax-supported institutions in which lay boards of control constantly affected by political, social, economic, and demographic changes determine overall policies for professional educators. Superintendents, as the top appointed school officials, inevitably learn to twist, turn, and finesse the conflicting roles embedded in the position itself.

DNA is a metaphor, and we are speaking of organizations, not the human body. Can these dilemmas not be resolved by reorganizing, by eliminating the conflicts — or to push the metaphor — by gene splicing? Such thinking has occurred in the past. Proposals to divide the principalship into two positions, one for instruction and one for administering the school, have surfaced and receded. Hiring superintendents who have no background in education — recent superintendents in Milwaukee and Minneapolis come to mind — is another way of trying to outflank these dilemmas. Such solutions will fail to eliminate these conflicts because they are deeply embedded in the purposes of the organization, its administrative roles, and the inflated expectations of those who hire principals and superintendents.

Beyond an organizational explanation for these persisting dilemmas, strong societal attitudes favor viewing problems as solvable, not intractable. Strong social beliefs that individuals make a difference, that simply working hard can solve any problem — the can-do approach to all problems — permeate school organizations. Hence, every problem has a solution. It just needs the right person to find and implement the right solution. The attitude that leaders can conquer all constraints and get the job done contradicts the more obvious realities that there are intractable situations that require unattractive choices and compromises that satisfice and place limits on leaders. These societal attitudes also help explain the durability of these dilemmas (Lindblom & Cohen, 1979; Majone, 1989; Schön, 1982).

Dilemmas are unsolvable, but they can be managed. They need to be coped with imaginatively; they just will not go away. But if professional educators, parents, taxpayers, and school board members persist in seeing dilemmas as merely problems waiting to be solved, then the expectation for crisp, sure-fire solutions will remain strong and inexorable. Assume, for purposes of discussion, that these strong social beliefs harnessed to these organizationally anchored dilemmas explain the durability of these conflicts. What, then, can those who prepare and work with experienced administrators do?

WHAT SHOULD BE DONE?

For university professors in educational administration the problem becomes how to prepare students to understand, survive, and thrive in such dilemma-ridden settings. For professional associations, academics, and entrepreneurs engaged in helping principals and superintendents grow in their jobs the problem is how to help people who want to be effective administrators better understand the dilemma-rich situations in which they work.

Preparation Programs

Programs aimed at examining personal, occupational, organizational, and societal values will lay the foundation for understanding the work that newcomers to the job will face. Such programs include ways of acknowledging the durability of dilemmas, reasoning through distinctions between problems and dilemmas, and differentiating one from the other. Such programs spend more time helping students think through different ways of managing dilemmas. No doubt there are individual courses at various institutions that take up assorted pieces of what I am suggesting. No doubt existing state certification requirements limit how far existing programs can stretch or even change. Whatever the constraints that professors and university administrators face, the larger point is that adding courses to the formal curriculum is insufficient to help newcomers reach these practical understandings. More comprehensive curricular and pedagogical reforms have to be forged to overhaul existing preparatory programs.

There have been, of course, some moves in these directions. Professors, for example, have experimented with problem-based learning, case-method teaching, problem reframing, and closely-supervised intern- and externships. An acute awareness that different ways of teaching are as important as the content itself will help graduate students see more clearly how their personal values, the nature of school organizations, and the larger society are connected in the dilemmas that they will inevitably face (Bridges & Hallinger, 1993; Hart, 1993; Kelsey, 1993; Silver, 1986).[10]

Professional Development

Working with experienced principals and superintendents suggests different strategies than working with newcomers to the occupation. For those who have worked in schools and districts, reflecting on those experiences through teaching the concepts of dilemmas, and creating situations where making choices, satisficing, and reconstructing earlier compromises is essential. The lack of time to reflect is an obvious issue, but so is the way individuals reflect on their daily work. Using case studies as a primary form of instruction where administrators can bring their experience to bear on a specific dilemma suggests alternatives for managing it, and appraising the consequences of actions gives both the professor and students opportunities to extract concepts that may be applicable in their work settings.

The obstacles that block such changes in preparation and experienced administrator programs are both formidable and well-known. State certification standards, inertia among professors of educational administration, and other hurdles keep such actions at a minimum. The enduring dilemmas that university professors and administrators face in their own organizations would be the subject of another entire chapter. There are, then, directions that those who prepare administrators and work with experienced principals and superintendents can take to bring an increased awareness of these persistent work-embedded dilemmas that just will not go away.

These enduring dilemmas are at the core of administrative work and have to be acknowledged, understood, and worked through if both new and experienced principals and superintendents are to cope with the strong impulses for school reform. Without this intensely practical understanding of the deeply-rooted value conflicts in educational administration, and the varied ways administrators have learned to tame these perpetual struggles, schools and districts will continue to be administered as they are and face dim prospects for engaging in timely, meaningful, or significant reform. Such a practical understanding is a necessary, but insufficient, condition for improvement. It is neither more nor less than survival knowledge for those administrators who desire to last long enough in these posts and, of equal importance, who seek to improve their schools and districts.

NOTES

1. "Satisficing" is a term invented by Herbert Simon. It merges "satisfy" and "sacrifice" to create the notion of a good-enough compromise and tradeoff (Simon, 1957: 204–205).

2. There are, of course, other types of dilemmas that many administrators face that go beyond the purposes of schooling, strategies of change, and results, although they do get entangled. For example, virtually all administrators have to cope with the career versus home dilemma. The principal who is expected to attend most evening football and basketball games, school board meetings, and parent-sponsored events may also have a wife who is in a doctoral program and two preschoolers at home. Juggling his work schedule with his wife's academic responsibilities and care for his children while maintaining the marriage is one of the frequent dilemmas that principals and other administrators contend. I exclude such dilemmas.

3. These dilemmas over results are fairly recent rather than durable ones. Since the mid-1960s, when the assault upon the credibility and effectiveness of schooling, especially in big cities but ultimately for all public schools, began in earnest, measurable results have become highly prized. The passion for using standardized test scores as signs of academic success escalated in the 1970s with minimum competency tests, accelerated swiftly with the *Nation at Risk* report (1983) and, since then, has forged strong linkages between school

productivity — as measured by test scores — and the performance of the larger economy. Schools are now seen as serving the economy. Results pay off and schools have heeded the call. But not without costs to their administrators (McDonnell, 1994).

4.   Robert Crowson questions whether conflict is as central to the work of superintending as I and others claim. He raises the issue by pointing to the cross-institutional research comparing schools and city governments and other organizations that reveals little conflict. See Robert Crowson, (1987). The local superintendency. A puzzling administrative role. *Educational Administration Quarterly, 23*(3), 49–69.

5.   While here I use examples for the superintendent, I could have just as well used instances for the principal. The dilemma of identity applies to both positions (Wolcott, 1973).

6.   Of course, elsewhere in the nation, county and state superintendents of instruction are elected to office. While these are often nonpartisan positions, still these are political offices sought by professional educators, in many instances, and for such posts the political setting takes precedence.

7.   Superintendents' actions, of course, are perceived as political by others regardless of the motives of the particular school chief. For example, Joseph Fernandez, Chancellor of the New York City schools (1990–93), ended up leaving his position for many reasons of which one was the "Rainbow" curriculum for sex education that had sections dealing with gay and lesbian families in what was viewed as too positive a light by antagonists of the Chancellor (Hiss, 1993).

8.   The best evidence for these extravagant expectations for superintendents being both problem solvers and reformers is often seen in the brochures that school boards prepare for soliciting candidates to apply for a superintendent vacancy in their district. For a brief history of the criteria used to select District of Columbia superintendents in the 1960s and 1970s see Mary Hunter, (1977, April and May). Looking for superperson. *Bulletin Board* (District of Columbia Citizens for Better Public Education), *9*(3).

9.   The following data have been collected and analyzed by Gary Yee, a former Oakland, California, elementary school principal and currently a graduate student in the Stanford University School of Education. He took a database of 25 big cities and their superintendents between 1900 and 1975 that I collected 20 years ago for a study I had done on three urban superintendents (Cuban, 1976). He filled in the missing information in that database and updated it to 1990. It was his insight about the different questions that one could ask to calculate tenure that provided the basis for this analysis of tenure. His work revealed both cycles and trends about which I had been unaware. I had been concentrating on turnover rate in my work on superintendents. Yee pointed out that we could analyze the data from how many years school chiefs actually served and then calculate completed tenures, a concept that is far more accurate about term in office and the potential for reform.

10.   The case-method for teaching has had a long history of being applied to educational administration courses but few programs, if any, depend upon that form of pedagogy.

2

Managing Dilemmas in Education: The Tightrope Walk of Strategic Choice in Autonomous Institutions

Ron Glatter

In this chapter I take as my starting point Cuban's (1992) reflections on managing dilemmas developed in his penetrating and provocative presidential address at the 1991 annual meeting of the American Educational Research Association and in the first chapter of this book. These ideas mesh very well with my developing thinking over a long period about administrator preparation ("management development" in the United Kingdom) and administrative practice (for example, Glatter, 1972, 1991) and also with ongoing research that I am directing on the effects of recent market-based reforms in English education.

After a brief discussion of Cuban's ideas and some of their implications, I shall apply the notion of managing dilemmas to the current reforms in England and Wales, both at the macro (policy) level and, particularly, at the micro levels of schools and individuals.

MANAGING DILEMMAS: IDEAS AND IMPLICATIONS

Let me review briefly Cuban's basic argument. He distinguishes between "problems" and "dilemmas" (or "predicaments"). The former are relatively routine, structured situations that can be overcome by the application of standard problem-solving approaches: he gives the examples of students failing to cooperate over getting classes to start on time and a researcher meeting obstacles in gaining access for a research study. Dilemmas are different (although whether only in degree or actually in kind is not quite clear) in that they are "conflict-filled situations that require choices because competing, highly prized values cannot be fully satisfied" that are "far messier, less structured and often intractable to routine solutions" (Cuban, 1992: 6). They involve balancing competing claims, striking bargains, and making trade-offs between values in reaching decisions. "We invent a tightrope to walk, knowing that to cross the tightrope juggling the competing claims will still leave us uneasy" (Cuban, 1992: 7).

Cuban acknowledges that the distinction is far from original. However, he makes at least two noteworthy points. First, he suggests that researchers often overlook the tension-ridden dilemmas that policy makers and practitioners continually have to manage in their organizations. Second, in a "can-do" culture that often generates a guilt-inducing "mirage of simple solutions" (Cuban, 1992: 10), it is important to recognize that many situations do not lend themselves to clearly defined solutions. The best we can do is to reframe the dilemmas through explicit analysis and thus seek to "create better compromises and more elegant tightrope walks. Reframing and managing dilemmas are art forms, filled with doubt but at least free of corrosive guilt" (Cuban, 1992: 8).

Holmes (1993) distinguishes between open-ended dilemmas, for example, the allocation of a new resource, and closed dilemmas, such as reallocating an existing resource, maintaining that the former are much easier to tackle.

Cuban and others assume that managing dilemmas is an activity much concerned with making moral choices, and, indeed, Maclagan and Snell (1992) claim that their own research and that of others on managers outside education "demonstrates *the everyday nature of many moral dilemmas faced by managers*" (p. 166). However, we need to be clear what "moral" includes in this context. Such dilemmas may have none of the clarity and certainty that the term often seems to imply. Handy (1994) makes the point sharply: "Most of the dilemmas which we face in this time of confusion are not the straightforward ones of choosing between right and wrong, where compromise would, indeed, be weakness, but the much more complicated dilemmas of right and right" (p. 83). He suggests further that most compromise is in any case not about our principles but about our interests (although the two may presumably overlap). The dilemmas we face may be analyzed and understood at least as well from a micropolitical perspective (Bacharach & Mundell, 1993) as from a moral one.

Unfortunately, much of the discussion about values and ethics in educational management is at the level of abstraction and generalities. Writers about moral aspects rarely examine real situations of conflict and tension in which there are genuine dilemmas to confront, for example, decisions about the allocation of scarce resources or about the exclusion of disruptive pupils from school.

Some dilemmas of leadership appear to be perennial. In the personnel field, for example, dilemmas concerning the management of the under-performing or embittered teacher, the staffroom rebel, the arrogant disciplinarian, and so on are the stuff of many case studies and role plays in educational management development. Other kinds of dilemmas are broader and more pervasive, and are concerned with the connection between the organization and its environment (or in Bacharach and Mundell's [1993] terms, between micropolitics and macropolitics), which is a key focus of this chapter. Drawing on the work of Hoyle (1975) and Hughes (1985) concerning leadership by education professionals, Busher and Saran (1994) characterize headteachers as confronting the dilemma "of two sets of potentially conflicting values. On the one hand, they act as managers taking decisions in the interests of the stakeholders of an organization, on the other, they support the values of their teacher colleagues which define good professional practice" (p. 11).

A particularly graphic description of leadership dilemmas is given by an unnamed superintendent in the transcript of a reflective interview published by Osterman and Kottkamp (1993). The superintendent is commenting on his leadership style in dealing with staff who will not go along with a particular course of action. He says that, in such instances, he used to take a confrontational line too often in the past, but has now modified his style: "I am sure there are people who would like to see the superintendent say, 'You, change or get out!' However, that can't be done. . . . What you learn on the job is that there are no either/or's. There are degrees of either this or either that. [pause] I call it ambiguities. The ambiguities we deal with at work (which are probably the most important elements in the long run for effectiveness) I now share with people frequently — which I didn't do before. I take assessments more frequently of those ambiguities, unclear pathways" (pp. 168–169).

It is possible that these "unclear pathways" and "ambiguities" are relevant to the familiar distinction between espoused theories and theories-in-use (Argyris & Schön, 1974). Perhaps the discrepancies often noted between them in individual behavior arise as much from the dilemmas, ambiguities, and compromises intrinsically involved in the decision-making process as from other causes, such as weak or unclear basic values and convictions or conflicting theories-in-use. (Even so, as I suggest later, the doubts and compromises that led to a particular decision often may not be articulated, and perhaps not even recognized, once it has been made.)

A number of general points can be made at this stage. First, using the language of dilemmas and predicaments holds some dangers, even in cultures that are not as determinedly can-do as Cuban considers the United States to be. This language carries the implication of paralysis, of leaders being constantly torn between alternatives, or "dithering" (a word that has been effectively used recently as a term of abuse in the British political sphere). As Holmes (1993) has suggested, it is the task of leadership to confront dilemmas and ambiguities, not to let them fester and multiply. There is evidence that teachers value a decisive approach. From their large-scale study of new heads of secondary schools in England and Wales, which included collecting nearly 300 teachers' views on their preferred style of headship, Weindling and Earley (1987) concluded that "Most teachers wanted heads to be consultative and listen to the views of staff, but then make a clear decision. They disliked indecisiveness and slow decision-making" (pp. 175–176). This is likely to be the expectation of other stakeholders also. When we talk of the management of dilemmas we must not imply that practitioners should adopt the styles and timeframes of scholarship in reaching their conclusions.

Second, however, focusing on dilemmas and ambiguities has significance for management development and administrator preparation, particularly in such contexts as the United Kingdom where much stress is currently being placed on detailed frameworks of measurable and relatively mechanistic management competences (Esp, 1993). An intriguing study by Cave and Wilkinson (1992) based on in-depth work with a "focus group" of educational leaders over an extended period concluded that, as well as specific areas of knowledge and skill, provision needs to be made for the development of "higher order capacities" of which the following were identified from the study: "reading the situation," "balanced judgement," "intuition" (based on experience and reflection), and "political acumen." Reed and Anthony (1992), writing from a general management perspective, also emphasize the limitations of technically-oriented, competence-based approaches and argue that managers must be helped "to cope with the contradictory pressures and conflicting priorities which they will inevitably confront as professionals working within, and to some extent dependent on, complex organizations" (p. 609). This involves challenging an "unreflective pragmatism or 'hucksterism' poorly suited to the spirit and condition of the times" (p. 610).

Third, there is a need for those writing in this area, particularly (but not exclusively) from a moral or ethical standpoint, to examine actual situations where decisions are made "at the crunch," in which the reconciliation of conflicting pressures is attempted and priorities are determined, in order to relate these to their broader frameworks of analysis.

This preliminary general discussion has been intended to provide a backdrop for the following commentary on, and exemplification of, dilemmas and ambiguities in some aspects of the process of school reform, with particular reference to England and Wales.

TENSIONS IN THE REFORM ENVIRONMENT

It is almost a truism that schools face a host of complex and often inconsistent pressures from their environments. These pressures interact with one another to produce even greater complexity and to make prediction at the micro level of the school a hazardous and uncertain activity (Levin, 1993).

If this is an accurate assessment in relation to the contemporary scene in general, the recent espousal of radical reform strategies by governments in many countries has accentuated the uncertainties. The policies that have been adopted contain numerous tensions and contradictions. The paradox most frequently remarked upon is probably that between greater and less regulation: the simultaneous demands for more central control and checking for purposes of accountability, and for more devolution of authority, diversity, and choice in the interests of autonomy (Guthrie, Cibulka, & Cooper, 1989).

Cooper (1991), a strong supporter of the contemporary reform movement in general, nevertheless draws attention to three dilemmas or "cross-tensions" that need to be understood and at least partially resolved if the process is to move forward. The first dilemma is how to provide high quality, equitable, and appropriate education for all without creating an unresponsive state bureaucracy. The second relates to the possible effects on parental involvement of the weakening of the concept of the neighborhood school within a geographic community: "Parents-as-consumers may be in conflict with parents-as-participants, since heightened choice may send children off to far away schools, distant from the neighbourhood, community and families with whom children grew up. Thus, a dilemma of school reform lies in the conflict between individual families' choice on the one hand and the need for concerted, community involvement in schools ('social capital') on the other" (p. 239). Cooper goes on to suggest that "schools of choice must be aware that as their catchment area grows, their natural and easy access to parents diminishes" (p. 248). The third dilemma is concerned with the increasing role of parents on local school governing boards, how they can operate as both clients and formal decision makers at the same time, and how they can be both a provider and a consumer.

Shapira and Haymann (1991) also use the language of dilemmas in analyzing school reform policies, but they focus on competing values (pluralism versus integration and excellence versus equity) whereas Cooper's emphasis is more on management processes and role conflicts. The central point, however, is that these tensions and dilemmas do not remain locked in the wider system environment but are reflected within individual schools and localities.

In analyzing the market-oriented reforms in Britain, Cole (1992) refers to what he sees as "the contradiction between the free market, consumerist approach to education and the authoritarian drive for social order [as reflected in the imposition of a National Curriculum]" (p. 141). Writing with reference to England and Wales, Simkins (1993) argues that the task facing schools is to reconcile at least three different perspectives on effectiveness:

(a) that of central government, with its clear mandatory requirements on curricula, testing, and inspection and on the publication of information about examination results, truancy levels, and other matters;

(b) that of parents — whose expectations are not monolithic and pose difficult choices for schools about which groups to seek to attract;

(c) that of staff working within schools, who will bring both professional and interest-group considerations to bear on their judgements.

There may be some overlap between the three sets of definitions of effectiveness, but Simkins suggests that they will often be contested and hence may not be easy to reconcile. This is a key task for school managers, working within a context in which the balance of power has recently been significantly changed in favor of the external stakeholders.

In making their responses within this contradictory, ambiguous, and dynamic environment, schools (or those within them) must seek to reconcile the conflicting pressures. This is the subject of the next section.

DILEMMAS OF REFORM AT THE SCHOOL LEVEL

Some consideration has been given to the respective contributions of environment and organization in determining responses (Hrebiniak & Joyce, 1985). Greater significance has recently been attached to the importance of subjective perception and human agency in shaping events. In a powerful article, Daft and Weick (1984) stressed the complexity and importance of the process of interpretation: "Managers literally must wade into the ocean of events that surround the organization and actively try to make sense of them. . . . Interpretation is the process of translating these events, of developing models for understanding, of bringing out meaning" (p. 286). Morgan (1986) goes so far as to suggest that organizations in effect create their own environments, and argues for the need to overcome the false impression that they are "reacting to a world that is independent of their own making." This would at least help them to understand "that they themselves often create the constraints, barriers and situations that cause them problems" (p.137).

An illuminating recent review of the concepts and literature in this area argues for a balanced view of responsiveness: "Clearly, a simple response model, whether it sees schools as heroic actors or hapless victims, does not do justice to the complexity of the situation. Rather, we need to think in terms of a complex interplay between so-called external features, features of the school as an organization, and the specifics of a given time, place and group of people" (Levin, 1993: 15).

Levin looks at available research both within and outside education. On the whole, this shows organizational actors' limited capacity or willingness to understand, anticipate, and adjust to change. Often they seem to take steps to change as little as possible, although they are not always successful in this endeavor. Of particular interest, in view of our earlier discussion about schools' need to reconcile differing definitions of effectiveness, is the suggestion that, because as public organizations they "are fundamentally subject to competing interests," they will exhibit "a pattern of response which stresses placating interests over achieving goals" (p. 13).

It might be argued that the new environments of radical reform have been designed precisely to change this situation, by forcing schools to respond effectively and to keep a clear focus on achieving goals (as defined by the architects of the reforms) rather than on placating interests. Thus, considerable stress is currently placed, in England and Wales, on the concepts of strategic and development planning (Hargreaves & Hopkins, 1991; Office for Standards in Education, 1993; Weindling, 1993) in spite of the problems frequently identified with such approaches (Mintzberg, 1994; Wallace, 1992). As Levin (1993) suggests, "Organizations may face simultaneous pressures in quite opposite directions, so that it is not at all clear what strategy might be most effective" (p. 14).

Some schools in England and Wales have taken strategic positioning decisions of a fairly dramatic kind because the new competitive market arrangements, in which funding is linked largely to the numbers and ages of pupils attending the school, were introduced. In particular, schools that opt out of local education authority control and become grant-maintained can make quite wide-ranging decisions about their future organization, usually subject to the approval of the Secretary of State. This might include lowering the age of entry to the school, introducing a Sixth Form to offer programs to 16 to 19-year-olds, teaching boys and girls separately for the first time, and introducing selection tests for applicants. There are current examples of all of these. The motivation in all cases appears to be at least in part to obtain competitive advantage over nearby schools. Sometimes these pioneers receive the bonus of national media coverage. Without research, however (which we plan to undertake in at least one of the above cases), we do not know what dilemmas were confronted in making the potentially fateful decision or what its outcomes will be in educational and marketing terms.

For our Parental and School Choice Interaction (PASCI) study[1] we are using both quantitative and qualitative methods to focus on the dynamics of parental choice and school response in three contrasting areas in different parts of England. Each of these areas resembles as closely as possible what we call a "local competitive arena" in which secondary schools draw from a largely common population of parents. The factors affecting parental choice and school response can only, in our view, be adequately understood within the specific local context in which they operate and this includes the nature of the particular "competitive environment" (Kotler & Fox, 1985) in the locality.

Indeed, our early findings suggest that schools are often more responsive to what competitor schools and feeder schools are doing than to any clear perception of "consumer" expectations; there is little formal assessment of the latter by the schools in our case study areas (Woods, Bagley, & Glatter, 1994). Overall there appears to be considerably more evidence of responses of a purely promotional kind (concerned with publicity and image enhancement) than on what we have called substantive change (concerned with the school's central educational activities and the way it organizes itself). Moreover, where there is evidence of the latter it tends to be mostly in the direction of safe or traditional academic practice (such as examination performance, homework, and setting by ability), apparently in the hope of attracting more middle class and academically able children. If these tendencies are confirmed, they would support Levin's (1993) assessment that organizational responsiveness is something of a myth. However, our study is a longitudinal one and the jury is still out. The projected loosening of the hitherto highly prescriptive National Curriculum may release new energies for change.

In the next section I look at one of the three competitive arenas included in the study to see what light it throws on the central themes of this chapter.

EXAMPLES OF STRATEGIC CHOICE DILEMMAS

The examples that follow are drawn from three schools in a local competitive arena to which the PASCI study has given the fictitious name "Northern Heights." It is an area that displays many of the forms of social disadvantage characteristic of parts of urban Britain, with above-average proportions of working-class households, poor-quality housing, and high rates of unemployment. There is a small but identifiable ethnic minority community, which is mainly of Bangladeshi origin.

This arena contains three secondary schools, although, as we have pointed out in another paper, "Local competitive arenas are not discrete entities. Their boundaries will tend to overlap and individual family perceptions of the area in which they may choose schools will vary according to such factors as access to transport" (Woods, Bagley, & Glatter, 1994: 2). The following brief sketches of the schools (taken from field notes prepared by Carl Bagley) should be read with this caveat in mind.

Braelands School is at the top of the "league table" of school examination results that the government publishes annually for this area (and all others), and it is oversubscribed. It is rurally situated in a middle-class area at the boundary of Northern Heights. The headteacher and senior managers are committed to maintaining, expanding, and promoting the academic nature of the school. It is financially secure and supported by a wealthy and active parent-teacher association.

Newcrest Technology School (which changed its name last year from Newcrest High School after receiving some extra funding from a government initiative on school technology) is in the lower half of the examination league table and struggles to maintain its planned admission number. It is situated in the urban center of Northern Heights and serves a multiracial working-class population. The headteacher and senior managers fully recognize the competitive environment and are working hard to consolidate and, if possible, increase the school's market share. The school is financially insecure, and the parent-teacher association struggles to raise money.

Leaside School is at the bottom of the examination league table and is undersubscribed by 50 percent. It is understaffed and has financial difficulties. It is situated at the center of a large isolated public housing estate and relies for its admissions on the support of parents from its immediate feeder primary schools. The school makes little or no attempt to market and promote itself outside the estate. The headteacher is resigned to the school having a low roll and skeptical about any strategy being able to increase pupil numbers.

It is possible to identify some dilemmas of strategic choice based on interviews conducted with senior staff of the three schools as part of the PASCI study. However, this is probably not the best source of information on dilemmas because, as Levin (1993) points out, individual respondents tend to rationalize their behavior and to give events greater coherence retrospectively in relation to goals than they had at the time. We will, therefore, need to look for other sources of evidence of conflicting pressures on strategic decision making as the study progresses.

Given the relatively fortunate circumstances of Braelands School, it might not be expected to have significant dilemmas of strategic choice. This is, indeed, the case, but despite the strong and successful emphasis on academic excellence, uncertainties remain. Parents who have chosen the school are asked to fill in a form giving the reasons for their choice and, somewhat surprisingly, the reasons given most frequently relate to the school's ethos and the child's happiness, rather than to examination results. Although the questionnaire only obtains the views of those who have already selected the school (and who may, therefore, be taking their preference for an academic orientation for granted in their replies), the headteacher feels he must continually strike a balance between the school being too informal, on the one hand, and being too strict or authoritarian, on the other, which could alienate some parents.

Newcrest Technology School's dilemmas are more serious. The school has decided to try to raise its academic profile because, in the words of the headteacher, "If we attract less able children our exam results are poor, our position in the league table is poor and we attract less children the next year. . . . It's a downward spiral." A major vehicle for this effort is the association with technology provided by the extra funding obtained from the government and the change of name. It will be important, while making this push to attract more of those families who tend toward a "rational academic" value perspective (Woods, 1994), not to alienate the majority of parents who are currently attracted to the school for "human warmth" reasons.[2] The headteacher also points out: "I can't cut off my remedial support because that is my bread and butter." There are personal as well as institutional aspects to this dilemma. The headteacher regrets the pressure to emphasize academic features at the expense of, for example, extracurricular activities and school trips, so that: "the width of education, the whole balanced person, is suffering. I've always taken the line here that our niche in the market is with confidence, a bit of bottle because we haven't got the academic front. Now we're having because of competition, to market the academic side so much so that the last year staff were pulling kids back in at night time and insisting that they would complete their homework."

It is not clear how successful this strategy will be for Newcrest, given the school's resource deficiencies (such as buildings in a poor state of repair) and the character of the existing pupil intake. For example, it is said that some white, middle-class parents in the area will never send their children to Newcrest because it is "classed as a black school." The strategy is not a response to an expressed need by parents, although the school feels it can sell it to them. As the deputy headteacher said in interview: "We talk to our parents and we convince them that that's what they want. . . . People are malleable."

Cuban uses the terms "dilemma" and "predicament" interchangeably, but perhaps they should be distinguished. Leaside School seems not so much faced with dilemmas as in a predicament. For example, the school has numerous financial problems, including a sports hall needing repair; if money could be found to repair the hall, it could be hired out to raise extra funds for the school. Turning around parental preference statistics in situations like this has been compared to "turning an oil tanker round in an estuary." Arbon (1993), who drew this analogy, went on to comment that it can be done and is being done in certain instances. (Deem, Brehoney, and New [1993] report the case of a school that even contemplated solving — or avoiding — the problem by moving to a site in a more congenial area.)

In the case of Leaside School, however, the headteacher considers that there is no realistic way that pupil numbers could be significantly increased. No doubt there is a personal dilemma for school managers in such adverse circumstances: whether to choose the path of acceptance, and be thought to display weak leadership, or to take a more optimistic approach and perhaps raise false expectations. Ironically, in spite of its chronic undersubscription, this school has a lifeline: Braelands and Newcrest do not attempt to attract parents from the estate in which Leaside is situated (which has a poor reputation) because they feel it is in their interests to ensure that Leaside stays open, otherwise they would receive the kind of pupils that currently go to Leaside, which they are keen to avoid.

A competitive climate, such as that now existing in many areas of England and Wales, creates numerous dilemmas of strategic choice for those guiding the affairs of schools. One of the most sensitive and difficult is what balance to strike between acting separately and acting collabora- tively with other schools (Glatter, 1993b; Levacic & Woods, 1994), requir- ing school managers to exercise fine judgment based on educational, political, and managerial understanding and a shrewd reading of the local situation — precisely the kinds of "higher order capacities" identi- fied by Cave and Wilkinson (1992) and discussed earlier in this chapter. (For example, in our work we have come across cases in which an appar- ent agreement between schools not to compete in certain areas has been breached by one of the parties, requiring some form of response by the others.) Greater school autonomy and heightened competition produce both sharper challenges and a more ambiguous context: in Cuban's terms, more tightrope walks.

CONCLUSION

Most of the examples presented in the last section suggest that dilem- mas can be addressed through striking a balance, by attempting to recon- cile apparent opposites — what Handy (1994) has referred to as "managing paradox." (He quotes Schumacher: "For constructive work, the principal task is always the restoration of some kind of balance" [p. 19].) Elsewhere, I have suggested that "Managing for school effectiveness requires at least three delicate balancing acts. It involves seeking to reconcile: the complex- ity, uncertainty and fluidity of the environment with the unique character and culture of the school as a social institution; strategic planning with daily problem-finding and problem-solving; creativity with accountabil- ity and discipline" (Glatter, 1993a: 29).

One merit of such formulations, as suggested earlier, is that they direct attention to some of the key capacities or competences with which prepa- ration or development programs should be concerned. For example, they provide an important rationale for the use of structured, reflective approaches in such programs (Osterman & Kottkamp, 1993). Another merit is that, by employing the terminology of balance and reconciliation, they suggest how the indecisiveness associated with the idea of dilemmas may be avoided. At the same time, they emphasize the strengths of the approach: for instance, one study in the business sector suggested that the more creative, dynamic companies tended to be better at recognizing and resolving dilemmas, whereas the less innovative ones tended to oversimplify situations and make sharp choices, often rushing from one extreme of policy or organization to another (Baden-Fuller & Stopford, 1992).

However, they should be treated with caution in at least one respect. Satisfying though these formulations implying the possibility of harmony may be, they are perhaps overoptimistic in paying too little regard to the degrees of severity in different dilemma-filled situations. The problems faced by Newcrest Technology School and, particularly, by Leaside School in Northern Heights appear much less tractable than those encountered by Braelands School. It is important not to be beguiled by notions of the reconciliation of opposites, nor to allow them to foster, in Cuban's terms, "the mirage of simple solutions."

I hope to have shown in this chapter that the study of organizational dilemmas, including how they arise, the ways they are perceived by different actors, and varying approaches to their resolution, should receive closer attention in educational administration and management, both in the context of the implementation of structural reform and more generally.

NOTES

In writing this chapter, I have benefited greatly from the ideas and investigations of my colleagues working on the PASCI study, Philip Woods and Carl Bagley. The shortcomings of the chapter, of course, are all my responsibility.

1.   This study is supported by the Economic and Social Research Council (ESRC) reference R000234079.

2.   Parents who tend toward a rational academic value perspective attach importance to academic standards, examination results, and so forth. Parents who tend toward a human warmth value perspective place importance on personal relationships, a caring environment, and so forth. Clearly these are not mutually exclusive, nor are they the only ones parents or children bring to bear in choosing a school (see Woods, 1994).

3

Persistent Dilemmas in Administrative Preparation and Practices in Underdeveloped and Developing Countries

Earle H. Newton

As they endeavor to develop or reform, restructure or energize, and manage and direct educational systems and institutions, educational planners and administrators are confronted by numerous problems and issues. These problems and issues can have many historical, cultural, political, and economic dimensions and may be caused by factors and circumstances that are indigenous or exogenous to the particular locale. They may assume such magnitude and have such serious consequences for individuals, groups, or the wider society that they take on alarming proportions and appear insurmountable and insolvable. Some of these problems and issues are universal. Some are specific to certain contexts, cultures, or regions. This chapter will identify and discuss some of those factors that are specific in some way to underdeveloped and developing countries.

Before one can proceed, however, this formidable topic must be brought within manageable proportions. The parameters within which it will be approached must be carefully delineated and defined. The focus of discussion will be small developing nations and states; the term "under-developed" will be subsumed under the concept of developing. The chapter first discusses and defines the terms "small state," "developing," and "dilemma," on which a proper understanding of the content of the chapter hinges.

A FRAMEWORK FOR DILEMMAS

Dilemmas, according to Cuban (1992) and the first chapter of this book, involve conflicting moral choices that are deeply rooted in who we are and in our practices as administrators. They are often distinguishable from routine, structured administrative problems because they are complex, untidy, and insolvable.

Aram sees dilemmas as situations in which people are forced to choose between equally attractive or equally unattractive alternatives with no way of rationally calculating the better choice. He states "A dilemma is a predicament — a complicated and perplexing situation that requires choice between equally valued alternatives" (Aram, 1976: 9).

Katz and Raths (1992) suggest that a dilemma is a predicament that has two main features. First, there must be a choice of two or more courses of action, each, in turn being problematic, and second, the choice of any one course of action sacrifices the advantage that might accrue if the alternative were chosen. In summary, a dilemma is a situation in which a perfect solution is not available.

These three definitions have been selected as our framework because they reveal different approaches that reflect the predicament in which administrators in small developing states often find themselves. It must be observed, however, that the choices do not always involve purely moral positions, nor indeed are the alternatives necessarily equal, in any or every way. They may involve conflict, various desiderata, and considerations but they are always dilemmas or predicaments where decision making is not straightforward and uncomplicated. Educational administrators in small developing states have to make hard choices in a variety of areas and over a variety of issues at the macro level. At the micro level, they are expected to be all things to all people. They have to nurture and balance organizational and individual growth and development in situations fraught with difficulties not experienced by their counterparts elsewhere — at least not to the same degree.

CHARACTERISTICS OF SMALL
DEVELOPING COUNTRIES

What are the characteristics that make small developing states stand out and create peculiar problems for the development and administration of education? The major features of developing countries are lack of adequate financial resources; inadequate technical and technological resources, knowledge, and skills; limited and inadequate provision of education across the recognized, basic and primary, secondary, and tertiary levels, and especially in the technical-vocational and special needs areas; inadequate and inappropriately trained and qualified teaching and administrative staff; inadequate provisions of social services (health and sanitation, education, transportation, water, and welfare); and infrastructural arrangements that are generally too limited and too weak to initiate and sustain a meaningful and relevant development thrust.

These problems have been fostered and exacerbated by the pervasive and iniquitous influence of a dependency syndrome and a misguided concept of development. The former has its origin in the historical master-colonial, dominant-dependent relationships of colonial days and is kept alive today by the developed world and its lending agencies. The latter is the progeny of the former (the dependency syndrome) and was inflicted on the developing world by the developed world to serve its own trade and financial interests when the growing forces of nationalism and independence caused the demise of its empires. Development is measured by the standards of the developed world and the extent to which a country mimics and approximates it, receiving its exports-consumables, technology, values, and culture.

Graham-Brown observes: "Despite the achievement of political independence, the vast majority of countries in the South have remained locked into positions in the international economic order which impose constraints on national decision-making of a quite different magnitude from those which affect most countries in the North" (Graham-Brown, 1991: 13).

As we approach the twenty-first century, we notice a deterioration in the position of the developing countries. In many of these poor countries, there has been a serious decline in the per capita rate of gross domestic product, public expenditure, and private consumption. This has been accompanied by an increase in the debt service that now claims a greater share of their export earnings. The plight of the developing nations has been further exacerbated by a decline in trade for primary agricultural and mineral products, and the protectionist policies of Europe and the United States that led to attempts to exclude certain products of the developing world from the markets of the developed world. There is no doubt that the economic and policy decisions of the developed world and the international financial and lending agencies that they dominate continue to hold serious implications for the developing world.

All developing countries suffer in some way, but the most severely affected have been those that depend more on primary commodity production. The key economic problems affecting these developing countries are both the producers and the products of the dual demon of the dependency–misguided development notion. As the developing countries under the impulsion of the developed world strive to be more like it, they achieve greater degrees of dependency, often to the point where they approach the undignified state of international mendicancy and are forced to sacrifice or prostitute their values and norms.

Naturally, the factors discussed above do not apply in every particular to all developing countries nor indeed do they necessarily have the same impact. However, this general picture of the plight of developing countries is necessary if we are to understand the context and intricate nature of the issues and problems of educational development, management, and administration.

The problems and challenges of poor developing countries become magnified and more perplexing for the small developing countries. These countries cannot produce many of the goods they need, their factories and other means of production operate on a small scale and generally cannot use the most efficient production methods, and they are always at the mercy of outside forces, in whatever sphere.

There are few approaches to the definition of what constitutes a small state. The demographic approach uses simple statistics, such as population, area, or the magnitude of the national product. Sociological interests define small states in relation to the nature and number of relations and roles that exist within the society. Another approach involves measuring the structural dimensions of an economy, both the level of diversification of economic functions and the degree of complexity of relations among the agents. There are merits and demerits in all these approaches that must not detain us at this time. Suffice it to say that the demographic approach, which is the one most commonly used, will be used here. One million inhabitants is the generally accepted upper limit, but a UNESCO Conference in Mexico in 1990 on Planning and Management of Educational Development decided to raise this threshold to 1.5 million. This, with some fluidity, is the threshold to hold in mind. However, as Atchorena points out: "The reality of small states is not limited to demographic size, and to grasp the concept of small state it is necessary to have a vision including the dynamics of development. Small size often ends up being associated with concepts of dependence, vulnerability, viability or even isolation" (Atchorena, 1993: 17).

Small states have been described as "transparent" societies. In transparent societies everybody knows everybody else and what they do. Indeed, it is often said (quite erroneously) that everybody is related to everybody else. Be that as it may, relationships (family and friends) and affiliations (social, religious, and political) are important, and political influence and consideration impinge more directly on official action and decision making. The point here is not that these factors are nonexistent in larger developing or developed countries, it is simply that the impact can be greater, more pervasive, and more obvious in smaller societies.

In small societies, there is a greater tendency to centralization and bureaucratic control, and status and power assume a greater significance. The size factor, limited resources, and the need to be cost-effective have combined to create multifunctionalism in small states. With respect to education, for example, whatever its size, a country needs to establish an education system to provide an efficient education service, and any system requires an administrative and managerial organization. The same tasks (perhaps more) as those in larger countries have to be done. As Farrugia and Attard observe: The actual number of people working in each branch . . . of small education systems will be fewer, sometimes much fewer than in larger states. However, the difference is not proportional to population or school enrollment. The pressures on personnel expected to fulfill a number of roles and responsibilities are proportionately much higher than those in larger countries" (Farrugia & Attard, 1989: 19).

This background to the circumstances and situation of small developing states is useful, perhaps even essential, for an examination of some of the administrative dilemmas in education. However, the picture is not complete without some reference to those factors that influence educational provision in all countries — large, small, developed, or developing. Educational provision in all countries must be based on some feasible and defensible concept of social justice. The various social, cultural, and other elements of the society must be reflected in and provided for in the planning and administration of education and due consideration must be given to issues of equity and equality with respect to gender, class, ethnicity, religion, and other areas. As societies become more multicultural, multiethnic, and more stratified, the greater the problems and challenges become.

The conditions in developing countries, revolving mainly around the dependency-development concept, the special circumstances of small states, and the more general issue of social justice all combine to influence and determine educational policy, planning, and administration in small states. It is also at the confluence of all these elements that major problems and dilemmas are created. It is, therefore, to a consideration of some dilemmas and problems that attention will now be turned.

It might be useful to point out that the term "educational administration" is used in a broad sense in this chapter. It embraces both the traditional executive functions of the administrator — decision making, planning, communication, allocating roles and facilities, supervising, coordinating, evaluating, and so forth — and policy making and planning at the macro or systems level.

EDUCATIONAL DILEMMAS IN DEVELOPING COUNTRIES

Many dilemmas are encountered and hard choices have to be made in the administration and management of education in small developing countries. These dilemmas and choices manifest themselves at the general system level, at the institutional level, and at the individual level.

Education has been seen as the major, if not the only, means of uplift and salvation for both the individual and the nation in most developing countries. It has been proclaimed as a right and efforts have been made by governments to provide free, universal primary education. Many small states in the Caribbean and indeed countries across the Commonwealth have gone farther, providing free secondary education; some have provided free or heavily subsidized postsecondary education. Public support for education has become a given. Public education is the norm, certainly across the Caribbean. It is seen as a means of protecting the rights of the poor and disadvantaged groups to quality education.

Today, public education is under threat. The ever-increasing demand for more and better education, escalating costs, the worsening world financial situation, and pressure from lending agencies have all combined to force policy makers, politicians, and administrators to pay more attention to sources of funding. There are renewed discussions as to who should pay for education. Lending agencies are demanding that some sort of cost-recovery mechanisms and cost-effective strategies be put in place to bring educational costs under control. Policy makers and administrators fear that user fees will hurt the already disadvantaged groups and affect their life chances. On the other hand, cost-effective strategies, such as reduction of teacher-pupil ratios and limited spending on texts and equipment, will result in a decline in the quality of education provided. This, in turn, could lead to an upsurge in private education that would have implications for the concerns of equity and equality. The way ahead is not an easy one. Inequities, disadvantages, and perceived injustices can assume greater significance in small transparent societies than elsewhere.

The situation is further complicated by the equity-efficiency conflict. Equity in the provision and delivery of education recognizes that more resources (time, equipment, and teachers) are needed for groups or individuals that are disadvantaged — slow learners, the mentally and physically handicapped — or at risk by virtue of class, gender, ethnicity, or geographical location. It is, therefore, deemed legitimate to employ a variety of measures and approaches to ensure wherever possible acceptable standards of learning. The efficiency approach advocated by the developed countries and their lending agencies for the developing world rejects as economically wasteful such approaches as repetition of a year and individualized or small group learning. This overemphasis on efficiency is anathema to the legitimate aspiration of people in small developing states to quality education. Hard decisions have to be made in this domain. Educational planners and administrators often find themselves caught between the rock of the politician's desire to be seen as a fair champion of the people's aspirations and the hard place of the financial reality imposed by the lending agencies.

An area of great concern in all developing countries, but one that has special implications to small states, is the extent to which they can develop national institutions instead of continued dependence on overseas institutions at the higher levels of education. Education at the postsecondary and tertiary levels is very expensive, hence, expenditures must be carefully considered and there must be a reasonable expectation of commensurate benefits and returns. The need for education and training at this level may be strongly felt by both the individual and the state. However, the numerical demand is seldom enough to justify significant outlays and recurrent expenditures to cover a wide range of needs. Decisions, therefore, have to be made. But decisions cannot be based purely on financial considerations, important though they may be. Social, historical, cultural, religious, and moral aspects must be considered. In today's world, there is great cultural awareness; small states are alert to the fact that their cultures are constantly under threat from rich and more powerful nations through the electronic and print media and other sources. They are conscious that overdependence on large powerful countries in such vital areas as education puts their cultural and values heritage under siege.

When, for example, the majority of key personnel in education planning and administration in small states is being trained abroad, many questions must be raised, even if satisfactory answers cannot be immediately found. What guarantees will there be that the training will be appropriate for the particular purpose? How can one tell that the individual's and the state's best interest will be served by the training? What assurances will there be that the theories and philosophical tenets of the course will be transferable between the cultures involved? How can one be assured that there will be no major dissonance between the culture, values, and aspirations of the state in question and the teachings and practices in the course? These and similar questions have been treated elsewhere (for example, Newton, 1985; Marshall & Newton, 1983) and it is not appropriate to elaborate on them in this forum. However, it must be borne in mind that educational goals, aspirations, and expectations are closely bound up in the historical, social, cultural, and values orientation of the people involved. Therefore, the assumptions of the theories developed for the Western developed world may not necessarily apply in the developing world.

Regional cooperation, although not necessarily the preferred solution, may be a workable and more fruitful alternative. The University of the West Indies and the University of the South Pacific, each of which serves a number of small states, are good working examples of what can be achieved in this regard. Fortunately, many small states are archipelagoes with considerable similarities and close geographical location that facilitate collaboration and cooperation. Even here, however, administrative predicaments abound. In small island states, transportation and communication can be problematic and solutions carry a high cost factor. Insularity and parochialism can assume alarming proportions, and require delicate and sensitive handling, lest they get out of hand and operate to the detriment of good educational decisions. Great care has to be exercised with respect to the cultural and national aspirations of each contributing territory. The University of the West Indies has had to grapple with these and similar problems, but has adjusted from time to time, and still continues to retain the confidence and support of the people and to serve the region well. The advantages of such regional cooperative ventures are obvious. It is recognized, for example, that a doctor trained in his own region will have a better understanding of the environment and context of his patients and should, thus, be better placed to offer help.

However, returning to the overdependence of small developing states on the developed countries, there is yet another aspect to it — one that is often neglected or ignored by the developed world and its lending agencies. It is the national pride of the small country that is compromised in many different ways. No country can stand proudly and defend its rights if it constantly occupies the dependency end of the dominance-dependency relationship. Recognition of this important fact could bring about a change of attitude that could lead to a change of policy and greater efforts by the developed countries to help the developing world generally, and small states in particular, to develop their own capacities on a number of different points. There is a strongly held view that it suits the purposes of the developed countries to maintain this dominance-dependency relationship. This position is manifest when the developing country is required, against its convictions, to support a stand taken by a developed country that provides some form of aid.

The curriculum, textbooks, and examination system also pose a dilemma for educational administrators and planners in small states. For a long time, questions have been raised and dissatisfaction expressed over many aspects of these questions. The relevance of the curriculum has been questioned, textbooks have been seen as expensive, irrelevant, containing unfamiliar content and ideas, and, in some cases, misrepresenting minority and disadvantaged groups and presenting them in a patronizing or derogatory manner. A curriculum that has been tied to foreign examinations has been unable to respond to the needs of a society as it evolves in a quickly changing world. The examinations naturally reflect the foreign textbooks, test material, and knowledge that are often outside the experience of the local student. Administering the foreign examination also has a foreign exchange implication for the small state, even though it may be argued that what is lost here is more than made up for in international currency and credit worthiness of the related certification.

Would it be to the advantage of small states to develop their own curriculum, produce their own textbooks, and design their own examinations? Would this be more cost-effective? Do small states have the expertise in sufficient depth and numbers and over a sufficient range of specializations to make such a venture a worthwhile undertaking? Is the relevant technology available or can it be attained at reasonable cost? Would local examinations be as readily acceptable on the international market as the recognized foreign ones? These questions would have to be answered on an individual basis and decisions made accordingly. The obvious gains in developing local syllabuses would be curriculum relevance; familiarity of content; authenticity in social, historical, cultural, and values orientation; and the removal of foreign currency outflows.

The Caribbean Examinations Council is a good example of a regional effort that was established to tackle some of the problems described above. The council was set up by a number of Caribbean governments to prepare syllabuses and texts in a range of subjects to replace the British Ordinary level (O level) examinations in the secondary schools. The council brought together teachers from across the region, resulting in an examination more oriented to the region. By careful communication with and involvement of existing foreign examining boards the council was able to tackle the problem of international currency and acceptance.

However, the council has created what some teachers term a dilemma for them. The O level examinations were deemed to be heavily content-oriented and to pay insufficient attention to thinking, creativity, application, problem solving, and divergent thinking. The curriculum developers seem to have gone overboard in most subjects. While they have been catering to those areas insufficiently addressed in the O level exams, they have been criticized for increasing the content as well. The result, in the opinion of many, is an examination too challenging and demanding on average for the 16-and-over age group for whom it is intended. It is fairly typical of countries seeking to free themselves from a dependency situation to hold greater expectations, set higher standards, and make greater demands of themselves.

This leads to yet another dilemma that small countries have to confront — that of training education. The question of whether small states should be primarily concerned with training individuals to operate certain procedures and technologies efficiently or with educating them to be creators and designers is not easily resolved. In spite of what politicians and governments say, they are more likely to be influenced by programs that lead to improvements in material wealth during their regimes: the rapid results syndrome. This is often more easily achieved by adopting and adapting foreign technologies than by developing indigenous ones. The products of foreign technologies are more likely to be marketable both inside and outside their territories. Hence, training programs that teach people to perform routines efficiently may be the most attractive. The resulting increase in wealth from these programs is likely to sustain this type of activity at the expense of more creative pursuits, at least in the short term. This has serious implications for what is taught, how it is taught, and how it is tested, particularly at the secondary and postsecondary levels of education.

Nowhere perhaps is there more talk of democracy or more claims made for democratic practices in the management and administration of education than in small developing states. Equally, perhaps nowhere is the tendency to centralization and bureaucratic control more manifest than in these very states. Ministries of education proclaim that their principals have the authority and discretionary powers to act. Principals, on the other hand, claim that, when they dare to exercise authority and discretion in their schools, they come into conflict with the ministry. Clearly this conflict over the locus of change and decision making constitutes a dilemma for all concerned. What has been noticeable, however, is that, in times of severe social and financial problems, there is a tendency to talk of decentralization, of placing greater authority and autonomy in the school. This may simply be a way of shifting the pressure away from the central body by placing a greater measure of accountability on the principal. Principals are, thus, being called upon to do more with less. In some places, they are expected to operate on market principles without the resources, the tradition, and the training necessary to make such principles workable. The problem for the principals is that they dare not resist, because, in so doing, they put at risk all aspects of their professional autonomy for which they have been striving for so long.

Within the schools themselves teachers experience similar difficulties — whether to act or speak in staff meetings — because any action on their part easily prompts such reactions as "This is my school. I make the decisions. What I say here goes." from their principals. It is as if principals believe that the involvement of teachers diminishes their authority .

These situations are experienced across the small states throughout the world. They are rooted in the false notion of status and authority that considers discretion, judgment, and knowledge to be hierarchically distributed within the organization and that it would be an admission of failure or an abdication of authority if people lower down the ladder were seen to be contributing in their realm. This approach is by no means peculiar to small states, but it takes on a particular significance here where the bosses have high visibility and are always (often by their own choosing) under scrutiny. The bosses must be assertive and no one and nothing must be seen to diminish their authority or status.

The concept of multifunctionalism mentioned earlier must now be revisited. We must recognize and accept multifunctionalism as a way of professional life in small states and prepare our administrators and other officers to function efficiently and effectively in their multifunctional roles. It must not be seen as a problem or a nuisance that we have to live with but would rather be rid of. This latter approach is the cause of some of the problems associated with the concept.

Farrugia and Attard (1989), elaborating this multifunctional role, noted that it is quite usual to find many areas of responsibility centered in one post. They cite the example of a director-general of education who also has responsibility for youth, culture, sports, public libraries, and museums. There are cases where the lone secondary school principal may also be the education officer responsible for all the primary schools. They observe: "Education Officers in small states often cover the pedagogical and curricular development of several subjects taught in all sectors of the education system. . . . In addition they are likely to be called upon to monitor teachers' work in schools, run in-service courses, lecture in teacher education institutions, prepare budgets, sit on purchasing committees, chair selection and promotion panels, attend policy meetings, meet parents and teach their subject specialisation in one or more secondary schools" (Farrugia & Attard, 1989: 23).

How do persons so placed get through their professional day? Imagine the predicaments they must face each day as well as those they must create for other personnel in their organizations. Is the alternative to designate posts and assign personnel on the basis of specialisms even when there is insufficient work to occupy them? There can be nothing less cost-effective for the state and more soul-destroying for the individual than to have every professional day filled with bits of nothing. Sound and practical approaches to multifunctionalism must be arrived at. It must not be left to happenstance, accretions, or the whims of individuals. Every effort must be made to reduce the number of tasks — especially highly demanding, specialized, or conflictive tasks — assigned to any one post and careful job descriptions must be provided to assist the post holders. Above all, training based on the shared experience of the post holders should be provided.

Relationships, affiliations, and political concerns have a profound influence on policy decisions and administrative actions in small states in ways that are not experienced in larger countries. Recognize however, that this statement does not imply that nepotism, political patronage, or interference are rife in small states. Administrators and decision makers know that whatever action they take will be subject to scrutiny and interpretation according to their known or ascribed affiliations and attitudes as well as the connections and dispositions of those who judge them. Often people in authority seek to find out (more by inference and surmise) the will of their superiors so that it can be done. Thus, important areas for decision making that affect both individuals and institutions — appointments, promotions, evaluations and assessment of teachers, disciplines, locations of schools, and educational reform — are placed in a sphere where objective professional judgment, vital as it is to these areas, is submerged in a sea of other considerations. The basis for action, therefore, becomes not, "All things considered in my judgment this is the best," but "This is the one likely to cause the least stir, the least reaction." This may be illustrated in these examples: promote not necessarily the best but certainly the most senior candidate; go for the one with the most support; write nondescript reports on teachers (they may say nothing but they'll cause no stir and raise no questions). In many small states the way around these difficulties is to establish cumbersome bureaucratic decision-making structures so that no one individual can be blamed for the decision.

The strong academic orientation in the curriculum in most developing countries is a legacy of their colonial past. For some time now, questions have been asked about an approach to education based on a metropolitan model designed to serve a small elite. Is this competitive, examination-oriented, academic approach relevant and should its dominance be allowed to continue? The response has been a thrust, apparently not very powerful, toward vocational education to prepare students for the world of work by providing them with marketable skills. Thus, a tension has developed between those who see education as improving the mind and creating the "cultured individual," and those whose "human capital" orientation values only those skills that have a direct bearing on the labor market.

The reality is far more complex than is reflected in either of these simplistic positions. Technical-vocational education is costly and the demand for certain skills is not static. Skills that are valued and essential today are not necessarily those that will be required tomorrow. Furthermore, most ex-colonial societies do not place a high value on manual and technical skills. More importantly, the value of education cannot be dichotomized in this way. While education can make a contribution to the achievement of social equity and a more democratic society, it cannot of itself achieve such goals. Education cannot be too closely tied to economic considerations or separated from them. Education is much broader. It is inextricably linked to social, cultural, moral, and intellectual development. Education in most societies is identified with people's hope for change. A country's education system and the curriculum and organization of its schools should reflect all these interests. Therefore, as Graham-Brown (1991) suggests, "It is not only a question of assessing the economic demand for particular skills, but also of questioning the society's assumptions about both work and educational achievement" (p. 279).

Clearly then, decision making about reform of the school curriculum in developing countries, particularly in small states, is not easy. There is often a wide gap between statements about the aims and objectives of education and the application of these aims in the school curriculum. There has been a great deal of rhetoric in the developing world over the introduction of technical-vocational education with little practical results to show. In one Caribbean state, there have been many recent studies by foreign consultants on the need for technical-vocational education and many recommendations have been made. Yet another study has been planned and is, in fact, being carried out. Today, the curriculum has remained virtually unchanged and there is hardly any provision for the training of teachers in the field.

CONCLUSIONS

This chapter has examined a number of dilemmas in developing small states. It was not intended to be exhaustive, but the hope was that it would serve to provide some insights into and raise questions about the peculiar situation of small developing states. This section of the chapter will attempt to draw out a few implications and make some suggestions that might provide useful guidelines for the way ahead.

It should be clear that the training of administrators in small developing states is crucial and cannot be left to chance. People who operate within these dilemma-ridden, multifunctional contexts cannot be promoted primarily on experience or seniority. It must be obvious, too, that the traditional approaches to the training of administrators in the developed world, with different values, experiences, and constraints, is unsuited to the needs of the small developing states. How can training from a totally different philosophical orientation, in a technologically advanced setting, with different interpersonal relationships be used to train people for other contexts? Consider the findings of some researchers on this question: "This research demonstrates that cultural factors affect organisational processes in ways that render universalist statements of the effects of organizational structures on individuals seriously deficient. Organizational structures may be loosely coupled to formal goals but they are closely tied to the social and cultural orientations of the people involved in them" (Lincoln, Hanada, & Olson, 1981: 114).

In general, each time the environment is involved, the theory developed for Western settings does not apply, because it assumes contingencies that may not be valid for developing countries (Kiggundu, Jorgensen, & Hatsi, 1983: 81).

A further problem, of course, is that, even when the training is not done in the metropolitan country, the books, materials, and theories are still imported from them. What is needed is the collaboration of colleagues across the cultures to develop practice-oriented theories, texts, and materials suited to the needs of the developing states. Such a collaborative effort would require that educational experts — planners, administrators, philosophers, and practitioners — from the developed and the developing world, work together as equals in research activities, seminars, and other professional ventures. Opportunities should be provided for the movement of academic and practitioner scholars in both directions for professional activities. Frank and open communication in an atmosphere of mutual respect and good interpersonal relationships would be of paramount importance. Associations, such as the Commonwealth Council for Educational Administration and its partners and affiliates, and programs like the International Intervisitation Programme already make a tremendous contribution in this regard. Perhaps an attempt should be made through these existing channels to formalize an arrangement that would allow a more continuous and sharply focused set of activities in this direction.

The reality of multifunctionality demands that training be broad based and provide insights and understandings in a wide range of activity. It should be problem based and practice oriented and the explorations of values and valuing should play an important role.

The simple process of living and working in small transparent societies emphasizes the importance of understanding and practicing good interpersonal and communication skills and the necessity of understanding the political process. These should, therefore, feature significantly in training programs in educational administration.

Superior officers must be taught to understand the value of empowering and involving their professional subordinate staff. This serves the best interests of the individual, the institution, and the community and ensures that the best use is made of expertise that is often limited. This is particularly important in schools and other educational institutions. Strong school leadership is often equated with control and the disenfranchisement of teachers by principals. It has been observed that the distribution of authority does not necessarily diminish principal authority nor does supervision necessarily diminish teacher authority.

It is considered that, in poor countries, higher education is elitist and benefits only a very small part of the population. This, together with the fact that costs per student are high, is used as an argument, especially with respect to small states, to concentrate funds into basic rather than higher education. However, it must be borne in mind that access to higher education is an important aspiration in developing countries and "no nation can be truly autonomous unless it has its own autonomous cultural and educational institutions" (Graham-Brown, 1989: 278). Graham-Brown further argues that all countries, even the most underdeveloped, need an appropriate pool of highly skilled people and a locus for critical analysis of their history, economy, and society. Indeed, if societies in the developing world are to design their own models of development rather than continue to copy models from the developed world, their own higher education institutions must be the cradles where curricula can reflect histories, traditions, and cultural values appropriate to their own societies. Regional cooperation of states similarly placed may, indeed, provide a workable alternative to undue dependence or excessive expenditure.

ACKNOWLEDGMENT

The author thanks his postgraduate students who contributed to some of the thinking in this paper: Vere Parris, Keith Glasglow, Carolyn Sinckler, and Bonita Thompson.

II

SOCIETAL AND ETHICAL DILEMMAS IN SCHOOL ADMINISTRATION

4

Administering for Diversity: Dilemmas in Multiethnic Schools

James Ryan and Rouleen Wignall

Over the past century educators and policy makers in North America, Britain, and elsewhere have responded to student ethnocultural diversity in a number of ways. Some have employed a melting pot metaphor to guide their actions while others have followed a mosaic model. In the earlier part of the century, however, policy and practice were dominated by assimilationist ideologies. School systems overtly encouraged students to relinquish their own cultural heritages and embrace the dominant Euro-Western ways (Barman, Hebart, & McCaskill, 1986; Sutherland, 1976). In more recent times, however, many of those responsible for the education of both young and old have abandoned this direction in favor of what is typically referred to as multicultural education.

Generally speaking, the various models of multicultural education (Gibson, 1976; Sleeter, 1989) differ from assimilationist education in a number of ways. In contrast to assimilation, most multicultural approaches value diversity. One popular variant, for example, displays this value by attempting to reflect the diverse cultural backgrounds of the community in the school environment, curriculum, and pedagogical practices, and by promoting an awareness and understanding of various cultural groups (Banks, 1981; Bullivant, 1981; Gibson, 1976). Central here is the concept of understanding. According to this model "schools should be oriented toward the cultural enrichment of all students, that the multicultural education programs will provide such enrichment by fostering under-standing and acceptance of cultural differences and that these programs will in turn decrease racism and prejudice and increase social justice" (Gibson, 1976: 9).

Among other things, those who support multicultural approaches assume that learning about other cultures will reduce students' prejudice and discrimination toward those from different cultural and ethnic backgrounds (Bullivant, 1981). Recently, however, scholars have identified a number of shortcomings in the multicultural approach (McCarthy, 1988; Olneck, 1990; Troyna, 1993). Troyna (1993) and Bullivant (1986), for example, maintain that "cultural understanding" does little to reduce racism and fails to address the wider structural realities that limit the life chances of many minority students. A number of educators and policy makers have taken these criticisms seriously. The Ontario Ministry of Education and Training (1992, 1993), for example, acknowledges that systemic inequities of power and privilege generate inequities in the treatment of members of some cultures and races. Removing these barriers to achievement, then, requires more than understanding; it requires changes in current policies, procedures, and practices — changes that the ministry decrees must occur by 1995.

Despite this move beyond the cultural understanding model, individual school administrators facing challenges of diversity are likely to find themselves devoting considerable time to their attempts to understand the culture of groups about which they know little. This may be particularly true in schools that serve 50 or more ethnocultural groups, as is the case in some areas of Ontario. Although these efforts of administrators will have little to do with altering structural inequities, they frequently constitute an unavoidable and sometimes important part of their roles.

This chapter describes the experiences of two administrators as they encounter dilemmas that involve cultural beliefs and understandings that differ from their own.[1] First, we describe the elements of these two situations. Second, we draw the reader's attention to the current context for education. In particular, we outline the growing ethnocultural population both in Canada and in Canadian schools. We also describe the local context for particular schools in which moves are being made to develop antiracist policies. Next, we illustrate, with special reference to specific cases, the efforts of two administrators as they come to terms with the dilemmas they face as administrators of schools with ethnocultural[2] school populations. Finally, we discuss the limitations of understanding in addressing the challenges of administering schools with diverse ethnocultural student populations.

TWO DILEMMAS

In the day-to-day management of schools with diverse ethnocultural populations, administrators are likely to encounter situations that perplex them in various ways. Barbara and Joan are administrators who face such dilemmas in Ontario schools. Their quandaries are typical of the predicaments described by administrators we interviewed in the course of our ongoing research on principals' problem solving and ethnoculturally diverse schools (Ryan & Wignall, in progress). As they grapple with their dilemmas, administrators are limited by their own life histories and ideological frameworks. Even though they attempt to understand the meaning of these situations for all involved, they are caught within their own limited world views, which are in many respects culturally imposed. In the following paragraphs we present details of two selected dilemmas. Only after presenting these experiences do we begin our analysis.

Barbara's Predicament

Barbara stood as her five guests were ushered into her office. She had expected four of them and was somewhat surprised to see the fifth. Barbara recognized this additional guest, in spite of a black veil partially hiding her face, as the teenage daughter of one of the couples. Barbara was quite surprised to see the girl, because she had been told that the young woman had returned to India last week to care for her ailing grandmother. In her third month as an administrator in South Haven School, Barbara was already accustomed to these sorts of surprises. Even so, she realized that she had much to learn about, and from, the many ethnocultural groups that were represented at this suburban secondary school. Barbara knew immediately that this encounter was about to provide one of those learning occasions.

The group hesitated as they entered the office, apparently a little uncomfortable with what was to come. Barbara tried to put them at ease, offering them seats and coffee. They seated themselves quickly, but respectfully declined the beverage, as Barbara knew they would. The two families, one Muslim, the other Hindu, were from strict religious communities. Both of these communities had, by Canadian standards, rigid codes of behavior for their teenage daughters. Community norms dictated that young women not consort with members of the opposite sex. Among other things, they were forbidden to touch potential husbands or to make any sort of eye contact with them. Dating was out of the question; marriages were always arranged by the parents.

One of the fathers spoke first. Barbara could tell by the strain in his voice that he regarded this matter as extremely serious. In hesitant tones he explained to Barbara that, over the past week, his family had received four phone calls from a young man who claimed that his daughter had been dating young men, skipping classes, and "doing this and doing that." The other family had received two similar phone calls. Despite vigorous denials from the two young women, both families viewed their problem as extremely serious. In fact, the young women's denials were quite beside the point. Apparently, if news of their daughters' indiscretions spread — whether it be fact or fiction — the young women would be seen as unmarriageable in the community. So concerned were the parents about confidentiality in the matter that they insisted that no translators be present at the meeting and that the matter not be discussed beyond the office walls. They believed such talk could sabotage their daughters' chances at marriage and they wanted it stopped at once. In the end, the father of one young woman, who sat silently with her head bowed, threatened to take the matter to the board if Barbara could not solve the problem herself. This was no simple or straightforward problem for Barbara, particularly because she did not approve of gender-related beliefs that tend to subjugate women.

Joan's Quandary

Across town, Joan was experiencing another kind of dilemma. Although the specific details were substantially different from Barbara's experience, the situation also involved an encounter with a group who did not share the beliefs and understandings of many Canadian educators. Not long ago, Joan was appointed principal of a new school. In the first few weeks she was delighted with the warm welcome that the community gave to her and her colleagues. One of the many community members who stopped in to greet her was the father of a First Nations student at the school. He brought with him a gift of sweetgrass. While Joan sincerely appreciated the gesture, she did not completely understand the significance of the gift and so she asked the man about it. He responded to her first question by telling her that, if hung on the inside of the school wall facing east and blessed by an elder, the sweetgrass would protect the school from evil spirits and bring good fortune. Wanting to know more, Joan then inquired into the history of the tradition. Her visitor's response to this second question, however, took her completely by surprise. Instead of answering he became, in Joan's words, "agitated, very agitated." She confessed that, at the time, she was completely bewildered by his behavior. The man left a short time later, leaving Joan uneasy about the encounter, and particularly disappointed because the man had come in good faith but had left in anger. Joan was most uncomfortable, however, because she had no idea why he had left in such a state.

Unwilling to let things hang, Joan pursued the matter further. She contacted the man and he agreed to meet with her. At the meeting, he explained to her that he had perceived her inquiries as a questioning of his gesture, and he told her, "In my culture you do not question gifts." Joan explained that her intent was not to question the gift but rather to understand the custom. "My intent was genuinely one of wanting to understand the custom. I always have this need of knowing why, it doesn't matter whether it's technology or culture or whatever." When the man left the second time Joan felt that she still was not much wiser, even though she now understood that, in his culture, gifts are not to be questioned. She now faced a perplexing dilemma. She wanted to learn more about aboriginal beliefs so that in the future she would be able to respond in appropriate ways. However, if she attempted to learn more, she also risked offending the gentleman once again. Joan continued to wonder: "When is it okay to ask something? How do you know it's okay to ask?" But even as she asked, Joan was bewildered about how she could go about finding answers to her questions.

THE CHANGING FACES OF
OUR STUDENT POPULATION

The above dilemmas are by no means unique to administrators in Central Ontario. Indeed, many administrators in North America are likely to face similar situations on a daily basis. The composition of the student population in North American schools is currently changing, and these changes are affecting school administration. No longer do young people of western and northern European heritage constitute the majority in many schools. Moreover, where a European majority remains, many students with other ethnocultural backgrounds typically attend the school. This changing school population reflects changes in the larger North American population. Immigration patterns have, to a large degree, accounted for these changes. In Canada, for example, patterns changed substantially following the adjustment in immigration policy in the 1960s. Until this point, discriminatory immigration practices made it difficult for non-Europeans to enter the country. From 1913 to 1957, for example, the United Kingdom accounted for 37 percent of all immigrants (Statistics Canada, 1993). By 1974, however, these numbers had changed. At that time immigrants from the United Kingdom comprised 17.6 percent of the total immigrant population while such places as India, Hong Kong, Jamaica, and the Philippines accounted for 5.8, 5.8, 5.1, and 4.3 percent, respectively (Statistics Canada, 1993). The next two decades brought yet more change. By 1989, Asian immigrants outnumbered Europeans by almost two to one, with 94,645 immigrating from Asia, 50,725 from Europe, and only 7,045 from Great Britain (Statistics Canada, 1990). In 1991, the largest group of immigrants came from Hong Kong (9.7 percent), followed by Poland (6.8 percent), China (6.0 percent), and India (5.6 percent). Other immigrants reported such countries as the Philippines, Lebanon, Vietnam, El Salvador, Sri Lanka, Guyana, Iran, Greece, and Italy as their place of origin. At the same time, the United Kingdom only accounted for 3.3 percent of Canada's immigrant population in 1991 (Statistics Canada, 1993). Typically, immigrants settle in urban areas. In 1991, for example, immigrants accounted for a large proportion in major cities: Toronto, 38 percent; Vancouver, 30 percent; Hamilton, 24 percent; and Kitchener, 22 percent (Statistics Canada, 1993). Immigrants, however, do not constitute all of Canada's ethnocultural population. For example, in 1989, Ontario included 167,375 and 108,710 people of aboriginal and African heritage, respectively, who were born in Canada (Statistics Canada, 1990).

The immigrant population by itself is producing major demographic changes in school populations. Data gathered from one Toronto school district in 1988 indicate that one-third of the total school-day population and two-thirds of the mothers of this same student population were born outside of Canada (Handscombe, 1989). The Ontario Ministry of Education and Training (1993) indicates that nearly 70 percent of all foreign-born immigrant youth live in greater Toronto, over half are of single non-European ethnicity, two-thirds are visible minorities, 50 percent have a mother tongue that is neither French nor English, and one-third arrived in Canada since 1981. The age of immigrants is also significant — many of them are either of school or childbearing age. In 1987, 28 percent (42,970) of the total immigrant population were 19 years of age or younger, while 50 percent (76,834) were between the ages of 20 and 39 (Statistics Canada, 1990). This age distribution, coupled with a generally high immigrant fertility rate (Kellogg, 1988), points to a future in which the ethnocultural student population will continue to increase at an even more rapid rate.

ETHNOCULTURAL EQUITY AND ANTIRACIST EDUCATION

This changing demography presents educators, such as Barbara and Joan, with new challenges. Many of these arise because newer students often bring to school different experiences, values, and understandings than those that educators have traditionally expected of students. These differences may be reflected in conceptions of, beliefs in, and practices associated with, patterns of language and communication (Corson, 1992; Erickson & Mohatt, 1982; Philips, 1983), teaching and learning styles (Appleton, 1983; Cazden &, Leggett, 1981; Ramirez, 1989; Ryan, 1992a), testing (Deyhle, 1983, 1986); cognitive processing (Cole & Scribner, 1973; Das, Kirby, & Jarman, 1979; Gay & Cole, 1967; Tharp, 1989), self-concept (Clifton, 1975), family traditions and commitments (Divoky, 1988; Gibson, 1987; Olson, 1988), locus of control (Tyler & Holsinger, 1975; Zenter, 1971), attitudes toward cooperation and competition (Clifton, 1975; Goldman & McDermott, 1987; Ryan, 1992b), aspirations (Gue, 1975; Grygier, 1977), and space and time (Clifton, 1977; Ryan, 1991). While educators and social scientists may disagree over the precise ways in which differences between the dominant Euro-Canadian tradition and other traditions play themselves out in schools and classrooms (see for example, Erickson, 1987; Ogbu, 1987; Trueba, 1988), most agree that these differences contribute to problems for both ethnocultural students and the educators responsible for their education.

One response to the difficulties associated with cultural differences has been to view these differences as deficits for which the school must compensate. Such an approach typically reinforces and sustains the marginalization of minorities. A more equitable approach has been the initiation of antiracist education. The Province of Ontario, for example, where both Barbara and Joan administer schools, has declared that all school districts must develop antiracist and ethnocultural equity policies for their schools (The Ontario Ministry of Education and Training, 1993). By 1995, all districts are expected to have policies and practices in place that address leadership, school community relationships, language, curriculum, assessment, counseling, harassment, and staff development issues. These moves are based on a recognition that "Ontario's education system has been primarily Western European in content and perspective, reflecting the original patterns of settlement in the province" (The Ontario Ministry of Education and Training, 1992: 2). These Western European schooling practices, in turn, act as barriers that often prevent students of other cultural heritages from developing their individual potential. Unfamiliar patterns of classroom interaction or subject matter that either ignores or devalues (implicitly or explicitly) certain heritages, often penalizes students who are not of the majority culture. Antiracist education begins by acknowledging that some "existing policies, procedures, and practices in the school system are racist in their impact, if not their intention" (The Ontario Ministry of Education and Training, 1993: 5). Such education seeks to correct past biases at the system, school, and classroom level. From this perspective, educators must "recognize how discrimination, distortions and omissions occur . . . [and take steps] to correct distortions and remedy omissions and discriminatory conditions" (The Ontario Ministry of Education and Training, 1992: 2).

Both Barbara's and Joan's school districts have adopted antiracist education, developing antiracist and ethnocultural equity policies well before most other districts in the province. Quite beyond this institutional assurance, both Barbara and Joan are personally committed to a philosophy of equity. Both believe schools have an obligation to accommodate the various cultural practices and beliefs of the schools' client groups and eliminate subject matter or schooling practices that denigrate, devalue, or discriminate against particular groups of students and their families. Barbara, for example, explains that "we are a multicultural nation. It's not a melting pot. We're a mosaic and we have to accommodate as much as we possibly can."

Joan also actively promotes diversity in her school. She goes out of her way to include the community in school activities, to sensitize teachers to the complexities of diversity, to encourage teachers to critically scrutinize curriculum and reading materials, and generally to make life in school more comfortable for all students. Such initiatives can be complex, even paradoxical. Indeed, there are situations, as we have seen, where ethnocultural equity may conflict with other deeply held beliefs about other kinds of equity, or where attempts to achieve an understanding may be frustrated by the very efforts made to attain it.

DEALING WITH ADMINISTRATIVE DILEMMAS

How do administrators handle these challenges of ethnocultural diversity? What initiatives can they take to promote equity in their schools? In the cases at hand, how did Barbara and Joan deal with their own dilemmas? Let us first consider Barbara's experience. Asked what she does in situations like the one described above, she replied: "You fly by the seat of your pants, you really do. And you . . . get information." Flying by the seat of one's pants is not something unique to Barbara. In fact, many of the administrators we talked to approach these challenges in much the same way. Barbara and other administrators do so because, with few exceptions, they have little experience in similar situations. They are generally unable to rely either on their personal experience or on conventional wisdom in administration to work their way through the challenge; they are often confronted by understandings and beliefs that they do not totally comprehend. Therefore, in many of these cases, a first step in addressing the situation is to understand. To do so, administrators need to acquire information about the particular ethnocultural group in question and the circumstances surrounding the situation in question.

ETHNOCULTURAL AND GENDER EQUITY

Barbara conducted what she described as her research both before and after her meeting with the parents. Because she had a general sense of the issue in advance, she was able to consult a number of sources and use the information as she prepared for the meeting. Barbara approached several teachers and students and spoke with a board consultant. From the students and teachers she learned details of the specific situation and developed a general overview of the religious sects in question. The consultant, on the other hand, supplied her with further details about the practices of the particular sects. On the basis of this information, Barbara was able to establish that the callers were in all probability young suitors who had been rejected by the daughters of the two families. The calls were, in her estimation, acts of retribution. These young men apparently knew "how to press the fathers' buttons" and did so with the intention of retaliating against the girls. Barbara also learned more about the particular religious groups, and this knowledge was subsequently confirmed in her meeting with the parents. While the parents were obviously concerned with the actual behavior of their daughters, they were apparently even more concerned about the impression left with their communities. If word spread about their daughters' indiscretions, these parents would have little or no chance of arranging marriages for them. In other words, the parents' priority was to save face in their communities. When it came time to meet the parents, Barbara felt she knew exactly what the parents were talking about. In her own words, Barbara recalls her efforts to understand the situation: "I hastened to understand their perspective. And I did. I did understand that it had little to do with the girl, that it had a lot to do with her reputation. So now we know what we're talking about. And if these boys do not stop these phone calls, these girls could have to go back to India because there is a chance that the community will know."

Barbara's understanding helped her resolve this dilemma, at least on a temporary basis. The resolution, however, allowed her to avoid what she believed to be a central issue in this dilemma — conflicting equity prerogatives. On the one hand, Barbara, her school, and her school district are committed to ethnocultural and gender equity. On the other hand, however, Barbara perceived that the particular religious groups hold strong patriarchal values and beliefs. To fully accommodate the wishes and beliefs of these sects, Barbara and her school would have to violate their commitment to gender equity, or so it appeared. Barbara herself is a strong advocate of gender equity, and while she makes every effort to acknowledge and respect beliefs of all cultural groups, she readily admits that she finds these gender-related practices personally offensive. In this case, the actions of the parents, in particular the father, made her "sad" and "enraged." She had particular difficulty with what she perceived to be the relationships of the fathers to the mothers and daughters and the kinds of restrictions that were placed on the women. Indeed, Barbara was upset by the way that one mother apparently deferred to the father rather than standing up for the daughter, and by the father's lack of trust in the young woman. She also objected to the fact that these young women were not permitted to mix freely with other students in the way that most other students were. She freely admitted wanting, at one point, to "crunch this little man." Referring to one of the girls, Barbara maintained that "this is a 14-year-old girl. She just turned 14. She's just a kid." In the end, however, Barbara felt that it was her responsibility to emphasize the commitment to gender equity to the parents. She explained: "I think my responsibility is to reiterate to the parents what Ontario public schools are all about and to let them know we believe in gender equity and let them know we encourage boys and girls in different cultures to mix." Barbara bluntly admits that when it comes right down to it, she sometimes takes a stand against particular ethnocultural values that contradict the ones that she favors, however difficult taking such a stance may be. She explains directly that:

When you're not accommodating you feel somehow you've failed, because we are a multicultural nation. . . . We're a mosaic and we have to accommodate as much as we can. It really does hurt not to be able to do that. And in some cases you want to take a stand. [But] I can't accommodate that kind of abuse of young women. It would be the same thing if I found out a young girl was to undergo circumcision. . . . I couldn't stand it. I wouldn't give a damn about their culture or what they believe is important. There comes a point where you have to say: "This is wrong, you're in Canada now."

How, then, does Barbara reconcile her personal beliefs with the wishes of the parents in her office? Is it possible for her to satisfy the parents without compromising her deeply held beliefs? To achieve her goal, Barbara took two separate tacks. First, she reiterated her philosophy about gender-related freedoms to the parents in their meeting. "Our major concern in school," she maintained, "is the academic progress of your daughter, as well as her physical growth and well-being. And we encourage girls and boys to talk together." Anticipating pleas from the parents to isolate her daughter, she went on to tell them she "could not make false promises. There [are] 2,000 kids in the school and I certainly can't walk around after their daughters and make sure they don't talk to anybody." The parents claimed they understood, but they still wanted to ensure that their daughters acted appropriately and to prevent any talk about their alleged indiscretions.

Barbara also took other measures for her own peace of mind. First, she kept from the parents much of what she knew of their daughters' activities at school. These young women, like many others in their situation, according to Barbara, take advantage of their new-found freedom. She maintains: "What I perceive when I walk around the halls are these girls who are absolutely going wild as a result of the strict behavior they have to maintain at home. And they're flirting like crazy with these boys and they're kissing each other and throwing snow at each other and rolling on the ground. And I know if their fathers saw them, they'd be flogged. I know that. And here I was sitting there with [this] knowledge. . . . And you know, it's a terrible thing to know."

Barbara chose not to reveal these details to the parents. Doing so, she obviously felt, would compromise her personal belief that these young women had the right to partake in certain interactions, not to mention the harsh punishment she felt would be forthcoming were their habits discovered. Barbara was also engaged in what she referred to as "a conspiracy" with the two girls in question, albeit after the fact. In the course of a conversation with one of the multicultural assessment officers in the school district, the woman offered to consult with the young women. Desperately wanting someone to talk to about their situations, both jumped at the chance. Barbara was well aware that their parents would not approve, but felt it was the least she could do to assist these young women with the injustices she believed were being perpetrated against them.

How did Barbara placate the parents? For her, a key was in her understanding that the parents were first and foremost concerned with stifling rumors about their daughters. For this reason, Barbara concentrated on issues associated with the circulation and curtailment of information rather than on the behavior of the young women. In the meeting she told the parents about what she believed to be the origin and reason for the phone calls. She also took care to attribute the improprieties to the boys and not to their daughters. Barbara stated: "I did suggest . . . to the parents that their buttons were being pushed [and that] perhaps they could consider changing their phone numbers, [or] perhaps they could consider hanging up. But I let it be known that I was much more annoyed with the activities of these boys than I was with what the girls were doing."

She did not, however, ignore policing measures. Acknowledging that she could not ensure conformity to the parents' rules, Barbara suggested that one of the mothers, who had a master's degree in mathematics, could tutor in the learning center at the school. In this way, she would be able to supervise her daughter during the lunch hour. The woman seemed very interested but ultimately declined because she had to care for her four-year-old at home. In the end Barbara believed that the parents left the meeting "happy," apparently satisfied that she was doing all she could to help them out. The parents seemed now to understand more about the disturbing calls they were getting — that it wasn't necessarily their daughters' indiscretions that were prompting these. Most importantly, they seemed to believe that the calls did not necessarily mean that they would lose face in their communities or that they would have to send their daughters back to India to ensure their marriages.

DIFFICULTIES IN UNDERSTANDING

Like Barbara, Joan places a high value on understanding other cultural perspectives. Among other things, she believes that understanding can prevent the type of stereotyping that can be so harmful to many individuals and groups. Joan says: "I think that a lot of the stereotypes come about because we don't understand. And it's that fear or that ignorance that creates negative stereotypes." She also believes that the key to understanding revolves around the collection of information. For her, understanding is very much an empirical enterprise. Joan has initiated a number of strategies to gather information, including sending out questionnaires and highlighting different cultural heritages within the school. She elaborates:

Other cultures were brought in. Information was brought in through that. We initially celebrated things like, you know, let's find out where we're from. "Where did you come from? What school did you come from?" And now let's take it a step further. "Where were you born? Were you born in Canada? If not in Canada, let's find it on the globe, let's locate it on the map. What language do you speak?" Some of the typical things that probably a lot of schools do. Beyond that, through our "emergency" form that goes home at the beginning of the year, we also made parents aware that if they had any information that they wanted to share with us about their family life, about customs, to please feel free and come in.

Joan's data collection strategy, however, as we have seen in this particular case, proved to be insufficient to cope with the situation. Ironically, the strategy itself proved to be part of the problem. Indeed, Joan admitted that her previous knowledge of First Nations people — obtained largely through university courses — left her with the faulty impression that she had an adequate grasp of First Nations issues and cultural practices. But as she subsequently recognized, "a little knowledge can be a dangerous thing." Thus, when the man made his initial exit, Joan was completely bewildered. While she learned a little more during his second visit, she was then unsure how to learn more, as was her customary strategy in these cases. Certainly, direct questioning of the man was simply out of the question. At this point she called on the race relations officer at the central office and discussed the issue with another consultant as well. These discussions proved to be most helpful, and through them Joan began gradually to understand some of the conventions surrounding the prerogatives of individual men and women and intrusive behavior among this particular group of First Nations people (see, for example, Ryan, 1992b). Even so, Joan admitted that she was still far from a thorough understanding in this case. Fortunately for her, the father was also dissatisfied with the current state of their relationship and decided to do something about it. As Joan tells it: "The gentleman must have thought about it as well, because he came back a long time later with two pieces of photocopied material on sweetgrass. Because the other thing I learned from that is that it's never written down, that the only person who could tell me that would be an elder. Well, he went and spoke to an elder and explained to him and I guess they said it was okay to give us some information."

In the end, Joan felt that she had made some progress. She understood a little more about her intrusive behavior, and her relationship with the man had improved to a point. However, Joan admitted she still had no answer to her central problem — how to learn more about such practices so that she could understand them and, thus, act in more appropriate ways when she was apparently not permitted to ask questions. She still had no answer to her question, a question she posed to the parent a number of times in their last meeting. Joan recounts: "I said to him, you know, 'Tell me, then' — I guess I said that 41 times — 'Tell me, how can I understand and how can I ensure that I treat someone the way they would like to be treated when I now feel that I can't ask any questions?'"

THE LIMITS OF UNDERSTANDING

Despite the apparent move away from a model that highlights understanding other cultural practices and beliefs, school administrators like Barbara and Joan may find themselves devoting considerable effort as they attempt to understand ethnocultural lifeways that differ from their own. Routine activities, such as accommodating the wishes of parents, satisfying their concerns or demands, or solving a problem unique to a particular ethnocultural group, demand that administrators grasp the situation and, therefore, understand the perspectives of various participants. What does understanding entail? What, for example, do Barbara and Joan mean when they refer to understanding? Does this differ from the processes of understanding in which each of us engages in our day-to-day activities? Schutz (1967) provides us with insight here.

For Schutz, understanding occurs in the course of making sense of our own experience. As we "get on" with our lives, we routinely attribute meaning to our daily experiences. In other words, understanding is a matter of interpreting the world we experience in order to decide on future courses of action. Doing so often requires that we come to terms with the meanings that others attribute to situations. This does not mean, Schutz contends, that we interpret experiences of others. Rather, we simply reinterpret our own experiences. We appeal to our own experience and knowledge and not to the minds of others, integrating what we perceive into our own pre-existing frames of reference and the particular life patterns with which we are familiar. As part of this process, we attempt to come to terms with what Schutz (1967) refers to as the "because" and the "in order to" motives of others. Understanding in this sense involves knowing why people are doing what they do — determining what caused them to act in certain ways and what they intended to do in the circumstances. For both Barbara and Joan, understanding involves making sense of the motives of others. They are able to do so, however, only within their own frames of reference. Sense is acquired when their perceptions correspond to, or are integrated into, familiar patterns of interaction. This is not to say that understanding is exclusively a personal or individual process. Rather, it always takes place in a social and cultural context that generates constraints and possibilities for the ways in which particular situations can be understood. In other words, men and women draw on resources that are provided by such phenomena as discourses and institutional arrangements, for example, to make sense of what they perceive. In the final analysis, Barbara and Joan can be said to understand a situation or a way of life if and when they are in a position to make predictions about the future behavior of individual men and women. They are only able to do so, however, by appealing to their cultural frames of reference.

This process, of course, is not unique to Barbara and Joan. All human beings are engaged in interpretative work of one sort or another. Every situation encountered demands interpretation. Men and women in administrative positions draw upon their experience and their current knowledge as they attempt to make sense of what they encounter (Wignall, 1992). Thus, novel and well-known experiences are integrated into familiar patterns and acted on accordingly. Well-known experiences, naturally, are less demanding than the novel ones. Here people fit familiar patterns easily into well-established typifications or categories. The process breaks down, however, when elements of new experiences cannot be integrated into these patterns. Such was the case with Joan's encounter. She simply could not make sense of the man's actions or his attitude toward questioning. Her usual tactic of gathering data was not possible in this case because she was unable to ask the man himself. In fact, her attempt at data gathering proved to be part of the problem. In the end Joan was unable to understand the man's motives. She could not comprehend what propelled him to do certain things — and perhaps, more importantly, she could not predict how he would respond to her conciliatory gestures.

Barbara, on the other hand, was somewhat more successful in making sense of her guests' motives. Her research proved to be helpful in this regard. It unearthed key details that enabled her to connect their motives to one with which she was most familiar: saving face. This connection made it possible for Barbara to anticipate their reactions to her tactics, and in the end the parents left her office happy. However, understanding in this case did not engender acceptance of the practice, as one model of multicultural education would have us believe. On the contrary, Barbara's understanding of the sect's religious beliefs, in particular those concerning saving face and marriage, repulsed her. She was particularly offended with what she regarded as the parents' apparent lack of regard for their daughters, displayed by their exclusive concern with saving face in the community, their unwillingness to accept the daughters' word, and the obsessive restrictions that they placed on the daughters' behavior. But because she believed she understood where they were coming from, she was able to satisfy their concerns without sacrificing her own beliefs about gender equity.

There is also evidence, however, that Barbara, like Joan, did not completely understand the situation at hand. In particular, it appears she may not have understood the gender relationships among and between the mother, father, and daughter. Like everyone else, Barbara's perceptions are constrained by her Western cultural frame of reference that, according to Brah and Minhas (1985), is often guilty of propogating erroneous stereotypes about Asian girls and their relationship with their parents and the school. For example, they maintain that often the two different generations are presented as warring against each other with the adult generally depicted as authoritarian, uncompromising, and oppressive. They maintain that this, in fact, is not the case. Contrary to these stereotypes Brah and Minhas (1985) maintain that the majority of Asian girls have strong, positive, and mutually supportive relationships with their parents. Furthermore, the intergenerational conflict among Asian families is not any higher than among "white families." Because Barbara understood little about the private sphere of Asian family life and its dynamic and vibrant female cultures, she may well have jumped to conclusions about what she perceived to be injustices and acted accordingly.

CONCLUSION

It is clear from these two instances that the assumptions underlying the cultural understanding model of multicultural education hold little water. First of all, understanding other ethnocultural perspectives is not always easy — or, for that matter, possible. Despite valiant efforts, educators may never totally comprehend ethnocultural perspectives that differ radically from their own. Second, acquiring a reasonable understanding does not mean that the understood practice or belief will be embraced. In fact, quite the opposite may occur, as we saw in Barbara's case. Her understanding of the religious group's beliefs only reinforced her own different beliefs, prompting her to engage in covert activity. Whether other administrators will react in similar ways remains to be seen. Even so, as part of their roles administrators will likely have to devote substantial efforts to understanding different perspectives, particularly in schools that serve a wide range of ethnocultural groups. Many of their basic tasks, such as communicating with parents, community members, and students, require at least a rudimentary understanding of other ethnocultural perspectives. Although their efforts at understanding may do little to address the structural inequalities that find expression in our education system, they will continue to be an important part of the administrator's role.

NOTES

1.   The conversations we had with these administrators are part of a current study that explores the responses of administrators to cultural diversity in their schools. We acknowledge the Social Sciences and Humanities Research Council for its financial support of this project.

2.   We use the term "ethnocultural" here to refer, as Churchill & Kaprielian-Churchill (1991) do, to those students who are not of Anglo-Celtic heritage and to whom English may not be their first language.

5

Suspended Morality and the Denial of Ethics: How Value Relativism Muddles the Distinction between Right and Wrong in Administrative Decisions

Elizabeth Campbell

Within a society where objective right and wrong are viewed often as suspicious concepts, decision making leads to a host of dilemmas that are seemingly unresolvable on ethical grounds. Consequently, while questions of morality and ethics may be basic and straightforward, the implementation of right by inherently good-willed individuals, bogged down in contemporary organizational life, becomes a muddled exercise in value relativism and strategic decision making. Persistent dilemmas and choices are identified as practical, political, technical, and professional problems to be organized and managed rather than concerns that are rooted in fundamental moral and ethical principles (Campbell, 1992). Within the context of an increasingly relativistic and subjectivist world, the place of morals and ethics has grown obscure; because of value relativism, responsible ethical choices become a matter of chance, and, even in the most basic moral and ethical sense, right and wrong become issues of contention and debate.

The troublesome issue of persistency does not lie solely in the fact that moral and ethical dilemmas continually surface and present problems that must be dealt with on a case-by-case basis; such dilemmas may be recurring or, indeed, ongoing. Nonetheless, the real problem of persistency rests on the one dilemma that endures as the overarching dilemma that frames and enables all other dilemmas: simply, it is that we cannot, or will not, resolve the problem of defining right and wrong. How can we identify — let alone resolve — with any conviction and certainty daily moral and ethical dilemmas when the contemporary emotive tendency, reflective of value relativism, is to deny that right and wrong exist as objective governing principles?

Once we have lost the philosophical dedication to do what is right because we know it to be right, we are left to flounder in a confusion of questions that undermine, bit by bit, our lingering faith in justice, truth, courage, compassion, and other virtues that have stood for thousands of years, but now have become ridiculed, sneered at, attacked, and largely discarded. In dismissing what we have learned about ethics in both a positive and negative sense based on a tradition of moral philosophy and historical reflection, we have effectively abandoned the human quest for virtuous guidelines that point to fundamental goodness. Such a quest should be seen as an objective pursuit, not the self-serving attempt to impose values and wield power that relativism both condemns and, ironically, enables.

This central dilemma affects all individuals who grapple with daily choices in their personal and professional lives; however, the issue is addressed here as it influences educational administration. Following from a previous empirical study of ethical conflicts in schools (Campbell, 1992), this chapter has two objectives. The first is to explore the conceptual and philosophical question of defining right and wrong. The second is to relate this discussion to the administrator's responsibilities in modern educational organizations. Such concepts as suspended morality, false necessity, and compromise are examined as they typify administrative behavior.

THE PERSISTENT PROBLEM OF RIGHT AND WRONG

The assumption that right and wrong do indeed exist, not as subjective expressions of opinion and preference but as fundamental and objective concepts, raises contentious and conceptually thorny questions. Pertinent consideration of moral and ethical definitions and the ought-is and fact-value distinctions have been described as "among the most tangled controversies in philosophy" (Becker, 1973: 18), and "moral philosophy, as it is dominantly understood, reflects the debates and disagreements of the culture so faithfully that its controversies turn out to be unsettlable in just the way that the political and moral debates themselves are" (MacIntyre, 1981: 235). The area of moral and ethical conceptual theory is a vast one, spanning thousands of years of intellectual thought. It is certainly not the intention of this section to attempt to encapsulate this content. Nevertheless, it is useful to review definitions supported here and compare briefly differing theoretical approaches to morality and ethics.

While accepting that moral behavior implies "acting on a code that the individual has accepted as his own" (Peters, 1973: 24), one may assume that such a code should embody at least some element of universality. While an individual's perception of right and wrong may be a personal matter, morality must transcend mere preference driven solely by self-interest; moral persons would not justify their own behavior in ways that they would find unacceptable in others. Although some dismiss morals as mere "attitudes related to specific behaviors and actions" (Scott & Hart, 1979: 3), others rightly argue that moral claims "involve concepts such as right and wrong and express duties and obligations" (Strike, Haller, & Soltis, 1988: 37). Similarly, "that which is moral relates to principles of right conduct in behavior; the behavior conforms to accepted principles of what is considered right, virtuous, or just" (Rich, 1984: 122).

More or less synonymous with morals, ethics also concern principles of right and wrong in conduct. It has been noted that "the tendency to lump ethical judgments under the general class of value judgments and then to treat all value judgments alike is the source of much confusion about ethics" (Strike & Soltis, 1985: 9). Although morals and ethics are indeed part of the complex nature of values, it should be emphasized that not all values reflect right and wrong. Consequently, ethical standards of conduct should be distinguished from the "seductive notion that ethics merely describes the standards of behavior actually used by particular groups. Thus, the 'everybody-does-it' rationale carries no moral weight. Principles of honesty, fair play, compassion and respect, for example, transcend custom and practice" (Josephson, 1991: 52). In simple terms, values are "core beliefs which motivate our actions" (Josephson, 1990: 68). They may or may not relate to fundamental issues of right and wrong, morality and ethics.

How individuals, faced with moral and ethical dilemmas, interpret right and wrong may depend largely on their distinction between consequentialist and nonconsequentialist ethical theories. Consequentialist ethical theories maintain that the morality or immorality of an action relies solely on its consequences (Holmes, 1987: 43; Peters, 1966: 97; Strike, Haller, & Soltis, 1988; Strike & Soltis, 1985). These theories, closely related to the philosophical concept of utilitarianism (Beauchamp, Childress, & West, 1984; MacIntyre, 1981; Strike, Haller, & Soltis, 1988), gauge morality by that which produces the greatest benefit for the most people and is "capable of justifying immoral conduct in order to produce good consequences" (Strike & Soltis, 1985: 30). Certain aspects of this dark side of consequentialism support the claim that "no action is ever right or wrong as such. Anything whatsoever may under certain circumstances be permitted" (MacIntyre, 1981: 15). That the determinant of morality is not the action itself, but its consequences, is an appealing concept to moral relativists who shun the notion of absolute principles.

Nonconsequentialist ethical theories, on the other hand, maintain that an action is moral only if it is based on clearly defined moral principles

(Strike, Haller, & Soltis, 1988). Furthermore, nonconsequentialists "believe that the good life must be guided by fundamental principles such as truth, courage, justice, friendship and compassion" (Holmes, 1987: 43). The consequences, therefore, are not the decisive measure of morality. "Hence, if an action is objectively unjust, it cannot become moral because of good intentions or good consequences" (Ryan, 1988: 14).

One may agree that the optimal ethical theory "will embed a concern for consequences within a framework of nonconsequentialist ideals" (Strike & Soltis, 1985: 62); however, within schools, as in the larger society, individuals support both of these opposing ethical theories in different ways. Increasingly, the lure of provability behind outcomes (or consequences) combined with the moral uncertainty fostered by value relativism has rendered many either reluctant to take or incapable of justifying action solely on the basis of inherent ethical and moral principles (Campbell, 1992).

Those who regard questions of right and wrong from the perspective of value relativism deny the existence of any universal objective order or principles that define moral or ethical behavior. These values, like any other values of personal preference or opinion, are seen as being culturally or individually determined and can never be labeled "correct" in the way that a fact can be proven. Judgments regarding truth, goodness, and rightness, therefore, cannot be asserted from a fixed or absolute position; instead they are contingent upon numerous social variables pertinent only to the individual, group, or situation at hand.

Contemporary acceptance of relativism, defined by some as "modernity" (Holmes, 1984: 26), has been strongly influenced by the theories of Nietzsche, who believed that "what purported to be appeals to objectivity were in fact expressions of subjective will" (MacIntyre, 1981: 107), and Weber, who maintained that any value judgment is merely an expression of choice between human "goods" in general and, therefore, cannot be "reconciled in any single moral order" (MacIntyre, 1981: 133) as being either true or false. Hence, moral or ethical judgments are characterized as expressions of preference, feeling, attitude, or emotion.

This value perspective has been labeled the "emotive theory of ethics" (Peters, 1966: 110) or "emotivism" (MacIntyre, 1981). Emotivists extend their relativistic argument beyond the claim that moral judgments are nothing more than personal beliefs based on emotion; they further assert that because there can be "no valid rational justification for any claims that objective and impersonal moral standards exist" (MacIntyre, 1981: 18) there are, therefore, no such objective standards.

Such an assertion presents an ironic scenario for individuals who face choices and decisions in their personal and organizational lives. It acts as a liberating force for tyrants by providing them with the free license to oppress and manipulate, comforted by the knowledge that, because morality and ethics are not objective principles, their choices and actions may not be challenged easily. For moral individuals who strive to make good decisions, emotivism and associated relativistic beliefs enhance their dilemmas by blurring moral and ethical guidelines and muddling their confidence in virtue.

The distinction or separation of fact from value, advanced by both subjectivism *and* logical positivism, characterizes modern value relativism and has its origins, again, in the works of philosophers, such as Nietzsche, Heidegger, and, more particularly, Weber, who discussed the relativity of all values (Bloom, 1987: 150; Lovin, 1988: 145). This sharp distinction, which is quite alien to the theories advanced by classical Greek philosophers (Bloom, 1987: 154; MacIntyre, 1981: 79) and the intellectual inheritance of traditional moral philosophy, has been criticized for leading to an emotivist approach to values (Lovin, 1988) and morality (MacIntyre, 1981). Thus, lacking the criteria to evaluate right and wrong, one is forced to accept values that may be, in objective moral terms, unacceptable.

While one may acknowledge the relative and subjective nature of many individual, operational, and organizational values of preference, positivistic effectiveness, or efficiency, it is decidedly more difficult and ultimately unacceptable to apply similar emotive reasoning to fundamental issues of moral and ethical right and wrong. However, relativist theories do present, in part, a persuasive and appealing argument to those who value a tolerant and nondogmatic perspective on human interaction: clearly individuals do indeed have differing and often conflicting beliefs regarding social values, and personal righteousness based on one's subjective interpretation of the good is certainly not supported as virtuous behavior. Similarly, it is difficult to deny that values of preference, opinion, affect, and attitude that develop and shape social norms, customs, standards, and habits may be subjective reflections of individuals' or groups' interests.

However, to extend this perspective into the realm of the moral and the ethical and thereby equate principles of right and wrong with values of personal self-interest implies that even the most objectively appalling behavior can be justified under some circumstances. As mentioned, such an approach to values ultimately paralyzes any attempt on the part of individuals collectively to discern right from wrong and, thus, it renders moral and ethical concerns extraneous to the individual's pursuit of self gratification, a manipulative pursuit that may indeed be carried out at the expense of others.

Despite the dominant tendency in today's society to embrace value relativism and refute the notion of binding and consensual values that define ethics and morality, there are those who maintain the existence and relevancy of "fundamental beliefs about how human beings should treat each other" (Crittenden, 1984: 16). These beliefs may reflect core values identified as honesty, integrity, fairness, caring, and respect for others (Josephson, 1990: 68); such moral and ethical values are argued to be generally recognizable and capable of being upheld objectively.

Consequently, the ethical objectivist, in contrast to the relativist, the emotivist, the logical positivist, the consequentialist, and the utilitarian, believes that "there is a set of moral principles that are universally valid as standards of judgment. . . . Moral systems consist of beliefs and convictions about what is right and good in an ultimate as opposed to a technical, practical, or instrumental sense (Hatch, 1983: 8).

Following in part from MacIntyre's neo-Aristotelian discussion of an objective moral order, traditionalism articulates a belief in the human inheritance of moral and ethical principles of fundamental and basic objective value. Although no positivist or scientific criterion exists to prove the objective truth of traditionalist thought, the continuity and history of human development provide evidence that right and wrong, good and evil do exist not merely as subjective and relative expressions of individual belief or collective fashion but as truths that both connect and transcend individuals, cultures, and civilizations.

As a contemporary advocate of traditionalism in education, Holmes distinguishes between traditionalist theory and other paradigmatic positions. He writes, "the positivist believes patterns of behaviour in organizations can be predicted from an understanding of objectively determined variables. The subjectivist believes individuals manufacture their own truth. The traditionalist believes truth exists and must be deliberately developed and asserted" (Holmes, 1986: 43). Knowledge of such truth is drawn from the "best wisdom of our traditional cultural adherents . . . (and truth) is both known, if imperfectly, and emergent" (Holmes, 1991: 8). Reliance on the traditional concept of virtue, unreliable as it occasionally may be, provides a guide from which to judge and measure the moral and ethical adequacy of social and organizational life.

Institutions — and schools may certainly be classified as such — are "characteristically and necessarily concerned with external goods. . . . In this context, the essential function of the virtues is clear. Without them, without justice, courage and truthfulness, practices could not resist the corrupting power of institutions" (MacIntyre, 1981: 181). Despite his relativism, Hodgkinson (1978) expresses a similar warning and notes that "outwardly benevolent organizations can become latent collective forces for evil" (Hodgkinson, 1978: 173). Modern emotivism and moral and ethical relativism have not necessarily created this evil, but evil grows freely in circumstances where it is not challenged and checked.

Within schools, the relativist administrator becomes "concerned with how efficiently to accomplish pre-identified goals. Such individuals quickly become manipulators — of other human beings, unconcerned about the ethics of school administration and focused only on completing the tasks at hand. Such individuals also renounce responsibility for judging the educational and moral worth of the objectives and policies they are given by others" (Strike, Haller, & Soltis, 1988: 106). Contemporary acceptance of relativism and a rejection of traditionalism have had deeply significant effects on schooling; lack of moral and ethical consensus has obscured altogether any clear sense of right and wrong. By comparison, Holmes argues that it is the moral duty of the educational administrator (and indeed all who are concerned with education) "to become committed to a defined, common, moral endeavour" (Holmes, 1986: 40) as articulated by the framework of fundamental objective moral values.

In the "heroic society" of the classical philosophers (MacIntyre, 1981), from whose theories traditionalism has been derived, this common moral endeavor was clear — a conception of individuals' roles, fulfilled by adherence to the virtues, was an integral part of the local community. Members of the same community were accountable to one another, and support for a common moral and ethical pursuit was presumed (MacIntyre, 1981: 119–121). In contrast, the contemporary nontraditional school, consistent with the relativist character of modern society, "tries to cope with a host of conflicting desires and values, among parents and among teaching staff. As it has no agreed central purpose, it is a hostage to powerful single interest groups and even to persuasive individuals" (Holmes, 1987: 17). How then are individuals — in this case, educational administrators — expected to resolve daily dilemmas and make significant choices and decisions while maintaining some measure of moral integrity?

It may be suggested that true moral dilemmas are usually based on our inadequate perception of the good or on circumstances where no action can be good, because the situation entails a choice between two evils. This inadequate perception is fueled further by value relativism. How then does one discern blatant outrages and distinguish them from the morally insignificant amidst the grey areas of moral and ethical decision making? Josephson (1990), in citing Levin, maintains that "telling right from wrong in everyday life is not that hard; the hard part is overcoming laziness and cowardice to do what one perfectly well knows one should. . . . Honesty, industry, and respect for others form the gyroscope that stabilizes an individual on his journey through life, not an itinerary of policy positions" (p. 9). Is it simply laziness and cowardice that restrict individuals from making good moral and ethical choices? In some cases, the answer is likely yes: however, as stated previously, when one is immersed in a nonconsensual, emotivist, relativist, and consequentialist climate, the propensity to distinguish right from wrong, except perhaps in the most extreme incidents, let alone act on these principles, becomes muddled. The following section explores some of the theoretical strategies used by individuals (either intentionally or not) to cope with moral and ethical uncertainty or indeed, as suggested above, with their own personal frailties.

MORAL AND ETHICAL INDECISION: STRATEGIES FOR ADMINISTRATIVE CHOICE

Upon consideration of the administrator's responsibilities within modern educational organizations, one inevitably notes that the necessity to engage in decision making is a central expectation of the role. When that necessity becomes a burden, and the decisions become dilemmas, it is not difficult to imagine the moral and ethical significance of administrative choice.

When individuals believe that they are faced with moral dilemmas, it is often because of one of two reasons: first, because of value relativism, among other things, they become confused about principles of right and wrong and simply do not know how to respond to their problems. Alternatively, they may know clearly what the moral response should be — one that is honest and just, fair and courageous — but for personal reasons of convenience, efficiency, security, or advantage, they choose not to adopt it. In either case, the lack of a sound moral and ethical foundation as a guiding principle for action compels them to resolve their dilemmas and justify their actions by engaging in elements of suspended morality, such as false necessity, self-deception, and situational adjustment. While, in the positivist tradition, these approaches may be applauded as wise managerial strategies, in the moral philosophical tradition, they are ethically inferior.

The concept of suspended morality implies the existence of some middle ground between full acceptance of organizational values on the part of individuals and outright conflict among institutional members; an administrator, for example, may not buy into collective values advanced within the organization, yet behave in accordance with them as demanded by the role. Thus, when faced with a moral dilemma, the administrator may respond to it within the framework of policy statements, even if the policy violates his or her interpretation of justice and truth. Worse yet, the policy may also violate objective principles of morality and ethics, not merely one's subjective interpretation. Ball notes that individuals within organizations "are able to justify their actions as reasonable and normal" (Ball, 1987: 180). In a sense, individuals are able to suspend morality to suit their personal needs and choices.

In his research on obedience to authority, Milgram (1974) found that the moral judgments of individuals, who operate in the "agentic state" of carrying out orders, are "largely suspended" (p. 155). With reference to Milgram's work, Hodgkinson (1978) claims that "obedience or compliance can be construed as a way of abdicating responsibility. Conscience can be suspended" (p. 163). The concept of suspended morality, encompassing principles of false necessity, self-deception, and situational adjustment, is characterized by an individual's capacity to compromise moral convictions.

The "false necessity trap," as it has been called, is a method of justifying unethical or immoral conduct on the grounds that it is "vital," "crucial," or "essential," and that to do otherwise would yield disastrous results (Josephson Institute, 1989: 2). It denotes the belief that the necessary bureaucratic means may be used to achieve a desired end. Following from Nietzsche's observation that "necessity is not an established fact, but an interpretation" (Josephson & Josephson Institute, 1991: 52), critics who regard false necessity as an excuse note that "too often, getting the job done is treated as an ethical principle itself but this is simply rationalized self interest" (Josephson Institute, 1989: 2). False necessity enables individuals to take unethical shortcuts to accomplish something that could be achieved within ethical means, although such means could require some personal self-sacrifice of time, convenience, security, and expense.

Another aspect of false necessity stems from the doctrine that, within organizations, one simply "has no choice" (Holmes, 1991); this belief allows individuals to abdicate responsibility for their actions by maintaining that they do the only thing they can, given their positions in the organization. Within schools this doctrine is seen to "deprofessionalize" administrators and teachers who "must play the game and adopt a role in which they may not believe" (Holmes, 1991: 15). Their perceived lack of choice, reminiscent of Sartre's notion of *mauvaise foi* or "bad faith" in which individuals "attempt to escape anguish by pretending to ourselves that we are not free" (Stevenson, 1987: 96), provides both a motivator for action and an excuse for it.

Clearly, "educational administrators at any level may be subject to morally undesirable directives; . . . (while) it is not possible to say in advance precisely what educational administrators ought to do when confronted with a directive they believe is morally objectionable . . . they do have the responsibility to decide on moral grounds what action they should take" (Crittenden, 1984: 31). If one rejects on moral grounds the validity of claiming false necessity, then an appeal to a regulation is not always sufficient justification for taking a specific action. Of course, as explained previously, value relativism diminishes one's ability to know what is morally objectionable and, thus, on what moral grounds action should be taken; is it any surprise that administrators and others suspend morality and retreat from hard choices armed with the excuse of the organizational imperative?

Closely affiliated with the concept of false necessity is the state of self-deception in which individuals attempt to hide from themselves truths that they find unpleasant or untenable. Principles of self-deception may be misapplied "to explain away guilt. . . . Ignorance, even though self-imposed, is put forward as an excuse" (Bok, 1982: 66). In denying knowledge, individuals can deceive themselves and, thus, claim the false necessity of their actions with a more or less clear conscience. Once again, any moral or ethical evaluation of behavior is suspended.

Another example of the way in which organizational behavior is modified, and ultimately justified, has been called situational adjustment, defined by H. Becker (1970) as "the state in which individuals take on the characteristics required by the situations they participate in" (p. 276). Much of the literature concerning this socialization process centers around the individual's ability to adjust behavior and beliefs to match the ever-changing contingencies of the various social situations in which they operate.

These discussions are frequently value-neutral, but, even when values are addressed, ethics and morals are ignored. Surely if one "adjusts" oneself to suit the situation at hand, that individual must also, at times, adjust his or her perception of moral behavior. In the course of adjusting, the individual suspends this personal sense of morality. Therefore, to ignore the effects of situational adjustment on one's moral perspective is a serious omission. Perhaps a better term, reminiscent of the utilitarian notion of "situation ethics" (Noddings, 1984: 28), would be "moral adjustment" or "situational morality." In either case, individuals suspend concepts of morality by compromising ethical convictions.

Compromise is often interpreted to be an essential negotiating principle that enables individuals and groups to live and work together in reasonably mutual harmony. Some claim that all actions are the result of some degree of compromise between "motivation, situational conditions, available means, and the means and goals as interpreted in value terms" (Kluckhohn, 1962: 403). Nonetheless, if ethical compromise, more akin to suspended morality, leads to the rejection of objective and fundamental principles of right and wrong, then the act of compromise is generally undesirable. If one accepts that compromise, simply stated, is "the conventional opposite of standing on principle" (Nelson, 1984: 108), then, given that this definition of principle is objective and absolute, compromise is neither admirable nor beneficial. However, if standing on principle is merely a self-serving exercise to ensure personally advantageous consequences in specific situations rather than a defense of virtue, then the nature of compromise seems less objectionable.

Particularly vexing dilemmas confront administrators who are compelled to choose between issues in which their decision may support a value that they do not hold or compromise a value that they do believe to be worthy. In this sense, educational administrators may "faithfully execute policies of which they personally disapprove" (Merton, 1952, in Hodgkinson, 1978: 173). But this should not be. Instead, "the good leader moves the organization towards morally desirable ends and uses ethically acceptable means to accomplish those ends" (Holmes, 1988: 2). If the "faithfully executed policies" are morally wrong, then, again, the organizational imperative is not adequate justification for them.

Thus, suspended morality pertains to the compromising of individuals' subjective beliefs about right and wrong; however, in suspending their morality, they may also be suspending fundamental principles of objective right and wrong. A weak understanding of these principles, abetted by increased value relativism, accompanies such organizational behavior and, thus, provides administrators with managerial substitutes for solid moral and ethical decision making.

CONCLUSION

Moral and ethical uncertainty within educational organizations, as in society generally, stems in part from a lack of value consensus or standards with which to judge the daily problems of institutional members. They are individuals lost in big organizations in which clear ethical foundations have been muddled and replaced by bureaucratic imperatives and role expectations. Formal and informal norms of behavior determine emotivist values with which to evaluate action. Such values are communicated and modeled during administrator preparation programs, defined by means of policy statements and directives, and reinforced in the course of administrative practice.

Consequently, it seems likely that the prevailing belief among administrators is one that sees the raising of a moral perspective as being an attempt to force the individual's own values on others. Indeed, there are those who will argue that an apparent lack of a clear moral framework in education is a good thing; they may applaud modern tendencies to reject what they see as the rigidity of a moral framework in favor of consequentialist strategies. Such strategies may involve managerial problem solving, compromise, the suspension of morality, the denial of fundamental ethics, and decision making based on emotivist preferences and utilitarian aims. These critics also may argue that increased tolerance and flexibility are preferable to strong principles.

Yet, if flexibility permits the denigration of goodness, and if tolerance and compromise allow the denial of truth and the acceptance of injustice, then a lack of a clear moral framework should be a cause for considerable concern. If one accepts that there is objective right and wrong, then efforts to uphold strong principles are not the same as individuals forcing their own subjective values and beliefs on others.

Thus, if we, as a society, can recognize the persistent dilemma we created when we embraced value relativism as a substitute for a continuing quest for truth, rooted in moral and ethical philosophy, perhaps we can work to remedy our error; if successful, then we may find that other problems, commonly identified as moral dilemmas, may be resolved with greater clarity, integrity, and conviction.

6

Imagination and Character in Educational Administration

Susan Sydor

Study life. If you want to understand educational administration, study life.

— Thom Greenfield

Studying life, I look for a bent of imagination and character in educational administration. From the notion that we construct our realities, it follows quite naturally that we are writers of the texts that we experience and call life, although in some scenes we may have greater or lesser authorship. In schools and educational systems, administrators hold the pen and may be principal authors of other persons' narratives. Organizational narratives are concerned with problems of value, belief, and power, because they have "to do with the question of who holds the whip handle and who suffers the strokes of the lash" (Greenfield, 1993: 110). Answers to these questions and consequently preparedness to wield power come from experience that lends insight into human beings: "only those who have insight into life — its ironies, joys and tragedies — are fit to be administrators . . . it is life that must be understood and that life and the human spirit can take many forms and express itself in many realities . . . making administrators take a few journeys through the doors in the wall of reality in the hope that on their return they would see life in more complex, ambiguous and humane terms" (Greenfield, 1993: 112).

From this vantage point, the work of the administrator is literary: she works in language, plot, character, and mood and creates worlds that we understand as educational communities. All literary works are the product of the writer's imagination, but not all literary works are of the same quality, because some engage the reader to a greater degree because of their probability and human meaning, and these endure as works of art. These create educational institutions that resonate with human meaning and purpose, woven from an understanding of human nature and from personal will. In creating educational texts, what is required of the administrator is a particular bent of the imagination and a habit of value and care. Using Weber's ideal type, I will illustrate this idea by way of a case study into a reform program at a federal penitentiary (Sydor, 1993).

FREEDOM IN PRISON

The deep structures of our lives are the beliefs and values that we, and the others with whom we live, hold. As Amiel (in Gardner, 1965: 124) says, "Every life is a profession of faith, and exercises an inevitable and silent propaganda." These beliefs contain our activities and bind us in organization. We fill predetermined roles and follow routine behaviors that are enforced by institutional structures of power. As Goffman (1961a: xiii) puts it, "what is prison-like about prisons is found in organizations whose members have broken no laws."[1] So connected are the organization and the individual that individual behavior may be understood as a response to external conditions: "I speak now in relation between the Oppressor and the oppressed; the inward bondages I meddle not with in this place, though I am assured that if it be rightly searched into, the inward bondages of minde, as covetousness, pride, hypocrisie, envy, sorrow, fears, desperation and madness, are all occasioned by the outward bondage, that one sort of people lay upon another."[2] To the extent that the individual experiences the confinement of organizational life as dehumanizing, he is oppressed as though by a prison sentence. Changes in the organization of prisons have given inmates access to more freedoms — education, work, conjugal visitations, and participation in prison management.

Of the changes at Collins' Bay Penitentiary,[3] The Exceptional People's Olympiad (EPO) is regarded by prisoners as "in a class of its own," special and apart from those that are attempts to improve everyday living conditions. The idea of freedom in prison seems contradictory; in prison every aspect of life, even the trivial,[4] is controllable by authorities. For inmates the prison experience can be demoralizing, corrupting, and degrading, cutting into deeply held beliefs and values about individual freedom.[5] Yet, as a result of this innovative program, some prisoners say they experience freedom although they have not left their institutions. While some prisoners describe their experience as "free," "like a two-day pass," and that it is an occasion when "everybody wins," other participants say that the program gives them hope and that during the event, the prisoners are "fully human."

The EPO is an annual two-day program of athletic competition in which up to 150 developmentally handicapped people who live in institutions for the developmentally handicapped come from centers in Ontario and New York State to participate in a wide variety of games, races, and fun events, most of which take place inside the walls of the prison. Begun by prisoners and financially supported by charitable public donation, the EPO has a 15-year history at Collins Bay Penitentiary and has been a model for similar events in other correctional institutions.

During the EPO the organization of life changes; different routines remove some of the usual constraints of life within the institution and prisoners move about more freely, not confined by the regimens of "counts" and space, or by the hostile and mistrusting relationships associated with prison life. Inmates and prison staff voluntarily cooperate in the EPO, but the prisoners accept responsibility for its success; they organize the event, they "police" the activity, model the conduct necessary to maintain order and achieve EPO goals, and act as "godbrothers" to the handicapped athletes. Aside from the practical ways in which the EPO changes the organization of the prison in its relaxation of routine, two more significant features of the program make it substantively different — the legitimate empowerment of the inmates and the more open interaction of inmates with each other, members of the community and the developmentally handicapped athletes.

REDOING TIME

The inmates at Collins Bay Penitentiary created the EPO as a way of doing time. The event was intended to improve relations between prison administration and the inmate population. It was a reasonable plan, because the sentiments of the project were easily acceptable to both administration and inmate. Who could argue against caring for retarded children? However, the project had unintended consequences.

The EPO created new conditions and the possibility for human creative energy to seize these new conditions to transform itself. First, inmates were able to channel their energy in a different direction. Life in prison is predictable and the emphasis on control leaves little room for novelty, adventure, excitment, or creativity. Second, the event brought a whole new group of people into the prison and presented the opportunity for inmates to act in ways outside of the usual patterns of their roles. The EPO, in effect, created a crisis for the inmate population as a group and as individuals. Because we change through interaction with the environment, the EPO gave everyone involved the opportunity to change and to save face at the same time.

In choosing to organize the EPO, not for the first time, but every year, the inmate population accepts responsibility for the institution itself. This organizational change is rooted in a different understanding of time; the godbrother ideal creates the heroic image that connects the (previously isolated) individual to other individuals, beyond classification and limitation of role or type, to the human condition.

The EPO project is a modern day myth-in-the-making. Its theme is that, in the inmates' words, "labeled members of our world can and do transcend the limitations implied by the parameters of their specific handicap." For the offender, the EPO affords the opportunity to transcend the limitations of social disability and for the handicapped, the limitations of their physical development. The "Olympiad Newsletter" (1987) says that,

The Olympiad's main goal is now and always has been to identify, publicize, and (in our limited way) alleviate the plight of the Developmentally Handicapped in our society. As prisoners, we feel a kinship with those who are "locked away", and seek to draw on our own hard-won experience to help others even less fortunate. In truth, we light a torch! But this is not our only purpose; in addition to this principle aim, we wish to shed some light on the true potential of many prisoners locked behind the walls of Canada's prisons and afford them the opportunity to contribute in the most intimate and personal way imaginable — to society as a whole.

Through the EPO inmates create hope. They use images of light (the torch), affiliation (godbrother), and morality (helping the less fortunate) to symbolize redemption and truth. Institutions (both in the sense of the asylum and the practice of categorizing deviance) are the objective, abstract, and disconnected "enemy" of the personal, an enemy that can be defeated by the acts of individuals.

The event is a text continually recreated; it structures experience so that "readers" interpret its tacit meanings through sense perception, symbolism, and the vicariousness of the audience role (Bruner, 1986). As text, it offers direction (the mediating script) to the reader: in the words of one inmate, "No one gets hurt, give them (the handicapped athletes) what they want, don't get mad at them for what they can't do." Out of this, the individual inmate creates a "virtual" text of subjective interpretation.

TO SEE AN ALTERNATIVE

Some prisoners described themselves as "selfish" when they spoke about their criminal activities; they often spoke about their victims in the sense of nonbeings: the crime was not personal, the victim was nothing. For example, when one inmate talked about his criminal activity, he said: "When I steal from you it's not personal. I take the money, but it has nothing to do with you. You are nothing. It doesn't sound good, but it's true. I don't think about you. I just think about the money" (J.H.).

When the crime is not personal, both responsibility and the person are denied. That is, if it is not personal, it is objective — not animate — and, therefore, not of substance or value. If the act was considered substantive, it would have impact and "matter"; its causality in the self would require that the offender bear the terrible burden of a self who did harm to a person. By denying the personal, he also denies responsibility.

An organization ordered around technical rationality to the exclusion of individual worth, emotion, and value creates a criminal class in its own image. The deviant act, rather than alien to the social world, is totally consumed by it. This consciousness, based as Berman argues, in the Scientific Revolution and the split between fact and value, objectifies nature (including human nature), separates humanity from nature and places man in a position of dominance over nature. Berman (1981) says that the result of this is "a total reification: everything is an object, alien, not-me; and I am ultimately an object, an alienated 'thing' in a world of other, equally meaningless things" (p. 17) In this attitude, human activity is reduced to disconnected roles, in which the psyche creates false selves so that self and other do not engage in direct and meaningful interaction. As Barrett (1986) describes the phenomenon, "We can proceed, they tell us, as if the consciousness of the friend does not exist, and we shall find his bodily envelope and its behavior sufficient for all purposes of understanding" (p. xii).

The individual offender is not outside the social order, but is the social order incarnate and extreme. Similarly, as a society, we have proceeded in this way against forms of life that offend the techno-rational image. Any weakness, imperfection, or perceived threat is eliminated or dismissed as though it has no legitimate place in the world (Foucault, 1973; Hughes 1986). As Ignatieff (1978), in his historical analysis of the rise of the penitentiary concludes: "No attempt to raise the housing, educational, or sanitary standard of the poor was made without an accompanying attempt to colonize their minds. In this [Victorian philanthropic] tradition, humanitarianism was inextricably linked to the practice of domination" (p. 214).

Domination of the poor, the criminal, and the insane was tied to submission and the condition of moral improvement. Ferguson (1984) argues that modern forms of organization oppress men and women through similar forms of power and structure, particularly evident in bureaucratic capitalist society and its "appeal to efficiency [which] is largely a guise to conceal the control function that hierarchy performs" (p. 11). Modern society, based in an ideology that values functional rationality, power, and dominance, created institutions also based on rationality, manipulation, alienation, power, and dominance. When the social order so structures itself that people do not value themselves, it may then become the victim of those very beings it has made: "The creator of a robot or Frankenstein [monster] must suffer the consequences if its own creation turns on him while in that state."[6]

We are caught in a trap of our own making; the keeper, as prison life shows us, is as bound by the organization as the inmate. The created world holds values that make deviance possible; the thinking that creates the deviance also prescribes ways for dealing with it, so society creates prisons that it must maintain. Because institutions designed on a rationality of dominance create dependency, the modern social order has created a circle of dependent relationships that it may escape through transformation (White & McSwain, 1983).

THE LITERARY IMAGINATION IN ORGANIZATION

We experience life as the deep structure of narrative (MacIntyre, 1984), involved in its processes and contained by its mood. The narrative's structure imitates the beliefs of the actors who compose the plot and respond to their environment. To transform an organization, it is necessary to be able to conceive of an alternative to the current story. This narrative mode, according to Sutton-Smith (1988), "has little to do with objectivity, predictions, and verifications; rather, it has to do with consensual support, impartial readings, and verisimilitude. The science that derives from physics and mathematics is a science of verification; the science that derives from linguistics and narratives is a science of interpretation" (pp. 22–23).

For the EPO to take place, it was necessary to conceive of the inmates as godbrothers. The new language is associated with a reconception of the person; through the power of language, the literary imagination conceives of an alternative part for the inmate in the narrative that is created by the EPO. To imagine the inmates in the new role was to understand that they would agree to play the part of godbrother in the same way that they play the part of inmate. The capacity to imagine the alternative role and to create the story based on the alternative is an indication of the understanding the writer has for the subject.

Imagination is the faculty of mind by which we conceptualize. Through our imagination we are able to connect our direct experiences to reason and to examine, through language, oppositions and negatives. In imagination we may ask ourselves "what if" questions and challenge reality. Possibility and alternatives arise out of the capacity of the mind to imagine; it is in our imaginations that we are free. Imagination functions in all aspects of human activity, art, science, mathematics, logic, law, even in morality: "Consequently, our moral understanding depends in large measure on various structures of imagination, such as images, image schemas, metaphors, narratives and so forth. Moral reasoning is thus basically an imaginative activity because it uses imaginatively structured concepts and requires imagination to discern what is morally relevant in situations, to understand empathetically how others experience things, and to envision the full range of possibilities open to us in a particular case" (Johnson, 1993: ix–x).

It would be incorrect to assume that the imagination is without structure or rationality; that is, it would be a misinterpretation of the term in its present use to understand imagination as frivolous, trivial, or irrational, although these aspects of imagination have their place in human activity.[7] While the novel is the central feature of the imaginative faculty of mind, it is also necessary that plausibility accompany it. Nozick (1993) calls this plausible aspect of imagination its fruitfulness and Barrow (1988) argues that "unusualness and effectiveness" are criteria of imagination. To imagine in the realm of organizational reality would then be to conceive of an abstract representation of something that does not exist in the present but that may well exist for the betterment of the situation — something unusual and effective.

Nozick (1993) explains rather effectively the relationship between imagination and rationality, noting that even when decisions must be made among given alternatives, there is no mechanical way of doing so with certainty, simply because there is no mechanical way of locating unconsidered variables or choosing among alternatives that seem promising. Ingenuity and imagination, he says, must play a part, reminiscent, again, of Greenfield's admonition that, "ultimately, we must choose." In terms, again, of the relationship of imagination and rationality, Nozick does say that: "Without the exploration and testing of other imaginative possibilities, the procedures of rationality, by focusing on the given alternatives, will be myopic. Even when they do well by us, they may limit us to a local optimum" (p. 173). The danger, he warns, is that our belief in rationality may restrict us to the best of given alternatives and exclude the possibility of alternatives if the function of imagination is regarded as irrational. Yet, he also argues that it would be inefficient for everyone to try to explore possibilities in all areas. He notes, "Differences in opinion have an important function in the ongoing progress of science. . . . It is development along these diverse avenues that eventually produces the detailed knowledge of different theories' abilities and limitations and so brings about whatever general agreement the scientists show" (p. 174). What Nozick has to say about rationality and imagination is strikingly similar to the position that Ryle (1953) takes on the relationship of formal and informal logic in *Dilemmas*. The two faculties of mind serve different purposes; it is not a case of one doing the other's thing poorly.

What does this discussion look like if we take it back to institutional reform and the example presented by the EPO at Collins' Bay Penitentiary? Rothman (1980) takes the position that institutional reform efforts failed because of a failure of commitment or conscience. "Innovations," he says, "that appeared to be substitutes for incarceration became supplements to incarceration." This happened, Rothman argues, because the failure of reform was considered to be a failure of implementation rather than a fault in basic principles. Real institutional change, he says, required more than a change in practices, but rather a more fundamental change — a change from constructs that were more confining than were the institutions. In other words, true reform requires commitment to a clear set of values grounded in an appropriate understanding of human nature.

The founders of the EPO understood that the inmates were capable of caring for the handicapped athletes, of responding to the opportunity that the event offered, and of possibly learning through their participation. They also understood that there was a limitation to what could reasonably be expected of the event. There are no unrealistic claims of rehabilitation; the event is supervised and commitment to the EPO must be renewed annually. Because the population of the prison is continually changing, there can be no assumption of stasis. Consequently, the imagination must be continually engaged.

In this case, the imagination does not result in the kind of reform that Foucault (1977) criticizes as a disguised humanitarianism that confines the soul and the body. Rather, in the EPO participants experience a sense of freedom more of the spirit than the body. The administrative imagination in this sense has a particular bent. Its power and authority are nourishing rather than controlling.

To understand the difference, we can turn to Eisler's (1987) two basic models of society — the dominator and the partnership. The first is founded on the power to take, and the other the power to give, life. Modern social order derives from the first, and its present global crisis goes back to "a shift in emphasis from technologies that sustain and enhance life to . . . technologies designed to destroy and dominate" (p. xvii). Indeed, Merchant (1989: xvi) traces the problems of modern society to conceptions of nature "as dead and passive, to be dominated and controlled by humans" — a mechanistic world view. Deep in our psyches the image of the blade symbolizes the lethal power of control that, in our modern age, is characterized by nuclear warheads to socialize men and women into the dominator society that ultimately has the power to destroy itself.

This attitude of control and domination exists in human relationship no less than it does in the relationship of humans to their natural environment. It seems an understatement in times of apparent ecological crisis that Schaef and Fassel (1988) argue that establishing and maintaining healthy relationships is a problem in our society and that we are, instead, trained to live in addictive processes that are self-destructive (Schaef, 1990). To change these processes requires a trajection of the person (mind) into a different pattern of thinking and acting. "Transformation, break[s] through old limits, past inertia and fear, to levels of fulfillment that once seemed impossible . . . to richness of choice, freedom and human close-ness. You can be more productive, confident, comfortable with insecurity. Problems can be experienced as challenges, a chance for renewal, rather than stress. Habitual worry and defensiveness fall away. *It can all be otherwise*" (Ferguson, 1980: 24).

Nel Noddings (1992) captures the essence of what takes place in the EPO and the kind of transformation that must take place in schools, when she argues that the main aim of educational institutions should be moral. There are uncomfortable resonances between Noddings' critique of education and the critiques made of penal institutions. Both are founded in similar notions of discipline and control and a lack of true appreciation of the range and capacity of the human diversity that populates both types of institution. She prescribes a curriculum of care for our schools: care for self, intimate others, associates, the environment, and the human-made world of objects and ideas. A central point is that: "In trying to teach everyone what we once taught only a few, we have wound up teaching everyone inadequately. Furthermore, we have not bothered to ask whether the traditional education so highly treasured was ever the best education for anyone. . . . We cannot separate education from personal experience. Who we are, to whom we are related, how we are situated all matter in what we learn, what we value, and how we approach intellectual life" (Noddings, 1992: xiii).

THE REQUIREMENT THAT WE ACT

The educational administrator must not only develop the knowledge of when to seek out alternatives to the human narrative but also a knowledge that can be tolerant of new possibilities and patient when there can be no guarantees of their success. These are qualities of character or habits of conduct without which imagination cannot live (Booth, 1988). The character of the administrator brings new conceptions to life, protecting and nourishing them until their promise may be realized, or she stands apart from the tale, objective and detached as would be the narrator in a story. In either instance because choice, belief, and judgment are involved, there is a moral aspect to the administrative imagination. In referring to Wittgenstein, Greenfield found an analogy to the role of educational administrators. Wittgenstein granted philosophers the status of plumbers in their contribution to the social good. He saw architecture as both more rewarding and more challenging because it requires seeing, imagining, and acting on what is perceived. Similarly, argued Greenfield, the administrator's role is more demanding than that of the philosopher — he spoke of the true courage of leadership, giving form to the potential and to the possible (Personal communication, October 1989).

It is a special expectation of the administrative imagination that one act. The "efferent effect," not only of the new narrative but also of the story's characters, may well depend on the extent to which the administrator takes part in the story that he creates. Booth (1988) says that, "Readers who engage in a story, readers who enter the pattern of hopes, fears, and expectations that every story asks for, will always take on 'characters' that are superior . . . to the relatively complex, erratic, and paradoxical characters that they cannot help being in their daily lives. . . . We also 'behave better,' for the time being, on any given scale, in order to meet the invitation of the implied author" (p. 255).

The simplicity of the EPO is that the inmate is viewed not as a criminal but as a godbrother because he acts as a godbrother not as an offender. As a godbrother, he accepts responsibility[8] for his actions and uses his time, rather than merely "doing time" and distancing himself from others. The EPO, the self-help groups, the parties at Christmas for handicapped children, the charitable activities in which prisoners participate throughout the year, all worked for the prisoner to pass his time in a constructive way rather than in the destructive way of marking time. Each activity turned somehow back and over for the prisoner to create what was described as a "sense of freedom," but that freedom was, in reality, participation in community. Participants were then responding to the invitation of the new story, "behaving better" according to the standards set by the language and images of the new story.

Through narrative imagination the author invites others into her world. If the character that the administrator chooses to play has credibility for the reader, the administrator takes on the role of "leader" in the story (Kouzes & Posner, 1993). But knowing its power, the author also always recognizes its limitations: "The perceptual object 'man' has in it the possibility of transforming itself becoming a complete plant. The plant transforms itself because of the objective law inherent in it; the human being remains in his incomplete state unless he takes hold of the material for transformation within him and transforms himself through his own power. Nature makes of man merely a natural being; society makes of him a law-abiding being; only he himself can make of himself a free man" (Steiner, 1967: 138–39).

REASON AND IMAGINATION AS THE TOOLS OF ADMINISTRATION

The sense of security that comes from the notion that everything is predictable and rationally calculable is almost irresistible in the face of the unknown. Newton was the creator of the modern scientific method on which the notion of evidentiary reason is based. Out of these views of knowledge came the belief that man could control nature and his own existence. Hence, the modern values of individualism and self-interest stem from this attitude toward the world and become part of the notion of the modern age. Not only have modern discoveries caused a rethinking of the inherited practices of the science from the sixteenth and seventeenth centuries but also the notion of rationality as the basis of an objective knowledge is also cause for debate because different background assumptions lead to different hypotheses about reality. This is why we are able to retell a social situation from different viewpoints and hear veracity in both. This is why we are able to call both versions rational. Each represents a theory of the way things ought to be, based on an assessment of the way things are — based on the evidence as they see it. Imagination plays a part in both views.

Science alone cannot tell us what is important. That is a decision that must be made by people. Imagination plays a part here, too. It is the special imagination of educational administrators and teachers that their background assumptions be based in an understanding of people or, better yet, of life. The administrative science that would flow out of such understanding would be the science that Buber (1966) speaks of: True science is a loving science. The man who pursues such science is confronted by the secret life of things which has confronted none before him; this life places itself in his hands, and he experiences it, and is filled with its happening to the rim of his existence. Then he interprets what he has experienced in simple and fruitful concepts, and celebrates the unique and incomparable that happened to him with reverent honesty" (p. 98).

This science expresses itself in the art of administrative practice as a bent of the imagination and of character. To be human is to live with dilemmas (Billig et al., 1988). The true dilemma faced by the administrator, like the prisoner, is that what he must face is his own reflection in the text he lives and writes with others, and the choice he must make is power-based. For the administrator the choice is all the more demanding because the administrator must confront not only the self but also the self that has access to and acts out of institutional strength.

NOTES

1. Weber's "ideal type" theory allows a clearer view of organizational dynamics. See Rolf E. Rogers, *Max Weber's Ideal Type Theory* (New York: Philosophical Library, 1969).

2. Gerrard Winstanley, "The Law of Freedom in a Platform; or, True Magistracy Restored," in Carolyn Kay Steedman (Ed.), *Landscape for a Good Woman: A Story of Two Lives* (New Brunswick, N.J.: Rutgers University Press, 1987).

3. Collins Bay is a medium-security federal penitentiary. Its classification is "S-5." Maximum security institutions are classified "S-6." It is located near Kingston, Ontario.

    4. Goffman (1961a) uses this description in his general classification of the total institution, which includes prisons, mental hospitals, and prisoner of war camps.

    5. Michael Jackson, *Prisoners of Isolation* (Toronto: University of Toronto Press, 1983); Robert M. Carter, Daniel L. Glassier, and Leslie T. Wiliness, Eds., *Correctional Institutions* (Toronto: J. B. Lippincott, 1972); Gresham M. Sykes, *The Society of Captives* (Princeton, N.J.: Princeton University Press, 1958); R. J. Sapsford, *Life Sentence Prisoners* (Milton Keynes: Open University Press, 1983).

    6. John O'Driscoll and Maggie McDonald with Allan Gould, *The Violent Years of Maggie McDonald* (Scarborough, Ont.: Prentice-Hall, 1987), p. 142.

    7. As the cultural performance of festivals and carnivals, for example.

    8. Refers to the "personal." Responsibility is meant as Buber describes, the person who responds.

III

ORGANIZATIONAL DILEMMAS IN SCHOOL ADMINISTRATION

7

Monetary Incentives and the Reform of Teacher Compensation: A Persistent Organizational Dilemma

Stephen L. Jacobson

INTRODUCTION

It seems that whenever education comes under attack, school reformers turn first to private sector models of monetary incentives to increase what they perceive as a lack of teacher productivity. The use of monetary incentives in the private sector is predicated on the basic economic assumption that workers will increase their level of effort if they believe that their rewards will increase accordingly. The application of monetary incentives to education assumes that teachers are subject to the same income/leisure substitution effects as workers in other vocations. Advocates of monetary incentive plans argue that without such incentives there is little reason for workers, teachers included, to exert effort beyond the minimum performance requirements of their respective jobs.

During the 1980s, over 99% of the teachers in the U.S. worked in districts using uniform schedules that paid salary increments based solely on longevity and graduate credit accumulation (Murnane & Cohen, 1985). At the same time, a number of influential reports appeared that questioned the quality of public schools in the U.S. (see, for example, Boyer, 1983; Goodlad, 1983; National Commission on Excellence in Education, 1983). These reports raised the spectre that a deteriorating educational

Jacobson, S. L. (1995). Monetary incentives and the reform of teacher compensation: A persistent organizational dilemma. *International Journal of Educational Reform*, 4(1): 29–35. Reprinted with permission of Technomic Publishing Co., Inc.

system posed a serious threat to America's global economic pre-eminence. Indeed, some suggested that a causal relationship existed between the widespread use of the uniform salary schedule and "the rising tide of mediocrity" in American public education (NCEE, 1983). The issue received considerable public attention and led to calls for marked changes in the way teachers are compensated. Among the most often recommended compensation reforms were increases in entry-level wages, career ladders with differentiated salaries, and scarcity bonuses. But the most contentious reform proposals were calls for performance-related pay, more commonly known in the U.S. as 'merit pay' (Lipsky & Bacharach, 1983).

As we shall see, merit pay plans have been tried and tried again in public education, but their use has always been short-lived. Obviously, the question of whether the plans work needs to be examined. Not surprisingly, some plans work and others don't. But judging the vicissitudes of educational policy solely on the relative success of a few monetary incentive plans represents a limited perspective. There seems to be a regular ebb and flow in public interest in the use of monetary incentives for teachers, and the question of how to most appropriately compensate teachers is one that persists. As Cuban (1992: 6) points out, problems that persist often do so because they require choices to be made between "competing, highly prized values (that) cannot be fully satisfied." Cuban suggests that attempts to use the "template of technical rationality" to address administrative problems may hide conflicts in inherent values, leading to conflict-filled 'dilemmas' of administrative practice. In the first chapter of this book, Cuban points out that unlike problems that can be solved, dilemmas can only be managed, and the key to managing these persistent dilemmas is to recognize the values that are in conflict.

THE PURPOSE OF THE CHAPTER

The purpose of this chapter is to examine the conflicting values that underlie debates about the reform of teacher compensation. Elsewhere I have studied teacher compensation and incentive plans pragmatically, trying to understand what works and why? (see, for example, Jacobson, 1993, 1991a; 1991b; 1990; 1989a; 1989b; 1989c; 1989d; 1988a; 1988b; 1988c; Monk & Jacobson 1985a; 1985b). In this chapter, I re-examine the effects of monetary incentives on teacher recruitment, retention, and absence, focusing on the conflicts in personal and organizational values that cause problems with teacher compensation to persist. Two key issues to be considered are normative expectations of teacher behavior and differential responses to income/leisure substitution. I will argue that the way society views teachers and the way teachers see themselves are often at odds. At these times, changes in compensation and the use of incentives are introduced in order to bring teacher behaviors in line with public expectations. The public's perception of a 'dedicated' teacher is of an individual who is more concerned with the welfare of students than the attainment of monetary rewards. Teachers, on the other hand, desire to be treated like 'professionals' and not be compelled to compete for rewards. Yet, when monetary incentives are offered, they tend to adjust their labor market behaviors in relatively predictable ways, much like other workers in other fields.

I will argue that herein lies the root cause of a persistent organizational dilemma, i.e., school systems turn to monetary incentives to motivate teachers, yet they really don't want teachers who are primarily motivated by money. Teachers want to be respected for their dedication to children, yet they respond to monetary incentives and often demand extra compensation for activities school officials and the public perceive as being a part of their professional responsibilities. In other words, teachers and their school district employers both exhibit behaviors that seemingly conflict with their beliefs and values.

A case in point, teachers in the U.S. are presently being asked to become increasingly involved in site-based decision-making. The opportunity to participate as full partners in the governance of schools is perceived by the public as a professional responsibility that teachers should enter into without additional remuneration, i.e., teachers should volunteer their time just like parents and other community members who are involved in shared decision-making. Teachers, on the other hand, are questioning why they must subsidize these additional responsibilities by reducing their leisure time, i.e., why should they take on additional responsibilities without being offered additional income? Many teachers are asking that they be compensated for their involvement in shared decision-making activities, either through extra pay for extra work provisions, or release time from other professional responsibilities.

THE ORGANIZATION OF THE CHAPTER

In order to place this discussion in its political and social context, I begin the chapter with a look at teacher compensation in the U.S. and an examination of the composition of the American teaching workforce. Next follows a brief history of merit pay for teachers in the U.S., as well as a review of a number of studies of compensation reforms implemented over the past decade. I then examine what teachers value in their work and what society values in teachers. The reader will see that while monetary incentives can influence key labor market behaviors of teachers, their use tends to conflict with personal and societal expectations of what a 'good' teacher is and wants. There is also some misunderstanding about the income/leisure substitutions that teachers prefer. While monetary incentives plans assume that teachers will work harder for more pay, there is reason to believe that many teachers see the opportunity for more leisure time as a more attractive incentive than more money. These conflicting values and perceptions produce a persistent organizational dilemma caused in part by the very mechanisms employed to 'solve' it.

MONETARY INCENTIVES AND THE TEACHER WORKFORCE

Teacher Compensation in the U.S.

The reason salary is often singled out by educational reformers is that it is highly visible and easily amenable to comparison. As public employees, teachers' salaries are a matter of public knowledge and negotiated locally. This is particularly relevant in a decentralized system such as the U.S., where there are nearly 15,000 districts. Texas alone has over 1000 school districts. Each district has its own Board of Education which is responsible for determining the district's rate of pay, either unilaterally or through collective negotiations with teacher representatives. One consequence of local control is that teacher salaries vary markedly both across and within states. For example, in 1990-91, estimated average salaries for public school teachers across the U.S. ranged from a high of $43,808 in Connecticut to a low of $22,363 in South Dakota, a difference of almost 100% (Thompson, Wood, & Honeyman, 1994). Within New York State, average district salaries for classroom teachers in 1992-93 ranged from $62,406 at the 90% percentile to $28,187 at the 10% percentile (NYSED, 1994).

These wage disparities reflect regional differences in the cost of living, alternative employment opportunities for teachers, teacher union strength, and the average level of teacher experience and education. America's teacher workforce is very experienced and well-educated. Of a total teacher workforce of roughly 2.5 million in 1990-91, almost 65% had over 10 years of experience, 25% had been teachers for more than 20 years, and 47.5% had a Master's degree or above. In addition, the teacher workforce is 72% female, meaning there are 1.8 million women teachers in the U.S. (NCES, 1994).

Wage disparities are also a reflection of the willingness of the local community to support public education. It is important to note that in the U.S., local control also means local support. The National Center for Education Statistics (NCES, 1994) reports that in 1990-91, 46.5% of all revenues for public elementary and secondary education came from local sources, slightly less than the 47.3% provided by state governments (Federal sources account for only 6.2% of all revenues for public education). When one considers that professional salaries and benefits often account for 65-70% of a school district's operating budget, coupled with the fact that current per pupil expenditures have risen 33% since 1982-83 after adjustment for inflation (NCES, 1994), it is not surprising that American taxpayers have become highly sensitive to both increases in teacher salary and reports of declining student achievement.

The so-called 'first wave' reforms of the 1980s noted earlier, as well as a 'second wave' of reports (see, e.g., Carnegie, 1986; Holmes, 1986) led to significant improvements in teacher salaries. By 1992-93, the average salary for public school teachers in the U.S. was $35,334 (NCES, 1994). Adjusting for inflation, this is an 18% increase from a decade earlier, when the report *A Nation at Risk* (NCEE, 1983) first made educational productivity a national priority. But while their wages changed markedly over the past decade, the way that teachers are compensated did not. The vast majority of America's teachers still work in districts that pay increments primarily on the basis of experience. Yet this has not always been the case and the use of monetary incentives has a long but erratic history in American public education (Johnson, 1984).

The Use of Merit Pay

As early as 1903, teachers in Chicago fought the implementation of a merit pay scheme they felt would jeopardize their newly-won, longevity-based salary schedule (Urban, 1985). During the early 1920s, almost half of America's schools had 'merit pay.' There was considerable interest during that period in applying the efficiencies of industry to education, and merit pay was one manifestation of that interest.

Ortiz and Marshall (1988) contend that, "a misreading of Taylor's scientific management turned schools into competitive bureaucracies, rather than collaborative service organizations (p. 123)." Merit pay plans were, in fact, intended to foster competition, in the belief that competition can bring out a worker's best performance. But 'merit' in these early plans was more often determined by gender or level of instruction than by performance. By the 1930s and 1940s uniform salary schedules were becoming increasingly commonplace. Public interest in the use of monetary incentives was renewed in the late 1950s when the Soviet Union launched Sputnick, and by 1969, 1 in 10 (11.3%) districts enrolling more than 6000 students used performance incentives as part of teacher compensation. But once again interest waned, and within a decade, the number of districts using monetary incentives was down to only 1 in 25 (4%) (Porwoll, 1979).

More recently Murnane and Cohen (1985) tried to identify schools districts that had used merit pay plans for at least five years, had paid awards of at least $1000, and had an enrollment of more than 10,000. They could find only seven districts that met these criteria in 1985. And in these few districts, Murnane and Cohen found that merit pay did not appear to have much of an effect on the way teachers teach.

But while monetary incentives may not affect the way teachers teach, other recent studies suggest that they do have an important effect on other teacher labor market behaviors, specifically recruitment, retention, and attendance.

MONETARY INCENTIVES AND TEACHER LABOR MARKET BEHAVIOR

Recruitment: Occupation and Location Choice

A career in teaching can be demarcated by a series of critical choices, the first two, occupation and location choice are recruitment issues for the profession and school districts respectively (Jacobson, 1993). The first career choice, occupation, is particularly problematic and many of the reports cited earlier, most notably *A Nation at Risk*, expressed alarm at the lack of high caliber individuals entering teaching. During the 1970s and 80s, salaries in teaching, especially at the entry-level lagged behind those of other professions requiring equivalent educational preparation (Monk & Jacobson, 1985b). These national reform reports were unanimous in their recommendation that starting salaries in teaching had to become more competitive with those in other occupations. The resulting salary increases noted earlier indicate the influence of those reports.

After a person decides to become a teacher, s/he decides next where to teach, i.e., the choice of location. This is especially important in the U.S. because the decentralized nature of American education means that improvements in entry-level salary must be dealt with at the local level. As teachers choose among locations, they can be considered both buyers and sellers in the educational labor marketplace, simultaneously purchasing the job characteristics of school districts including starting salary, while selling districts their services (Antos & Rosen, 1975; Chambers, 1981). Given that salaries vary from district to district, one can chart the behavior of teachers to see whether their location choices are influenced by money.

I examined school districts in two regions of New York State to see how changes in starting salary affected the ability of these districts to compete amongst themselves for the services of beginning teachers (Jacobson, 1990). I found that school districts that improved the relative attractiveness of their starting salary vis-a-vis their regional neighbors subsequently improved their likelihood of recruiting the most highly educated novice teachers available. In other words, beginning teachers are responsive to monetary incentives, and districts, knowledgeable of that fact, use money to recruit these talented candidates as they compete with other districts for their services.

Retention

After deciding where to teach, the next critical career choice an individual makes is whether or not to remain in teaching, or more specifically, in a given school district. Even those authors who contend that teachers begin their careers with a willingness to forego high salaries in anticipation of teaching's intrinsic rewards recognize that over time frustration with salary becomes an increasingly critical factor in teacher turnover (Chapman & Hutcheson, 1982; Goodlad, 1983).

Using the same sample of districts I used in the recruitment study, I also examined the effects of salary change on teacher retention (Jacobson, 1988a). The findings revealed that districts that improved the relative attractiveness of their salaries, particularly salaries paid mid-career teachers, were the districts with the highest rates of teacher retention. In addition, women in these districts were more responsive to salary change than men, a finding that countered earlier studies that claimed traditional economic forces have little influence on female teachers (Charters, 1967; Lortie, 1975).

Attendance

What work to do, where to do it, and whether to remain represent choices made just a few times over the course of a career. But whether to go to work on a given day represents a decision teachers make regularly throughout their careers. In New York, a school calendar generally runs 180-190 days per year. On average, teachers in New York use 9 sick days per year, roughly 5% of available work time (Ehrenberg, et al., 1989). Some school districts have tried to use monetary incentives to reduce teacher absence. I studied teacher absence and found one attendance incentive plan that produced a significant, short-term reduction in the average number of days that teachers were absent from work (Jacobson, 1991a; 1989a; 1989b).

While it is not clear from these studies whether monetary incentives affect the quality of teacher performance, taken together the studies do indicate that monetary incentives have a significant influence on the way teachers behave in the educational labor market. I offer these findings to show the centrality of monetary incentives to the relationship between teachers and their public employers. When monetary incentives are offered, teachers tend to adjust their labor market behaviors in much the same way as other workers. But does society really want its teachers to act like other workers, or, do they hold teachers to a different standard? Next we look at what teachers value, and how these values match up with society's expectations.

What Do Teachers Value? What Does Society Value in Teachers?

Recall the central proposition of the chapter is that problems persist in teacher compensation because of conflicts in highly prized personal and organizational values. The studies reported above indicate that school officials use incentives to influence teacher behavior. Yet, the public's perception of a 'dedicated' teacher is of an individual who is more concerned with the welfare of students than the attainment of monetary rewards.

In a study of New York City teachers, Griffiths et al. (1965) categorized teachers based upon what they valued most in their work. The "dedicated" teachers in this typology were those individuals who are most interested in children — the "pupil-oriented" teachers. The values held by these teachers match most closely society's expectations of what teachers should value. "Subject-oriented" teachers represent a second category of teachers. The values these individuals hold dearest are not inconsistent with society's expectations. The public recognizes that schools need individuals who are concerned with the subjects they teach and not just those who take their subjects. On the other hand, "benefits-oriented" teachers — individuals who value their package of compensatory benefits, including the generous vacation schedule — are anathema to these normative expectations.

Benefits-oriented teachers are teachers who use the compensation system to their best advantage. Griffiths et al. write that these "benefits-oriented" teachers move horizontally "until they find a good deal" (p. 24). When monetary incentives are offered, these teachers adjust their labor market behaviors in much the same ways as the teachers reported in the studies above, i.e., they move to better paying districts, they remain longer in districts when their salaries become more attractive, and they attend more regularly when regular attendance is monetarily rewarded. And herein lies the rub, when money is offered, these teachers respond and school officials anticipate that they will. Yet neither side is entirely comfortable with the bargain. Teachers would prefer to be treated and paid like 'professionals,' and not 'bribed' with monetary incentives, while the public would prefer teachers who work to their full capacity without making additional monetary demands.

It would be naive to suggest that the categories in this typology are mutually exclusive. Certainly there are pupil-oriented teachers who are concerned about their benefits, and benefits-oriented teachers who are concerned about their subjects and students. It is as unfair to expect all teachers to be dedicated to their students as it is to suggest that all teachers are solely interested in their benefits. I believe that the relatively generous vacation schedule that teachers have accounts in part for public resentment over their attention to benefits. Let me offer one example of this resentment. I recall speaking to a dairy farmer in rural Central New York who was angry over teachers' demands for higher salaries. In his eyes, the teachers in his district were part-time employees. He pointed out that a teacher's workday begins well after his, and ends well before. And while children stay home on weekends, holidays, and ten weeks during the summer, his cows need to be milked twice a day, every day. From his perspective a teacher is a part-time employee. With so much time off, he would argue that teachers can find other employment if money is so important.[1] Which brings us to the second issue in conflict, i.e., income/leisure substitutions and how society views teacher time.

Income/Leisure Substitutions

Richards et al (1993) write that the income effect is, "The difference in the effort supplied at two different income levels" (p. 32). The relationship between income and effort is assumed to be positive, and the use of monetary incentives in education suggests teachers will work harder if they can earn more money. It also implies that unless these incentives are available teachers work at levels of effort that is beneath their capability.

In contrast, "the substitution effect occurs when an increase in earnings predisposes the employee to purchase more leisure" (Richards et al. 1993: 32). In other words, after attaining a certain level of income, workers are likely to seek more time rather than more money. To someone like our dairy farmer, the idea that increasing teachers' salaries could lead to their purchase of more leisure time runs counter to his basic work ethic. He would argue that if we are to give teachers more money, they had better produce more, and not ultimately convert increased wages into still more free-time.

Those who advocate the use of monetary incentives in education believe that teachers presently have plenty of free time, and therefore additional time and effort to be purchased. But teachers do not see themselves as part-time workers, countering that they already subsidize public education through low wages and the amount of preparatory work they undertake at home, on their own time, at their own expense. In fact, many teachers view time as a more attractive incentive than money.

Trading Money for Time: Deferred Salary Leave Plans

Deferred salary leave plans (DSLPs) allow teachers to voluntarily defer a part of their annual salary for a given number of years in order to self-fund a leave of absence. Teachers use the leave year for graduate study, travel, and other personal and family matters. The vast majority report a renewed enthusiasm for teaching upon returning from a leave, and quite a few opt into a second plan as soon as they return from their first. While some teachers use the leave year to improve their instructional skills, others simply want to escape the stress of teaching. These self-funded leaves are viewed by some teachers as an antidote to burnout (Jacobson & Kennedy, 1991; 1992).

DSLPs have been used in Canada since the late 1970s, but it wasn't until 1993 that the first plans of this type were negotiated in the U.S., in school districts in Muskegon, Michigan and Rochester, New York. Government officials in the Netherlands, concerned with high rates of long-term teacher absences related to stress, have also expressed an interest in implementing DSLPs.

The increasing popularity of DSLPs (13% of teachers in one Ontario school district are involved in one stage or another of a leave plan), indicates that the opportunity for release time may outweigh the attractiveness of monetary incentives to teachers. In other words, the premise that teachers have generous amounts of free time and are willing to use that time to increase their productivity in exchange for extra money, may underestimate the level of effort that teachers currently expend and the extent to which they value what leisure time they have. More time rather than more money seems to be what some teachers want, but allowing teachers additional free time runs counter to society's traditional work ethic.

CONCLUSIONS

Language can often confuse, as well as clarify, the way we look at our world. Much of administrative preparation and practice in education is concerned with the process of 'problem-solving' — identifying and framing problems, developing alternative solutions, and selecting among competing alternatives for the most feasible solution. When we have 'problems,' we seek solutions. But some problems seem to be more difficult to resolve. They defy a neat overlay of scientific rationality because they represent on-going struggles between competing values. As noted at the beginning of the chapter, the use of the "template of technical rationality,"is likely to ignore these conflicting values and therefore the problems persist (Cuban, 1992).

Educational reformers of the 1980s reported problems with American education, especially problems with its teacher workforce. According to these reformers, teachers were both the cause of and potential cure for deteriorating student achievement. These first wave reforms focused on market incentives and state mandates to solve the 'teacher' problem (see,

Farrar, 1990; Petrie, 1990; Jacobson & Conway, 1990 for details). Compensation reform was seen as a rational way to 'solve' the problem. There were few attempts to examine underlying values, and as Urban (1985) noted, current initiatives like those that had come before once again poured "old wine" (merit pay) into "new bottles" (compensation reform). Teachers rejected what they perceived as the demeaning treatment of having to compete for rewards, yet lobbied for substantial increases in salary. The public didn't necessarily object to higher wages so long as teachers worked harder for them. Both parties recognize the importance of money, yet both have reservations as to how important it should be. In many ways teachers are no different than workers in other professions, but in one very important way they are expected to be quite different, i.e., they are expected to be dedicated to their students, and place their own benefits second. But teachers question why they're expected to subsidize their employment in ways that other workers are not. Recall the example presented earlier, in which teachers and school officials disagree over whether teachers should be compensated additionally for their involvement in site-based decision-making. Should this be viewed as a function of good citizenship within a participatory democracy, or simply a case of extra work demanding extra compensation? As a result of fundamental disagreements such as this, the use of monetary incentives remains as much a topic of discussion as a practical reality.

The emerging wave of "systemic" reforms that have characterized the late 80s–early 90s, have become increasingly interested in the relationship between the social organization of the school workplace and teachers' commitment, performance, and productivity (see, for example, Mitchell et al., 1987; Reyes, 1990; Rosenholtz, 1989; Jacobson & Berne, 1993). In some ways, these systemic reforms are closer, conceptually, to Cuban's notion of managing the compensation dilemma than early reform attempts to solve it. For example, in order to make education more attractive to individuals contemplating teaching as a career, as well as to draw local stakeholders into educational decision-making, current reform initiatives in the U.S. have focused more on improving the school workplace and its relationship to its constituent community than on teacher salaries. Moreover, when incentives are successfully employed, they are used to reward collective rather than individual behavior (Richards et al. 1993).

Even with this heightened understanding of the systemic nature of the educational enterprise, policymakers continue to consider the appropriate role of compensation in school improvement. It is essential that we continue to explore relationships between monetary incentives and teachers' behaviors. The studies reported in this chapter suggest that monetary incentives can influence teacher recruitment, retention, and attendance, and that adjustments in compensation disbursement can allow teachers more leisure time which creates opportunities to alleviate job-related stress and burnout. But no less important to managing these persistent dilemmas is the need to study and try to articulate the personal and organizational values in conflict.

NOTE

1. The fact that the teacher workforce is predominantly female may also shape this dairy farmer's perceptions of their work and how teachers time should be spent.

8

Performance Related Pay and Professional Development

Harry Tomlinson

BRITISH GOVERNMENT ADVISORY GROUPS

The bodies in England and Wales that recommend teachers' pay to the government, the Interim Advisory Committee on School Teachers' Pay and Conditions from 1988 to 1991, and its successor, the School Teachers' Review Body (STRB) from 1992 to 1994, have increasingly insistently raised the issue of performance related pay (PRP) for teachers. The Interim Advisory Committee on School Teachers' Pay and Conditions (1991) in its Fourth Report stated uncompromisingly, "We believe the teaching profession needs to accept that a larger element of the pay bill . . . should be related to performance" (p. 52). The STRB in its Second Report explained:

The Review Body shares his (Secretary of State's) view that there is a need for a readier and more explicit reward for teaching excellence. . . . We acknowledge, as we were repeatedly told, that many of the incentive allowances awarded for extra responsibilities also recognised teaching quality. . . . We are also aware that some heads and governors devise new "responsibilities" because they are reluctant to identify and reward excellent classroom teachers per se, in case it should be viewed as divisive in the staffroom. In our view, this approach is counterproductive. It can also lead to a misallocation of responsibilities and to over-elaborate, ineffective management structures. (STRB, 1993: 18)

This fudging of the reward system lies at the heart of the discussion about PRP. PRP is allegedly unsuitable for the teaching profession, but it is also suggested above that we already use it, if somewhat dishonestly.

CITIZEN'S CHARTER

The government's Citizen's Charter (HM Government, 1991: 35) for public services requires:

more delegation of decisions on pay — the system of reward must be closer to the responsibility for the delivery of service.

extending rewards for performance — and equally important, penalties for failure — as part of the normal package of pay and conditions.

securing value for money for the taxpayer by tight cost control, with the net cost of performance rewards paid for by real productivity increases.

ensuring that rewards for performance are only given when demanding quality of service targets have been met.

The government is attempting to improve the quality of all public services for citizens. This involves creating a performance management culture in the education service, without, as yet, significant success. The teacher associations want pay to be determined nationally. They do not want pay for performance, partly because they allege high quality performance cannot be recognized. They believe, apparently unquestioningly, that the education service provides value for money. The unanimity of this antagonism to PRP appears to be unthinking and irrational, and not to be susceptible to challenge.

EMPLOYERS' ORGANIZATIONS

In 1989, four major employers' organizations with an interest in education all insisted that PRP was a necessary part of the process of raising educational standards in Britain. A local government employers' organization, The Local Authorities Conditions of Service Advisory Board, suggested that PRP could serve a number of management purposes including employee motivation, establishing equity in employee awards, and fostering the "performance culture" (1989: 8). The Confederation of British Industry, the major employers' organization, sought changes to the teachers' payment reward structure to create a high performance–high pay service (The Confederation of British Industry, 1989: 41). This should ensure that all teachers meet required quality standards through regular assessments, performance related payments, and flexible refresher and retraining schemes. The British Institute of Management (BIM), which represents all managers, looked for the introduction of individually based performance appraisal and reward schemes (Rycroft, 1989: 11). Coopers and Lybrand, frequently used by the government as consultants in the public sector, saw performance pay as part of a wider process of organizational change in the public sector (Coopers & Lybrand, 1989: 2). The emphasis should be on devolved management control and the fostering of a performance culture. Coopers and Lybrand noted that the overwhelming majority of organizations had devised target-based appraisal schemes, with the emphasis on the mutual setting of targets between the appraiser and appraisee.

The strength and coherence of the arguments as presented by all those with a clear interest in the raising of educational standards was unusual. The teachers' organizations remained obdurately opposed despite the expansion of PRP in the public sector, particularly the Health Service, and the growing acceptance that this would help in raising educational performance. What has been significant is the absence of any serious debate or discussion. The mutually contradictory assertions became increasingly strident with no thorough examination of the evidence of the alleged advantages and disadvantages of PRP. The teacher associations commissioned researchers to demonstrate that PRP could not work for teachers.

VIEW FROM THE (PERSONNEL) BRIDGE

A recent publication of the Institute of Personnel Management (Armstrong, 1993), takes the evidence from the public sector forward. Most of the contributors are personnel or human resources managers in public sector or recently privatized businesses.

Caines, writing about the National Health Service, says, "More damagingly, however the adherence to central pay structures has not allowed managers to use pay to reward good performers and penalise poor performers. The NHS pay scene . . . is distinguished by its flatness and overall greyness . . . and its drabness" (Caines, 1993: 28). He argues for the energizing force of a more imaginative and creative payment system. This is now developing in the National Health Service.

Griffiths, of Kent County Council, a local government authority, describes how the traditional reliance on rules, systems, procedures, and conventional hierarchy is being replaced by a focus on performance management and a flattening of the hierarchical structure (Griffiths, 1993: 40). The bureaucratic civil service model for public servants and the associated payment systems, Griffiths believes, are responsible for the inefficiencies of the public services. Kent is now developing new payment systems.

Connock, of Eastern Electricity, a recently privatized electricity distributor, explains that a major problem in introducing PRP is that managers have not been trained to make individual judgments on performance (Connock, 1993: 148–149). This is certainly the case in education. Indeed exploring the criteria for making such a judgment has been interpreted as unprofessional. We do not wish to know how to make such judgments lest the skill has to be exercised. Other problems within the electricity industry included a perception that managers' judgements were too subjective, that the introduction of PRP was only a cost-reduction strategy, and that it would detract from team achievement. Managers, Connock argues, need training in setting objectives, appraising performance, and understanding the link between individual and team performance. He recognizes that this is not straightforward. However if pay processes simply reinforce the notion of entitlement, irrespective of contribution, and of tenure, irrespective of skill level, the message is that achievement is less important than service. This describes the education service regrettably accurately. The emphasis, Connock insists, must be on results, recognition of contribution to objectives, innovation, and personal accountability. Teams operate in all other businesses where PRP is used successfully.

The privatized and privatizing public sector is using PRP to lever up standards. The teachers' organizations remain determined to resist what is happening elsewhere in the public sector. They argue that the tide has turned against PRP in the private sector, although the evidence for this assertion is doubtful. The personnel and human resources managers who have the capacity to view from the bridge make a strong case for PRP in the public sector.

DELAYERING AND DOWNSIZING

The Institute of Management research involving its members (Inkson & Coe, 1993) shows that the traditional management career is disappearing. Managers are changing their jobs more often. Sideways or downward moves are increasing and upward managerial moves are declining. Managers are changing jobs for different reasons, much less frequently for career and personal development reasons, and increasingly because of organizational restructuring. Delayering and downsizing are having an impact in the real world. Schools remain sheltered within their rigidly hierarchical and apparently ineffective bureaucracies. In secondary schools in England and Wales, with only 60 teachers, there are, in Kafkaesque interlocking hierarchies, eight responsibility levels.

Teachers continue to insist that these changes must not affect them. Career patterns should remain as they always have been, a scramble up the bureaucratic hierarchy, based on inadequately determined criteria for responsibilities often no longer appropriate. The present payment structure has, over the years, accrued additional bureaucratic layers even when these additional allowances were financed to pay for performance. There is a contradiction between the insistence that teachers have an unchanged career structure and the unsuitability of this structure for the needs of the education service.

SCHOOL PERFORMANCE

There is considerable evidence, particularly from international comparisons, that the performance of the English and Welsh education system, like that of the United States, is inadequate. In searching for an explanation the national debate is strongly polarized. The cause is either insufficient resources or the failure of the education service, in particular the teachers, to produce results. The now greatly reduced government inspectors of schools, Her Majesty's Inspectors, stated quite bluntly that management of schools leaves much to be desired (Department of Education and Science, 1990: 10). In only about one-third of schools inspected was senior management judged to be particularly effective. The proportion of middle management so assessed was judged to be lower still. They saw serious problems of low achievement and underachievement and of poor teaching. The analysis is detailed, thorough, and critical.

Research has shown that if schools were improved only within the current range of performance of urban comprehensive schools this would be sufficient to transform standards of secondary education (Smith & Tomlinson, 1989). There are massive and hidden differences in school performance. Perhaps, even more significantly, this research shows that, even though parents' attitudes to and views about the schools their children attend vary widely, these attitudes are statistically not related to the attainment and progress of their own child. Parents cannot identify the schools in which their children are developing particularly well. The vast differences in school performance are being kept hidden because it would undermine the teaching profession to reveal the immense variations in teacher performance.

There is, as yet, no clear evidence that teachers recognize their potential to greatly improve standards. The continuous whining about lack of resources in a climate where resources are inevitably going to be decreased is counterproductive.

At last some minor restructuring of the hierarchies within schools is beginning to happen. The role of the deputy head, and there are three deputies in large comprehensive schools, is changing because they have been administrators rather than managers or, even more important, leaders. As the Second Report from STRB states: "In too many schools deputy heads have a largely administrative role. That is not a cost effective use of a relatively expensive resource (a non teaching administrative assistant might offer better value for money) and may mean that the necessary management role is going by default" (STRB, 1993: 40). This again reflects the conservative failure to respond to new needs within the profession.

Local management of schools (the devolvement of at least 90 percent of the budget from the local education authority to schools) and a more competitive environment have meant that financial, personnel, and marketing roles are being taken over by nonteaching staff with training and expertise developed throughout their careers rather than learned inadequately by more expensive teacher administrators. This has important implications for career development for teachers. The management and leadership roles in schools, traditionally achieved by teachers who have climbed the hierarchy, may not be filled best by outstanding teachers, indeed, possibly not by teachers at all. The traditional career structure is starting to be eroded.

The implications for professional development, teachers' lives and careers, and the relationship of these to pay for excellence in teaching skills need to be recognized. If there is to be no PRP, then the rationale for any alternative payment system needs to be considered fully. The present pay structure is no longer appropriate.

APPRAISAL

In England and Wales, for the first time, a national teacher appraisal scheme is being implemented that focuses on professional development. There is an anxiety that any move toward PRP might undermine this. All teachers are required to have completed an appraisal by the end of the school year in 1995. The classroom observation was, in prospect, traumatic even in what is an excessively teacher development focused model. This illustrates the sanctity of the individual teacher's classroom associated with the professional ideal that existed in England and Wales prior to the development of this appraisal model. Classrooms had not been visited by managers for decades. Children's education had suffered from this ignorance, associated with a nineteenth-century model of professionalism.

There is an argument that appraisal should be about maximizing the individual teacher's performance and answering professional needs. Pay, on the other hand, should be tied to the structures and requirements of the school, its curriculum, and its unique objectives. It is not clear why these two should be contradictory and so deliberately opposed. They are, in principle, complementary. Unfortunately the first faltering steps toward a more rigorous appraisal system are only now being taken. Appraisal is not yet about improving performance, except as interpreted by the appraisee.

GENDER AND CAREERS

There are a number of issues related to teacher identity and teacher morale. There is still only the traditional model of a career structure. There is a recognition that there are problems for the mid-career teacher and tensions between hierarchies and collegiality. The self-actualizing professional, the reflective practitioner, and the extended professional are examples of conceptualizations of the teacher's role that are being explored in Britain. The issue of the associated payment structure is conveniently ignored in these discussions. It is not clear what the ideal payment structure would be for self-actualizing professionals. The relationship between personal growth and professional development, increasingly interpreted as self-management, is becoming a potent source for individual improvement. This is, however, also not perceived as a basis for payment, perhaps, thus, undermining the process.

The Institute of Management, which has evolved from BIM, has concentrated on two aspects of research among its members over the past few years. The first, discussed above, is the changing nature of careers. The second has been the role and status of women managers. An absurd and surprisingly strong sexism runs through all the evidence that BIM and the Institute of Management have collected from its male manager members. This is reflected in the education service.

The teacher associations present an interesting argument against PRP for teachers, based apparently on no evidence. They assert that it will further disadvantage women. The rhetoric of equal opportunities is used, not for the first time, as a weapon to oppose a new development. Women are underpaid in all forms of employment. The opposition to PRP is a manifestation of the male ability to distort a proposed change that aims at equal value for equal performance. Women should have greater rewards when they achieve superior performance. The male-dominated teacher associations, however, oppose PRP to maintain men's greater earning power.

The management skills appropriate for the 1990s, and teaching is about the management of learning, are essentially feminine. It is likely, therefore, that if pay genuinely were for management or teaching performance women would be paid proportionately significantly more than they are at present.

PERSISTENT DILEMMAS IN ADMINISTRATIVE PREPARATION AND PRACTICE

The 1994 International Intervisitation Program conference theme implies that some problems are amenable to solution by scientific principles and some are not. These represent ongoing struggles between such competing values as are inevitable in payment systems. In Britain, we have an education service where the quality of management is less than satisfactory and in which parents have inadequate information about which schools are better. They receive relatively worthless information, presented through league tables, of examination results and attendance. These provide no evidence of the "added value" that individual parents require. Teachers object to the inadequacy of this information but are not purposefully seeking to provide the more helpful information that would rigorously show which are the good and poor schools. Teachers pull back from this because it would also provide evidence of excellent and less than adequate headteacher and teacher performance. This information might then be used to help determine pay.

The professional associations are determined to protect what they perceive as the professional integrity of their colleagues. This apparently requires that there shall be no recognized distinction between the competent and the excellent, whether as teachers or as school leaders. Hence the wish is to sustain the bureaucratic hierarchical pay structure that is so manifestly inadequate for current needs.

The International Intervisitation Program conference planning team explored the categorization of the persistent dilemmas as organizational and structural; moral, ethical, and philosophical; and societal and personal. PRP in Britain is related to all of these. There are organizational (school) and structural (national) dilemmas. There are problematic government and professional association (a more delicate phrase for teacher trade unions) relationships. The fragmentation and centralization of the education system is occurring because of the government attack on the present forms of local democratic accountability. There will be a consequential devolution of pay structures. The English and Welsh education system is changing rapidly.

There are moral and ethical issues involved in any decision about payment systems, the relativities between teachers, between teachers and other staff in schools, and, indeed, between teachers and other workers. Both sides of the argument about PRP are seeking the moral high ground. I am not clear whether one could argue that money is a philosophical issue in this particular context. Certainly the discussion inevitably appears to be at the grubbier end of the philosophical. The Citizen's Charter is one of many examples that could have been chosen to show how this debate is taking place in a societal context. The STRB has to interpret the market and make a judgment about what is an appropriate structure and what level of annual pay increase, if any, is to be recommended to the Secretary of State. Maintaining the status quo is probably the easiest choice, and, perhaps, therefore, the most inappropriate alternative.

My personal dilemma is equally acute. I am conscious that apparently the great proportion of the teaching profession in Britain is opposed to

PRP, and that humility is allegedly a virtue. The arrogance of assuming the mantle of the unrecognized prophet seems somewhat daunting. However, I believe that teachers are motivated by money, certainly not only money, and possibly by money rather less than others. Nevertheless, I am paid four times more than the most junior member of my staff. Any differential should not be for having a responsibility but for carrying it out. Teachers should not be paid simply for being older but for having learned from experience, training, and professional development and, therefore, demonstrably performing better.

All this is to do with the management of schools, which, perhaps, can be relatively easily measured. Even more important and complex is what happens in the classroom. Headteachers may be such poor managers that they do not know which teachers inspire their pupils and which competently contain them. In that case, the children deserve better headteachers, trained to make such judgments. Those who inspire children in the classroom deserve recognition, including financial recognition. We pay outstanding teachers the same as the marginally competent unless they seek to leave the classroom to carry out administrative duties. At the higher levels of school management the responsibilities include those that they are not trained to carry out (for example, marketing, personnel, and financial) and can often be done better, and more cheaply, by others. This seems absurd rather than a dilemma. My personal dilemma is that few within the education service appear to agree with me.

REDESIGNING THE SALARY SYSTEM

There is the evidence that merit pay and career ladders have not been entirely successful in the United States. The discussion in Britain has concentrated on how models from the American education system, or British business, cannot possibly transfer to British schools. The proposed alternatives (Firestone, 1994) of knowledge and skills-based pay, job enlargement, and collective incentives for example, at least deserve consideration. They have the potential to enhance the motivation of teachers and to support other reforms. Knowledge and skills-based pay is not incompatible with teachers' views of their profession and with the flattening of school organizational structures. The complementary staff development of horizontal or vertical skills will help provide a culture of learning. Job enlargement is a less radical departure than knowledge-based pay. This involves developing a pay system that helps teachers take on additional, enriched tasks. The collective incentives approach in education focuses rather more on outcomes. This system also avoids the competitiveness and alleged divisiveness of individual incentive schemes.

In Britain the Secretary of State preferred individual PRP, whereas the STRB preferred whole school collective incentive schemes. The difficulty with this for the Secretary of State was that some inadequate teachers would be rewarded because of the excellence of their colleagues. There was also the problem that the worst schools would have the greatest potential for improving their performance. Both the Secretary of State and the STRB were clearly focusing on outcomes-based models. It seems increasingly likely that PRP will be imposed by the government, particularly for school leaders. There may be no additional money in 1995 except for PRP. This will ensure that the teacher associations are constrained to respond more positively to the government proposals.

PUBLIC OPINION

In a headline entitled "A black mark for the teacher conferences," an *Independent* (newspaper) editorial dated April 15, 1993, read:

Beneath these sentiments lies the underlying conviction among many teachers that any hint of competitiveness is anathema to the educational world. But nowadays nearly everyone works in teams. Those teams are no less cooperative if their members' salaries vary according to performance and ability. Performance related pay will help governing bodies retain excellent staff in the classroom. Indeed it is particularly important, during a period of inevitable and necessary public sector pay restraint, for employers to find ways of rewarding those staff who show initiative, enterprise and enthusiasm — and get results. Teachers are no different: they, like anyone else, will find that an extra point or two on their pay scale is a warming form of applause, even if it does not amount to much more cash. Good teachers have nothing to fear from performance related pay; on the contrary they have much to gain.

CONCLUSION

A systemic approach to educational reform requires that all policies be aligned to produce the desired effect. Pay policies are no exception. There has been no attempt in Britain to thoroughly consider how the national, or even locally determined, pay systems might be developed to complement and reinforce the educational reforms. Because the government is determined to pursue this approach, it would seem rational to at least consider rigorously the advantages and disadvantages of the various alternative approaches to PRP.

9

Equity and Efficiency: Tensions in School-based Management in England and Wales

Tim Simkins

THE CONTEXT OF REFORM

The Conservative Government's education reforms of the past six years in England and Wales, commencing with the Education Reform Act of 1988 and continuing with a number of further substantial pieces of legislation, embody a strategy designed to pursue its "five great themes" of "quality, diversity, increasing parental choice, greater autonomy for schools and greater accountability" (Department for Education, 1992: 2).

The reforms comprise a number of key components. At their organizational core lies the concept of school-based management. All schools — more than 90 percent of the total — which were previously administered by local education authorities (LEAs) are being given a substantial degree of autonomy. This takes one of two forms each of which, in Brown's (1990) terms, involves both organizational and political decentralization of power. In the weaker version — called local management of schools (LMS) — schools are given wide powers over the management of resources: school budgets and most aspects of personnel and premises management are managed at the level of the individual school. These powers are delegated to governing bodies containing representatives of parents, teachers, and the LEA as well as co-opted members; head-teachers are responsible to these bodies. Under LMS, however, schools remain under the umbrella of the LEA, which, among other things, is responsible for funding them through a local formula that has to be approved by the Department for Education, for employing the teachers (although governing bodies have full responsibilities for appointments and dismissals), and for managing capital works.

In contrast, under the other, more radical, form of school-based management — grant-maintained schools (GMS) — schools can "opt out" of local authority control to be funded centrally by the Department for Education. The governing bodies of such schools are effectively independent, owning their premises and employing their staff in addition to the powers that LMS governors have. To date, only a minority of schools have chosen the GMS route despite the government's preference for it.[1]

These approaches to school-based management are being introduced within a tightly regulated framework. First, all schools are being made much more explicitly subject to market pressures through a significant increase in the opportunities for parents to express preferences about the school they wish their child to attend. Second, however, this market is being firmly controlled through the implementation of a national curriculum through which the key elements of learning are being prescribed for all students aged 5 to 16 and a national system of testing and examinations for students aged 7, 11, 14, and 16 is being established. Finally, much more public information is being made available about schools. Examination and test results and other information — for example about non-authorized absences — is to be published regularly in a standard format on a school-by-school basis, schools are required to publish to parents a range of information about their philosophy and provision, and all schools are to be subject to inspection every four years with the results being published.

Taken together these reforms represent a radical and multifaceted attempt to address concerns about the effectiveness and efficiency of schooling in England and Wales. The theory underlying the strategy they embody matches quite closely that which Wohlstetter and Odden (1992: 530) argue underpins many school-based management initiatives in the United States: "Productivity and effectiveness can be enhanced if clear outcome goals are set at the top of the system, . . . implementation is decentralized to the school site where services are delivered, and accountability is structured either with rewards for accomplishing goals and sanctions for not or through parental choice of school."

As this quotation suggests, the prime stated purpose of the reforms is to raise the quality of education provision in schools. Success depends on a number of complex factors (Simkins, 1994; in press). However, it is important to recognize that the reforms also have important equity implications. Indeed, it could be argued that, despite the government's strong emphasis on the objectives of increasing effectiveness, efficiency, and choice in the school system, equity considerations are most likely to dominate the debate as we begin to work through the consequences of the reforms.

This chapter will attempt to provide a framework for considering these issues. It begins by exploring the meaning of the term "equity" with particular reference to its uses in relation to resource distribution in education. It then explores the central aspects of the reform from an equity perspective, arguing that such an approach raises a number of major issues that have received little attention because of the government's emphasis on the objectives of effectiveness, efficiency, and choice.

THE MEANING OF EQUITY

A useful starting point is to equate the concept of equity broadly with those of fairness and justice (Le Grand, 1991: Chap. 2). This in itself, however, does not take us very far. First, a distinction clearly needs to be made between procedural and distributional equity — the former concerning fair treatment in terms of rules and procedures, the latter concerning fairness in the distribution of resources. This chapter will concentrate on the latter.

Distributional equity can be treated in a number of ways, with terminology often being confusing and inconsistent. A useful starting point is the distinction between horizontal equity (the equal treatment of equals), and vertical equity (the unequal treatment of unequals). For those who value equity as an objective, this distinction is relatively incontroversial, and it highlights some key questions. For example:

How are "equals" and "unequals" to be defined? What categories are to be used and what criteria will distinguish between them?

What does "equal treatment" mean? Does it mean "identical" or "equivalent," for example? Should it be conceived in terms of access to resource provision, of the nature of the educational experiences that the resources provide, or of the outcomes or benefits that result for the individual?

How should treatment vary between unequals and why?

These questions are addressed in part by Wise (1967: Chap. 8) and Monk (1990: Chap. 2) who discuss a number of definitions of "equality of opportunity" that embody differing approaches to distributional equity. Drawing on their work, we can divide definitions of distributional equity into two broad categories. The first category, which defines equity in terms of resource inputs, comprises:

the "equal expenditure per student" definition;

the "maximum variance" definition: placing a limit on the permitted variance in expenditure per student;

the "foundation" definition: a prescribed minimum level of expenditure provided for all students; and

the "classification" definition: treating equally all members of specified categories,
whether these be defined in terms of need, ability to benefit, or some other
variable.

In policy terms, such expenditure-based approaches to funding for
equity are attractive, not least because they can be put into operation
fairly easily. Admittedly, the more sophisticated foundation and classification definitions do not, of themselves, resolve the questions outlined
above arising from the concepts of horizontal and vertical equity, but they
do make clear that the focus of attention is on the central policy concern of
expenditure levels. Viewed in economic terms, however, they leave a
good deal to be desired. In particular, they do not address the issue of the
relationship between expenditures, educational processes, and learning
outcomes. In other words, they do not account for the fact that the
distribution of resources in a particular way does not, in itself, guarantee that educational opportunities, let alone outcomes, will reflect this
distribution.

Divergence may occur for a number of reasons. For example, students
may be unwilling to utilize the resources offered or teachers and others
may not have the capacity to make the best use of the potential that the
resources provide. The first possibility raises a concept of equity that
relates to "deserts" or "merit." Why should those who are unwilling to
make good use of the resources provided receive them at the expense of
those who are willing? The second possibility draws attention to the
importance of the qualitative dimension of resource allocation that may
be embodied in such variables as teacher motivation, qualifications, or
school climate. Equal expenditure does not guarantee equality of provision in these terms.

To overcome such qualifications it is necessary to consider definitions
of equity that incorporate some view about the outcomes to which
the resources are intended to contribute. Wise (1967) suggests four such
definitions:

the "minimum attainment" definition: sufficient resources should be provided to
enable all students to reach a minimum level of attainment;
the "full opportunity" definition: resources should continue to be provided until
the marginal gains of all students are reduced to zero;
the "leveling" definition: resources should be distributed so that the least advan-
taged are favored most and variances in achievement are minimized; and
the "competition" definition: resources should be provided in proportion to the
students' ability to benefit.

If we consider the input- and outcome-based definitions together,
they fall into three categories (see Table 9.1). Two of the input-based

definitions (equal expenditure and maximum variance) are essentially concerned with resource equality rather than equity: they ensure that all are treated the same rather than treated fairly. Indeed, most would agree that such approaches are likely to be inequitable in their consequences unless the maximum variance is quite large. However, if this were the case, the definition would need to provide some rationale for determining and using the variance, and this would effectively transform it into a classification definition.

TABLE 9.1
Definitions of Equity

	Input-based	Outcome-based
Equality	Equal expenditure (strong)	
	Maximum variance (weak)	
Baseline	Foundation	Minimum attainment
Differential	Classification	Full opportunity
		Competition
		Leveling

The minimum attainment definition could be viewed as a stronger, outcome-based form of the foundation definition. It is unlikely, in fact, to imply an equal basic level of expenditure for all because different levels of expenditure will be required to enable students of differing abilities to achieve defined minimum levels of performance. Furthermore, its equity implications are strictly limited: all students are offered the opportunity to achieve a minimum level of attainment, but the definition says nothing about the distribution of opportunities beyond this. It can, however, provide an essential point of focus if there is concern about levels of achievement among lower attainers.

The remaining definitions embody more general rules for distribution. The classification definition is essentially a restatement of the concepts of horizontal and vertical equity, which leaves the key questions raised by these definitions unanswered beyond a requirement that treatment be defined in terms of expenditure. The full opportunity definition, in contrast, focuses explicitly on benefits. Such a definition is inherently attractive to educators. It bears some resemblance to the often stated goal of enabling each student to achieve his or her potential. However, as Monk (1990) points out, this definition is replete with problems. It is very difficult to operationalize; it places virtually unlimited demands on resources with no guidance about rationing if resources are insufficient; and its equity consequences are potentially serious if individual abilities to benefit vary markedly.

This leaves us with the leveling and competition definitions. These are particularly interesting because they provide clear rules for distributing scarce resources, and they also embody clear distributional values. They correspond fairly closely to distinctions made by other writers on the subject. Thus, Brown and Saks (1975) distinguish between individual teachers who are "elitists" and those who are "levellers" in their distribution of time and other resources among students, while Strike (1988), taking a more general position, characterizes "two general ways of thinking about justice in the allocation of education resources — utilitarianism and justice as fairness" (p. 174). The implications of the distinction made by all these authors are profound. If we assume that there is a fixed quantity of resources to be allocated and that students have different capacities to benefit in terms of learning from a given level of resources, then there is a clear choice available. We can attempt to maximize the total learning gain by directing resources to those whom we expect to gain the most, even though this may widen the distribution of learning outcomes (the competition, elitist, or utilitarian approach); or we can direct resources to those whom we judge to be most disadvantaged, thus, hopefully, reducing the level of variance in individual learning outcomes but at the potential cost of a lower total level of learning for the whole group (the leveling or justice as fairness approach).

Clearly it might be contested whether a competition definition could be said to embody any concept of equity at all. If we think of equity in terms of deserts or merit, rather than that of need, then, perhaps, it could. The argument, however, is fairly tenuous. Certainly, such an approach is inconsistent with Le Grand's argument that a situation is normally regarded as inequitable "if individuals receive less than others because of factors beyond their control" (Le Grand, 1991: 86). It seems more helpful to consider the competition and leveling definitions as reflecting resource allocation objectives that give different emphases to efficiency (defined in terms of maximizing the total learning gain from the application of resources) and equity (defined in terms of compensation for circumstances of disadvantage that are beyond the individual's control). In shorthand terms, the distinction between elitists and levelers is the relative emphasis they place on individuals' potential to benefit and on their need.

EDUCATIONAL REFORM AND EQUITY

How can these various concepts of equity be related to the educational reforms in England and Wales? As has already been indicated, the reforms are complex, comprising a number of components of change, some of which may be felt to be in tension. Their equity consequences, not surprisingly, are, therefore, difficult both to untangle and to predict. Broadly, however, they are likely to be a product of the interaction of three interrelated components of the reforms: formula funding, increased parental choice of school, and school-based management. This view may seem surprising; surely the key change is the implementation of a national curriculum whose purpose is to ensure for almost all children a basic curriculum entitlement between the ages of 5 to 16, accompanied by a testing regime designed to monitor the achievements that result. To some degree this is clearly true; the national curriculum does to a degree embody a kind of foundation definition of curricular content, but it neither prescribes nor guarantees the minimum level of resources that should be made available to make this curricular guarantee meaningful (National Union of Teachers, 1992a, 1992b). Furthermore, the national curriculum is currently being reviewed with the aim of making it simpler and less comprehensive. The prime determinants of the equity consequences of the reforms, therefore, are not likely to be the curriculum itself but the mechanisms through which it is resourced.

The prime determinant of the block budget of the school, which a child attends, is the funding formula that the relevant LEA is required to use to allocate resources among its schools.[2] At least 80 percent of the money allocated to schools must be distributed on the basis of the number and ages of students, with the remainder available to compensate for students' special needs and circumstances and for the diseconomies associated with small schools. Within these and other regulatory constraints, each LEA determines the formula that will be used to finance the schools in its area. The ways in which these formulae are designed — together with the overall level of funding within each LEA — are, therefore, the primary determinants of patterns of equity and inequity among schools both locally and nationally.[3]

The consequences of formula funding for an individual school, however, depend not only on the design of the formula — an essentially static concept — but also on the nature of the school's "market" where choices made by parents, and other factors, influence the size and composition of the school's student body. The formula and local market circumstances, therefore, interact to determine the broad distribution of resource opportunities among schools in a particular area and how these change absolutely and relatively over time. Such opportunities need to be considered broadly. Clearly budgetary levels are important, but, in addition, any full analysis of the resource position of a particular school — and hence of the degree of equity between schools — should also take account of such factors as the quality of resources it can attract (in terms, for example, of teacher experience and qualifications) and the characteristics of its student body, given evidence about peer group effects on achievement (Monk, 1990: 364–370).

The formula and local market circumstances, however, only determine the degree of equity between schools in the system and, hence, place constraints on the opportunities that schools can provide for individual students. The actual opportunities provided to any individual student within these constraints depend on a school's internal resource allocation policies and, in particular, on how the school chooses to use the freedoms given to it under the school-based management component of the reforms. Such policies will reflect the school's philosophy and objectives, including an explicit or implicit understanding of equity issues, but increasingly these are likely to be colored by perceptions of the effects of particular policies on the school's market position. It is the interplay between these factors that the rest of this chapter discusses.

SCHOOLS IN THE MARKETPLACE

The main reason why the government has chosen to tie school budgets so closely to student numbers is to make schools more responsive to parental wishes. Funding by formula is intended to enable popular (and, hence, good) schools to grow while unpopular schools contract and eventually close. Growth and decline, therefore, will depend in part — and sometimes substantially — on the degree to which schools can maintain their market position in terms of attractiveness to parents with the power to choose. There is a growing body of research on parental choice in the United Kingdom (Glatter, Johnson, & Woods, 1993), but only relatively recently has research begun on school responses to such choice and the interactions that occur in the "competitive arenas" that are developing as a result (Glatter & Woods, 1993; Woods, 1992). The issues emerging from this research can only be touched on here. Two points are of particular importance. First, parental preferences seem to be differentiated, among other things, by social factors (Glatter & Woods, 1993), suggesting that schools seeking to respond to parental preferences may need to make fundamental decisions about which parent preferences should receive priority (assuming, of course, that certain types of preferences are incompatible in terms of their policy and resource allocation implications), and, indeed, which groups of parents they wish particularly to attract.

Second, schools faced with increased competition have a number of strategies available to them (Glatter, 1993b; Woods, in press). As a minimum they are likely to pursue "promotional" strategies designed to raise the school's profile. Beyond this, however, they may pursue systematic "scanning" strategies to find out more about their markets and the factors that influence parent preferences. They may then use such information to change substantively what they do in an attempt to match more closely the perceived preferences of parents (more will be said about this). Alternatively, they may seek to change the characteristics of their student bodies through management of their admission policies or their policies in relation to the exclusion of students who are disruptive or have other behavioral problems.

Some schools have always had a selective intake; in some parts of the country students have been selected for the more academic grammar schools on the basis of tests at the age of 11 with the remainder of the age group (the large majority) going to secondary modern schools. In most areas, however, schools are comprehensive — they apply no formal test of ability or achievement at the point of entry and the primary determinant of the school a child attends is his or her place of residence. The introduction of open enrollment and increased competition, however, opens the possibility that the more "popular" schools will try to become more selective in their intake. Initially, the government was cautious about such a development because the idea of schools selecting students rather than parents selecting schools seemed inconsistent with the rhetoric of a policy of parental choice.

The position is subtly changing, however. Research on GMS (Bush, Coleman, & Glover, 1993) has found that schools that are oversubscribed are able to influence the socioeconomic and academic composition of their intake without using formal entrance examinations or tests.[4] However, it is too early to draw general conclusions about these kinds of effects for the majority of schools in England and Wales that are under LEA control through LMS schemes, not least because, for these schools, admissions policies are operated by the LEAs and not the schools themselves. However, one small-scale study of LMS schools shows how some may actively attempt to change the composition of their student body to improve their market position (Deem, Brehoney, & New, 1993). Such developments are likely to increase under new government regulations that will allow schools to introduce a limited degree of selection (up to 10 percent of their intake on the basis of ability in one or more of music, art, drama, and physical education) without seeking permission to do so. There is growing evidence, too, that the number of exclusions of children with behavioral difficulties is rising (Stirling, 1992; Imich, 1994), although it would be premature to link this trend to the effects of increased competition, and the government has recently discouraged exclusion except in exceptional cases.

The effects on equity among schools of the increased "marketization" of education has been widely commented upon elsewhere (for example, Jonathan, 1989, 1990; Ball, 1993b), and evidence is emerging only slowly. This is the arena in which the debate about the balance between efficiency and equity is likely to become sharpest, with the question of efficiency in the provision *of what* and *for whom* becoming major issues. It should not be assumed, however, that the broader school system is the only arena in which these issues will be played out. Much less researched and debated — yet also of considerable importance—is the "internal arena" of the individual school.

SCHOOL-BASED MANAGEMENT

According to the government "effective schemes of local management will enable governing bodies and head teachers to plan their use of resources . . . to maximum effect in accordance with their own needs and priorities, and to make schools more responsive to their clients" (Department of Education and Science, 1988: Para. 9). This will "increase the quality of education by making more effective use of the existing resources for teaching and learning" (Department of Education and Science, 1988: Para. 23). Whether school-based budgeting will indeed achieve improved effectiveness and efficiency of schooling is an important empirical question that cannot be addressed here (see Simkins, 1994, in press). Freedom to allocate resources internally in relation to their own perceived needs and priorities, however, also has potential implications for equity. Whatever the systems-level equity consequences of the reforms, school-based management gives individual schools the power, at least to a degree, to reinforce or mitigate these through the internal resource allocation policies that they pursue.

Very little has been written about the values, priorities, and assumptions that underlie such internal school policies. However, there can be little doubt that, for most schools, equity considerations play an important part. To explore such issues in more detail, a number of questions could be asked. For example:

Which groups of students and which aspects of the curriculum are resourced most favorably through smaller class sizes or other forms of additional resourcing?

What factors determine the ways in which teachers are allocated among groups?

How are special needs defined and resourced? What is the balance between provision for students with different levels of ability or differences in socioeconomic background?

How are choices about the allocation of resources discussed? Is the emphasis on need (particularly in relation to relative disadvantage, however defined) or in terms of the contribution that particular resources can make to increases in achievement? If the latter, whose achievement is emphasized?

In exploring such questions, a number of the concepts of equity outlined earlier are likely to be relevant. Many aspects of resource provision in schools seem to be predicated on equal expenditure assumptions — for example, the aim (which may not be easy to achieve) of equalizing class sizes in a primary school or the allocation of the teaching materials budgets on a strict per capita basis in a secondary school. Planned differentiation of resource inputs also occurs — for example, through differentiating class sizes among student groups with different perceived levels of ability or providing additional staff and other resources for students with special educational needs. Where such differentiation occurs, it is interesting to speculate (little evidence is available) on whether the rationale for such policies is based solely on input-based ideas about equity — most obviously through compensation for various forms of disadvantage — or on more sophisticated output-based ideas that attempt to relate, however vaguely, resourcing strategies to their likely learning outcomes. If the latter makes any contribution at all to resourcing policies then Brown and Saks' (1975) ideas about elitist and leveling strategies gain considerable potential relevance at the school, as well as the classroom, level.

How does all this relate to the consequences of the reforms? First, school-based management gives many schools much greater freedom to pursue their own equity values through their internal resourcing policies. Such values may be embodied in their general policies on resource distribution or in specific policies for meeting the special needs of particular student groups. With respect to the latter, the ability to make free choices about the use of block budgets means that schools will need to give particular consideration to the opportunity costs of educating children with special needs in terms of their provision for the student population as a whole. There is some evidence that rates of statementing[5] and of the number of students taught outside mainstream schools may be rising, and a number of authors argue that these trends are symptoms of increasing pressures on the ability of schools to provide adequately for students with special needs (Evans & Lunt, 1993). New regulations will require schools to specify in some detail their policies for identifying, assessing, providing for, and monitoring the 18 percent of students who have special needs that are insufficiently severe to require a statement (Department for Education, 1994). This will, no doubt, lead to equity issues receiving more explicit attention in school development plans. However, the resource demands of the proposed procedures are potentially considerable (Bibby & Lunt, 1994), and there is a "danger that the gap between well-resourced schools with comparatively few students with special needs and schools struggling with large numbers of pupils in need will grow wider than ever" (Peter, 1994).

Second, however, such policies must be pursued within the broader framework provided by formula funding and the market. It has been suggested in the previous section that one way schools may respond to their market circumstances is to change substantively what they do in response to their perceptions of parental preferences. Such changes may be designed to affect the school's performance in terms of the published indicators or of other factors that are valued by parents. One study found that such changes, drawn from a variety of schools, "include alterations to homework policy, the introduction of banding [tracking], emphasis on the caring and pastoral aspects of schooling, encouragement of staff to gain more qualifications, increased stress on extra-curricular activities and greater community access to school facilities" (Glatter & Woods, 1993: 15). Many such changes may be efficiency-enhancing as the government intends and hopes. However, it is also possible that a school's strategies may have equity consequences.

For example, the government clearly seems to intend that the increasing publicity being given to the publication of test and examination results has the effect of changing parent preferences so that these results dominate further their perceptions of the quality of education provided by particular schools. If schools believe this is happening, increasing numbers of them are likely to consider how their performance on these indicators might best be influenced. Several responses are clearly possible. The school might take the indicator as a given and attempt to influence the way in which it is interpreted by parents of existing and potential students, perhaps by providing contextualizing information to explain areas of apparently poor performance and complementary information about aspects of performance that the published indicators do not pick up. Such a strategy may or may not succeed. If not, there will be an incentive for some schools to explore ways of raising their scores on such indicators. This could move them to internal resource allocation strategies that are elitist (emphasizing ability to benefit) rather than leveling (emphasizing educational need).

CONCLUSION

The government's rationale for its reforms in England and Wales makes no explicit reference to equity. The twin issues of quality and choice are claimed to drive the reforms. Yet the very comprehensiveness of the changes being implemented makes it inherently implausible that they will be neutral in equity terms. Predicting their equity consequences, however, is far from easy. The concept is multifaceted, and the comprehensive nature of the reforms provides a variety of mechanisms through which equity might be enhanced or reduced.

Parental decisions and other factors in a school's market will determine whether a school's roll increases or decreases. Changes in school size may affect the range and quality of opportunities that schools can offer their students. However, beyond this, perceptions of a school's present and prospective market position may affect its ability to attract and retain high quality staff and may also have an effect on the social and academic composition of its student body. The equity consequences of these qualitative factors may be considerable.

Formula funding within a context of increased marketization, then, presents school managers with considerable challenges. The policies that they develop internally to address the issue of equity cannot be conceived in isolation from the changing environmental pressures to which the school is subject. Little evidence is available at present to predict how schools will adjust their internal resource allocation policies to their new situations. However, it does seem plausible to suggest that a major question for the future will be how schools in different circumstances achieve a balance between concerns for efficiency in terms of aggregate educational achievement — their potentially elitist implications — and concerns for equity embodied in a more leveling approach to resource allocation.

A comprehensive discussion of equity within a context, for many schools, of increasing resource constraint and increasingly complex and challenging environmental pressures will bring to the surface difficult, yet fundamental, questions about their core values and the degree to which these can, and should, be defended in an increasingly hostile world. Ball (1993a) argues that the empowerment of schools under school-based management and the parallel disempowering of the LEA is having the effect of "privatizing" to individual schools the means by which social values are translated into educational policy. One result of this could be that the degree of equity or inequity in the educational system as a whole becomes little more than an aggregate product of the individual policies of many thousands of independent schools in the marketplace. Such a diagnosis would be premature,[6] but it is certainly the case that school-based management, when coupled with increased parental choice, raises considerably the stakes attached to schools' internal resource allocation policies and the ways in which schools choose to respond to the increasingly complex and demanding challenges with which they are faced.

NOTES

A longer version of this chapter appears in Simkins (1995).

1. By the end of 1993, about 15 percent of secondary schools and 1 percent of primary schools had achieved grant-maintained status.

2. The LEA formula applies to LMS schools only. However, GMSs are funded by the Department for Education broadly on the same basis as they would have been funded if they had remained with their LEA.

3. For a consideration of these issues see the longer version of this chapter in Simkins (1995).

4. A common approach is to interview parents and students to determine their motivational characteristics in relation to schooling.

5.   Around 2 percent of students are assessed for "statements" that require LEAs to ensure that specific levels of resourcing are provided to meet their individual needs.

6.   LEAs retain important powers in relation to admissions to LMS schools and special needs provision in relation to schools under local management and GMSs.

IV

ROLE DILEMMAS OF
SCHOOL LEADERS

10

Principals' Dilemmas: Intraorganizational Demands and Environmental Boundary Spanning Activities

Jack Y. L. Lam

School administrators in Canada are facing many dilemmas in executing their responsibilities these days. Basically, these dilemmas arise as principals' responsibilities increase in scope and complexity. In a social environment marked by turmoil and constraints, school operation is embroiled in a continued controversy: the declining resources that the school receives clash with rising public expectations of what the school should achieve. The philosophical orientation of providing educational equality for all students, punctuated by the current mainstreaming movement, runs counter to the demand for academic excellence in the face of international comparison and competition.

In the context of these basic contradictions, this chapter intends to explore in detail two major dimensions of tensions and contradictions inherent in principals' roles — internal needs for greater coordination and environmental demands for more assertive leadership.

INTERNAL ADMINISTRATION

Within the internal dimension of administrative responsibilities, dilemmas are found in four levels of principals' operation. Details of these problematic areas must be fully scrutinized to develop an insight into the challenges and concerns current principals face.

School Missions

Amid the confusion of basic school missions, the school continues to receive unambiguous messages from the public that it should be restructured and reformed along the model of corporate business to achieve effectiveness. The ghost of the past, namely Callahan's "cult of efficiency" associated with the early Scientific School of Management (Etzioni, 1964) seems reincarnated and coated in new terminologies. Such a hard-nosed approach, while useful in shaking a domesticated enterprise like the school from a state of complacency, is certainly a misfit with the traditional humanitarian approach of viewing school as a nurturing and learning center catering to students' individual needs and capabilities. The search for a viable vision, so critical for preserving the vitality of professional leadership in school, continues to be distracted with tempting mirages and pragmatic constraints.

School-based Management

From another perspective, the ongoing process of decentralization, that is, school-based management with its diversified formats (Wohlstetter & Odden, 1992), is beginning to raise more questions among scholars and researchers in its intent as a governance reform to improve educational practice. While school-based management as a practice gains growing acceptance (Malen, Ogawa, & Kranz, 1990), the extent of decision-making responsibility devolved to the school is limited (Lam, 1995). In some situations, given the apparent need of the division or district to maintain some uniformity of goals (objectives), policy, and procedure, and to assure equitable allocation of resources, principals and their staffs have little to manage in critical areas, such as budget, personnel, and curriculum. Principals as middle managers, while attempting to adhere to the spirit of rhetoric decentralization, continue to be frustrated with the constraints of the deep-rooted centralization.

Another dilemma associated with school-based management is illuminated in two incompatible trends in the United States of advancing the professional autonomy, that is, teacher empowerment, and of resurrecting the lay democratic control to revive the ineffectiveness of the school board (McDonnell, 1991).

Literature on job satisfaction (Grier, 1988;), supervision (Gitlin & Price, 1992), and job commitment (Firestone, 1990) all point to the need for giving teachers a greater voice in improving educational practice. Teacher empowerment is deemed an appropriate remedy for correcting the first wave of U.S. educational reform that emphasized teaching quality improvement and teachers' compliance to regulations. The revival of community involvement in the school council to make critical decisions related to staffing, fiscal management, and curriculum changes is gaining momentum as a means of reversing the loss of grassroots contacts. This community involvement is in basic contradiction to the teacher empowerment movement, because both focus on the same jurisdictions and issues. Canadian school principals are in need of guidance from the U.S. lesson as to what model is more effective in improving school performance.

Staff Supervision and Termination

Educational reform, if it is to have a chance to succeed, depends heavily on how well teachers are upgraded and prepared. This is particularly important when the job responsibilities of teachers are increasing (Lam, 1984).

The term "supervision" has long changed its connotation from inspection (Bolin & Panaritis, 1992) to one of collegial clinical supervision and self reflection and improvement (Grimmett, Rostad, & Ford, 1992). However, the traditional practice of top-down supervision prescribed by provincial and state statutes and school division and district by-laws is still prevalent, creating unbridgeable dissonance among school administrators between what is advocated in professional literature and what is mandated by law.

We might argue that the traditional practice is justified in monitoring beginning teachers who need all the supervision and assistance they can get before they are formally assessed for tenure. Yet, the politically motivated Bill 77 in Manitoba, for instance, makes principals' decisions on staff tenure difficult because the probationary period has been reduced to ten months. Here the principals face another dilemma. Should their judgment err, either the candidates or students will suffer. Once the teaching staff are hired, principals will find it hard to remove the incompetent staff members in view of the legal demand for "due process."

The irony experienced by school administrators is that decentralization does not necessarily provide the kind of decisional autonomy they hope for. Rather, they are facing more of the legal and professional constraints that have been handed down to them by their superintendents. Thus, while school boards technically and ultimately are responsible for the legal wrangling, school administrators are now the frontline figures facing staff animosity while executing dismissal procedures. The dissonance of feeling powerless amid shouldering more responsibilities is indeed keenly felt by many school administrators.

Counselling and Disciplining Students

At the fourth administrative level, dealing with management of the student population, principals are confronted with perpetual problems of carrying out the incompatible roles of counseling and disciplining students. In brief, the counseling role deals with the provision of support, encouragement, and advice to students, whereas the disciplining role deals with dispensing of punishments, reporting to law enforcement agencies suspected illegal activities, and expulsion. With the decline of influence exerted by other institutions, such as churches and family, schools alone are left with the tasks of nurturing and educating the young. The lack of coherent social values, changing moral ethics, and complex social problems facing students have possibly adverse influences on students' attitudes toward study and the nature of their subculture. The continued need to deal with disciplinary problems, far more severe than they were decades ago, poses perpetual challenges to all school principals (Bowen, 1988).

EXTERNAL ADMINISTRATION

Nesting in the emergent role for school principals is the growing need to deal with the external dimension of school administration. The debates about the quality of public education (Williams & Millinoff, 1990; Lam, 1991a) and the recent empirical evidence of the substantial external constraint on the school system as a whole underscore the need for school administrators to focus on various stakeholders and external forces and to engage in boundary spanning activities more systematically. Inevitably, as a "resource dependent" organization (Aldrich, 1979), sensitive and susceptible to the political will of the public, the once "domesticated enterprises" that Carlson (1975) described must live up to the expectations of stakeholders in the pervasive movement for accountability. In this aspect, there are also four levels of dilemmas that should be explored.

School-parent Partnership

At the first level is a principal's persistent concern for cultivating amiable relationships with parents. Ironically, school-parent partnerships, with the common concern about children, are not always approached from compatible perspectives. In such a context, the partnership is fragile and unstable as formal allies can easily be turned into potential adversaries. Conflict between parents and teachers places school principals in a minefield. Support for their staff, as their leadership responsibility calls for, puts them at odds with parents who are seeking "justice" for their children. When the conflict spills into a courtroom, as it does sometimes, the principal is put in a lose-lose situation. Whatever the judicial outcome, the public relation function is damaged beyond repair. The management of partnership is, therefore, a tricky affair and it taxes principals' problem-solving and conflict-resolution skills to the extreme.

Publicity versus Vulnerabilities

As the public schools encounter greater criticism, many principals make their schools and classrooms accessible to the public. At the same time, more efforts are now devoted to publicity campaigns, making use of the mass media to disseminate good news from the schools. This open access, however, carries potential perils for critics to selectively examine their areas of interest and attack policies, procedures, and operational strategies that do not meet their expectations. The tendency for sensational journalism to exaggerate school ills is still prevalent. Open access is, therefore, a double-edged sword or a mixed blessing, forcing the school to operate in a transparent environment, subject to constant scrutiny.

Cooperation versus Loss of Control

Somewhat less apparent but, nonetheless, real is the dissonance for public educators in general and principals in particular to compromise their professional autonomy to solidify alliances with stakeholders and the public. The public school is forever dependent on the cooperation of parents to provide input into its goals and objectives, its policy formulation and implementation, its disciplinary measures, its numerous school functions, and its attempts to seek alternate sources of funding. The public school is also increasingly dependent upon social workers and law enforcement agencies to monitor and correct the antisocial behaviors of students. It is dependent on the goodwill of the Chamber of Commerce and business community for the success of its cooperative programs, for moral and fiscal support in raising special levies, in sponsoring educational events, in donating hardware and software, and in fundraising.

However, the more principals are successful in securing external support for personnel, curriculum, technical, and financial resources, the more principals have to engage in consultative processes and the less autonomy they possess in making administrative decisions. Dissonance is so sharp that no sooner have the principals been entrusted with greater authority through a school-based management model than they have to give it up for the purpose of consultative democracy.

External Constraints

With the increasing politicization of interest groups and stakeholders, the environment of the public school is becoming more turbulent (Wirt & Kirst, 1982) and is facing a multitude of external constraints (Lam, 1991b). Politically, the constant changes in educational policies and shifting locus of decision have thrown the school into a state of flux. Increasing government restraints in funding and resource allocation have compelled the school to continue the painful process of program and staff cutbacks. The lack of social consensus in values has greatly hampered the school's socialization effort. The enrollment fluctuation has pushed the school into an expansion-contraction cycle. The multiethnicity of student populations sets in motion new problems related to race relationships. The need for setting up second language and heritage programs creates logistical problems of personnel and resource redeployment.

Managing and neutralizing external threats is one of the most significant emerging roles of the school administrator. Without retaining some degree of internal stability, the core technology (Scott, 1987) will be gravely disturbed, and the domino effect will take place: the public school is unlikely to fulfill its basic mandates, public confidence in the system will be further eroded, and the ongoing search for alternatives (private school, home schooling) will be intensified.

POSSIBLE SOLUTIONS TO THE CURRENT DILEMMAS

Confronting the rising need for internal monitoring of school activities and for pacifying disruptive external forces underscores the greatest dilemma for school administrators. There are no easy answers to questions like: Which should receive priority? Which should be sacrificed to secure sufficient administrative time to deal adequately with an emergency? What consequences would follow if some administrative tasks have to be delayed or relegated to secondary importance?

In light of the complicated layers of dilemmas confronting school principals at present, the last section of this chapter is devoted to the search for strategies in managing the identified dilemmas. Pertinent literature and recent empirical evidence were consulted to develop and propose a plan of action for school administrators.

Some Conventional Approaches

The most apparent solution to current dilemmas is to train school administrators in time management. With greater ability to utilize the available time, principals can streamline their schedules, maximize their limited time for multiple demands, and minimize the downtime on routine tasks so that their entire operation will be optimized.

A similar approach is the prioritization of tasks principals have to deal with. Underlying this approach is the assumption that if principals recognize what is more important versus what is less so, there will be a more systematic attempt to rank issues that compete for attention simultaneously.

While the wisdom of these conventional means of dealing with dilemmas remains to be verified, we are doubtful about their overall effectiveness. For one thing, there is only so much time one can maximally utilize in a day, and no matter how much one prioritizes, there are always chances of running into a situation where all issues carry similar weight or significance. Both time management and prioritization are mechanisms addressing symptoms of administrative problems. Unless the deep-rooted problems are tackled, administrative dilemmas cannot be dealt with adequately.

For a more in-depth strategy for resolving dilemmas, a three-prong approach must be entertained. This involves:

an intrapersonal reflection of the existing and emergent roles,

an intraorganizational restructuring pertaining to the redistribution of power and
    responsibilities, and streamlining of school operation; and,

an extraorganizational initiative of taming the turbulent school environment.

Intrapersonal Reflection of Existing and Emergent Roles

Within the intrapersonal strategies of resolving administrative dilem-mas, principals must undergo a fundamental psychological reorientation to their emergent roles. With their operational parameter being modified by internal demands and external constraints, principals cannot hold on to their traditional responsibilities and at the same time rise to the chal-lenges of emerging demands.

More specifically, they should be aware that minimizing dilemmas necessitates a paradigm shift in terms of decentralization and empower-ment of others (Lam, 1994), particularly of their teaching staff. It is only when they are ready to share their traditional and newly found power can restructuring be completed harmoniously.

Intraorganizational Restructuring

Power Sharing and Teacher Empowerment

Reducing administrative dilemmas involves power sharing and teacher empowerment. When teachers are given greater opportunity for sharing decision-making power, problems related to the four major sectors of the school operation — school mission, school-based manage-ment, staff supervision, and counseling and disciplining students — can be controlled.

While the public school is getting conflicting signals from the commu-nity, the nature of students in different public schools should assist prin-cipals, staff, and, hopefully, parents in defining a set of appropriate and attainable goals that best serve the present clientele. When there is a consensus of priorities, teachers and principals can work with greater harmony and a clearer sense of purpose while, at the same time, enjoying greater community support. This, in turn, will lead to a more rational allocation of resources and some common base for assessing the performance of the individual staff and the school as a whole.

While school-based management has not empowered the school to do what this concept was intended to do, principals should view this as a transitional stage where the school division and district administrators have to get used to relinquishing their traditional power to their subordinates, and they must persevere until full autonomy is attained.

If the public at large expresses an interest in the governance of the public school, principals should not perceive this as a threat to professional power but, rather, as an extension of the boundary spanning activities in which they are now engaging. When representatives of the major stakeholders are directly involved in policy formulation for individual public schools, they are less likely to criticize the system. In this sense, the public representatives in the school committee will serve as a buffer against unwarranted attack and criticism that many public schools are now facing. Over time, the school should enjoy a greater degree of public support.

Greater decentralization in supervision should likewise be a blessing for the principal. With wider implementation of peer coaching and mentorship, principals are free from the traditional, and sometimes senseless rituals of classroom visitations of all teaching staff, and can focus on only the beginning teachers and those who are in need of special assistance in their professional growth. This should be most beneficial to all teachers in their various stages of career development.

In a similar vein, when the teaching staff is empowered to deal with all aspects of the school operation, the function of counseling and disciplining students does not necessarily come solely from the principal's office. Such a diffusion of power should minimize conflicting role expectations and resolve the dilemmas associated with role incompatibility.

Role Redefinition

With the shifting of power from the traditional base to a more diffused power base both within and without the school system, there is definitely an urgent need to redefine the role and responsibilities. Internally, role redefinition reduces ambiguity and confusion, and clarifies lines of communication in intraorganizational restructuring. Dilemmas arising from inconsistency in job demands can be resolved more effectively. Should all internal school responsibilities be assigned to the vice principals, the major constraints currently experienced by the principals will be brought under control, and the whole operation can be streamlined. Indeed, role redefinition holds opportunities for maximizing personnel deployment and diffuses the pressure that builds on the "focal organization."

When the power is more evenly disbursed within and without the system, directions and orders will be replaced with collective decision making and with interpersonal or intergroup negotiation, broadly termed "negotiated order" (Bacharach & Lawler, 1982; Lam, 1993; Martin, 1976). For principals, tough and unpopular decisions will be rationally worked out in a group situation. Principals will be facilitators rather than the ones giving orders; they are no longer vulnerable to criticism and attack.

Routinization

One of the major reasons that so many principals experience stress on the job is their need to search for fresh solutions to problems and crises. Because they do not have the luxury to study in detail the origin or the root of the problem, they are inclined to prescribe solutions to the symptoms of problems, only to find themselves further entangled in the endless cycle of firefighting or crisis management.

Routinization of the problem-solving process seems to be a panacea to this phenomenon. After sources of similar problems have been categorized by the school administrator and his or her staff, policies defining both the parameter and procedures for handling problems in the same category will be spelled out clearly in steps or stages. When issues from the same categories arise in the future, existing procedures in dealing with the same type of issues will be applied automatically. Principals will no longer squander their resources on revamping new solutions. This should also assist principals in reducing the stress of dealing with dilemmas.

Extraorganizational Initiatives

Environmental Scanning and Proactive Planning

Placed in a working environment of high constraint, school administrators must engage more than ever in environmental scanning so they will be fully prepared for what is going to affect the school. Included in environmental scanning is a closer contact with the provincial or state department of education and the semi-official professional bodies, for example, teacher and trustee associations, and principals' own provincial organizations. By keeping in close contact with key people in the government and professional organizations, current and emergent issues that usually formulate the basis of government policies will be tackled more thoroughly and comprehensively.

Proactive planning in the context of uncertainty will be most beneficial to the school; it will not be in a state of panic when disturbing news or changes arrive. Instead, there will be a more comprehensive set of strategies for internal adjustment to absorb or deflect disruptive external forces.

Boundary Spanning and Networking

While environmental scanning and related proactive planning are primarily defensive in nature, boundary spanning and networking must be conceived as offensive strategies that principals can take.

By aggressively networking, seeking, and nurturing political linkages with these special interest groups, new sources of resources for the school are identified. Furthermore, additional buffers have been erected against turbulence from the external environment. New partnerships with social and law enforcement agencies can be cemented to combat many of the social and disciplinary problems engulfing public schools.

Lobbying

Hand in hand with the boundary spanning and networking activities is the active lobbying efforts that school principals have to undertake at the local and provincial or state levels to ensure that the policies and regulations developed are school-friendly.

In contrast to the conventional thinking that lobbying is a subversive force, Renihan (1990) asserts that lobbying is a "healthy reconstruction of preference, a clarification of positions and a valuable source of information for policy makers." To engage in active lobbying either as individuals or groups demands that principals develop an understanding of political intricacies at all levels. In a highly volatile political climate, principals will find lobbying one of the best defensive measures for nipping disruptive policies in the bud.

CONCLUSION

In executing their responsibilities, principals are facing many administrative dilemmas. These dilemmas likely originated from global societal changes and knowledge advancement that have an immediate impact on principals' roles and role expectations while the school system retains the inertia of attempting to carry on its time-honored functions.

To reconcile the conflicting internal demands and external constraints, conventional quick-fix remedies are destined to fail and strategies transcending intrapersonal, intraorganizational, and extraorganizational dimensions must be contemplated. In brief, principals need to reorient to the changing demands of their job, to share power both with the school staff and community stakeholders, to streamline their internal operation, and to engage more aggressively in boundary spanning political activities if their leadership is to remain intact in a trying time.

11

New Principals' Experiences with Leadership: Crossing the Cultural Boundary

Robert B. MacMillan

People inside and outside of school settings have preconceived ideas about the principal's role — ideas that are based on their previous experience with individuals in that role and on community and societal expectations and assumptions. Unfortunately, unless they are principals themselves, these individuals have limited means to test their understanding of principals' work. Even candidates for the principalship who have acquired a knowledge of the role through experience in other positions and through administrative training programs do not have knowledge of administration in practice or of the increasing complexity of the role created by the meshing of contextual variables in unexpected ways (Cuban, 1994).

Newly appointed principals face a difficult dilemma: while learning to be administrators and how to cope with the complexity of the role, beginning principals often must do so without the luxury of time to reflect on what they are learning (for example, Roberts, 1992b). During entry, then, beginning principals face the difficult task of confirming or rejecting their preconceptions of administration while adjusting to new sets of responsibilities and expectations.

At the same time, new principals must try to unravel the complexities and implications of the culture of their new schools (Schein, 1989: 299) and make decisions based on their understanding of that culture. To be judged effective by teachers and other stakeholders, however, these decisions must be acceptable, or at least understandable, within the context of their organization (Blau, 1964: 201–202).

Often in the course of learning about the principalship, new administrators begin to perceive the development of a difference and distance or
separateness between themselves and their staffs. One possible source of
this perception may be the nature of the role and the demands placed on
it by teachers. As Ball (1987: 57) puts it: "Like prime ministers, heads
[principals] are people that their subordinates love to hate. The demands
addressed to the head defy satisfaction because they frequently contain
contradictory expectations."

While we may intellectually acknowledge the existence of a distance
and difference between administrators and teachers, Marshall (1991) suggests
that the "chasm" separating the two may not be as deep or as wide as
people believe it to be. In her study of individuals newly appointed to
various administrative positions and of their agreement with teachers
about schools, she found little to suggest that a chasm exists between
administrators and teachers. She suggests three possible explanations for
her findings. One she calls the "New Era" hypothesis, which states that
principals have actually changed and are closer to teachers in their
conception of schools. The second she terms the "Micropolitical" hypothesis, which states principals may have dissembled or deconstructed their
responses to mask their true sentiments and to present politically correct
rhetoric. In the third or "Methodological" hypothesis she provides possible reasons for not finding the expected conflicts, including wrong
research assumptions, participants too new to their positions, the use of
potentially biased interviewers and instruments, and the suppression of
conflict and self-deception by participants.

This chapter investigates further Marshall's conception of a chasm
separating administrators and teachers. The main differences between
this study and hers are: only beginning principals were involved; the
interviewer had no connections to the school district; and the interviews
used open-ended questions to permit an exploration of each principal's
experiences. Unlike Marshall's participants, the two participating beginning principals were very clear about the internal and external conflicts
they had experienced during their entry into the profession. For this chapter, then, the questions to be examined are: What is the nature of an individual's passage from the role of teacher to the role of principal? Is there a
separation between principals and teachers? If there is a separation, then
what is the nature of that separation? "Role distance" is used interchangeably here with "role separation" to denote the difference between the
teacher's and the principal's role.

THE STUDY

This study is part of a larger one focusing on succession. The data used
here were collected through semistructured interviews with two new

secondary school principals, Beth and Jim, both of whom worked in the same school district serving the fringes of a large urban area. While Beth's school was quite large (1,650 students) and had a particular programmatic focus on the arts, Jim's was small for the area (650 students) and had no programmatic focus. Although new to the principalship, both participants had experience in various administrative roles in other schools. They had been appointed to their latest positions as part of the school district's policy for the systematic rotation of its administrators. This policy, as the district saw it, helped to maintain a sense of expectation among its administrators and provided a pool of versatile administrators by requiring the rotation of principals at intervals of approximately five years.

Each interview lasted from one and one-half to two hours and excerpts from the interviews were transcribed from the tape recordings. The data were analyzed to isolate descriptions of practices used during the process of entry and to determine what the principals understood about the changes they experienced during this process. Wherever possible, reflections about practices were noted.

DISCUSSION

Role Distance and Status Passage:
The New Principal's Perspective

For her study, Marshall (1991) assumed that role separation exists between teachers and principals. In most other organizations, the distance between managers and workers is taken for granted and is believed to be caused, at least in part, by the uncertainty inherent in the managerial function (Kanter, 1977). In these organizations, the administrative structure appears to be quite stable, but new officeholders soon discover this is a facade. Almost as part of the price of entry, new administrators continue to perpetuate the myth of stability by helping to restrict access to information about the managerial role to maintain the appearance of being "predictable and routine" (Kanter, 1977: 48). To limit the effects of uncertainty, any aggression role takers may feel as a result of their frustration with the organization is often turned outward toward subordinates (Hirschorn, 1988: 55). Only through the "social similarity" of administrators' experience (Kanter, 1977: 48) is discussion of difficulties permitted between managers but not between managers and nonmanagers. Unfortunately, this action only serves to isolate them further from those under their administration, adds to the role distance between managers and their employees (Goffman, 1961b: 115), and limits severely any possibility for a comprehensive understanding of the managerial role by aspirants. This is no less true of beginning principals who at first may not believe in the existence of a distance between themselves and teachers;

later, when they have experienced that distance, they may have difficulty comprehending the extent of that distance (for example, Parkay, 1992; Hall, 1992).

Initially, for beginning principals, as with administrators in other contexts, their appointment usually creates a sense of excitement and of opening opportunities (Sarason, 1972). The prospect of effecting school-wide changes and of influencing the system as a whole looms large in their imaginations. Once in office, however, perspectives change and a reality different from initial perceptions intrudes, a reality that forces acknowledgment of the organizational limitations placed on them (for example, Hill, 1992; Roberts, 1992a).

On further investigation, these new principals often describe their promotion not only in terms of a status passage (Glaser & Strauss, 1971), but also in terms reminiscent of entry into another culture entirely. Once-familiar patterns of behavior are no longer as familiar or as understandable from the perspective of their new role. Assumptions they made about the principalship while still teachers are called into question by exposure to new norms of behavior and to new values and assumptions placed on them by their supervisors and by teachers. Added to this is a need to succeed, meaning that incumbents not only must *make* the right decision for their new cultural contexts, but must also *appear* to have made the right decision to create and to reinforce credibility in their leadership (Evetts, 1994).

To illustrate, Beth, the principal of the larger of the two schools, gathered information on entry, and on discovering that nearly all teachers complained regularly about one particular issue, she instituted a solution to the problem, based on her understanding of this issue. Given her earlier discussions with staff, she assumed that everyone would agree with her solution and that teachers would be pleased that she had dealt with the problem. She was very much taken aback, however, when she met with strong staff resistance and quite vocal criticism of her actions. Although she had followed administrative procedures correctly, she said that "the Old Guard went rangy" because she had not followed cultural procedures for such decisions, procedures of which she was unaware. To restore some semblance of trust in her administration, Beth had to rescind her decision; she had to conduct a workshop on the issue for the 105 teachers on staff; and she had to reinstitute the decision once agreement had been reached by the staff that her solution was acceptable. While Beth assumed that she had license to make changes in her new school, she had not understood the norms of behavior for administrators established by teachers through tradition, norms that were in conflict with her assumptions.

Once new principals like Beth begin to understand the implications of their appointment, the distance between their old role as teacher and new role as administrator becomes translated by them as a status passage. However, the distance travelled may cause changes in outlook and behavior that may not be understood by those who have not experienced it, including teachers, friends, or even the beginning principals themselves. Beth, for example, had been involved earlier in her career as a consultant to principals who had difficult entries, and was very aware of the problems associated with succession. Yet she said, "You'd think with all this background, that I wouldn't have made any mistakes. I did. I made some mistakes."

Of particular difficulty for some new principals is the change in the nature of the relationship they have with former colleagues. Jim, the principal of the smaller of the two schools, described the succession of an acquaintance: "I also saw from him that he was someone returning to the school where he had been a teacher. And I also saw for him the loneliness of office, the fact you couldn't be one of the boys the way it was expected that he could be. He was welcomed back by his 'cronies' thinking 'Terrific!' and he wasn't what had left the school. He had changed and I think they hadn't. And they were a little bit rough on him because he wasn't the person he had been when he left."

New principals often experience a feeling of isolation when teachers who were once friends and colleagues become subordinates who seek advice and guidance. Jim experienced this isolation and was uncomfortable with the distance placed between himself and teachers by the staff looking to him for expertise. He voiced his uneasiness with this aspect of his new role: "The number of people who look to me for answers still overwhelms me and surprises me and disappoints me sometimes. The answer is available in a myriad of other sources." Whether they wish to acknowledge the fact or not, principals begin to realize the distance they have travelled, the status they have been given, and the separation that now exists between their present and former roles.

ROLE DISTANCE AND STATUS PASSAGE: TEACHERS' INFLUENCE

While principals are making the passage between the classroom and the office, teachers add to the distance of that passage by restricting the flow and the type of information available to the new principal. In some cases, especially in schools that have experience with principal turnover, teachers often limit the potential disruption of a succession event by taking a "wait-and-see" attitude before endorsing the new administrator (Macmillan, 1992). Although acknowledging that an individual "has a right to some learner's license and a limit to formality of obligation" (Goffman, 1961b: 140), staff often test a new principal by trying to determine how the individual uses information. In these instances, staff may purposely withhold or downplay the importance of crucial bits of information required to make the right decision for that cultural context. Once judged to have passed the test, the new administrator likely experiences an ease of entry into the culture of the school and an acceptance by the staff. If the individual fails, however, access to information is restricted and the principal is denied an understanding of the culture needed to legitimate his or her administration.

During Beth's succession, this issue became a factor in her attempts to develop credibility in her ability as a principal. On arrival, her "aim was to learn as much about the school norms, concerns, and climate as I possibly could and get as wide a range of input as I possibly could." To do this, she interviewed all department heads, many key people within the support staff, and the vice principals. She even discussed her actions and perceptions with her predecessor, who was the founding principal and had hired the staff.

In all of her conversations, no one had impressed upon her the degree to which the staff assumed and demanded their right to speak on every major decision or the depth of some of the rifts between departments and programs. In one incident early in her succession, she described a meeting she had with department heads. By the end of the day, no agreement had been reached on anything, but people felt somewhat satisfied that they had the opportunity to express their views: "All of the undercurrents and disagreements were out on the table. I didn't have very much to look for any more. All the things people were discontent about surfaced." Beth was surprised by her accidental discovery of rifts, the depths of which she had not suspected. Fortunately, she used her information accordingly to modify her perceptions of the school and her practices.

Like other beginning principals (Hall & Mani, 1992), Beth and Jim had collected a substantial amount of information about their schools and based their practice on this information. However, the piecemeal and jumbled nature of this information created some degree of uncertainty about the proper interpretation of this information. Based on their previous experience and the need to act, Beth and Jim made decisions on their interpretation of the standards of behavior expected by staff. In effect, they acted as other new administrators who are "concerned with maintaining the impression they are living up to the many standards by which they and their products are judged. Because these standards are so numerous and so pervasive, the individuals who are performers dwell more than we might think in a moral world. But, *qua* performers, individuals are concerned not with the moral issue of realizing these standards, but with the amoral issue of engineering a convincing impression that these standards are being realized" (Goffman, 1959: 251).

Beginning principals often make the mistake of trying to live up to these standards, not knowing which are artificial to the context and potentially hazardous to the acceptance of their administration by teachers. For example, Jim assumed that teachers had legitimate reasons for requests and tried to honor as many requests as possible. "I've always tried to say 'Yes' to teachers. I've found, to my horror, the job demands I say 'No' often. In terms of the future, I might have been better if I had said 'No' more often in my first year. But I'm not too critical of myself because what that staff needed in its first year was pleasantry, was social consistency, was to be made to feel important again."

Once he realized what they had done, Jim did not penalize the staff. Instead, he let them know that he was aware of their actions; he used the situation to build staff support and he was careful in the future to filter and to check carefully the information he was given.

THE NATURE OF THE BOUNDARY:
A POSSIBLE DESCRIPTION

To teachers in the beginning principal's school, status passage is not the issue, but role distance is, especially if the new principal is appointed from outside of the organization. In many instances, staff limit the impact of the principal by considering the individual as just another administrator with a reputation to build (Macmillan, 1992). For beginning principals, the appointment *is* a status passage, one which may cause a feeling of isolation from a once familiar school culture, from easy access to the teaching milieu, and from the support of comrades who might help to ease the adjustment to the administrator's role. A principal's first school, then, is special because it represents to the appointee a potentially dramatic change in status and career orientation.

Consequently, when appointed to a school, a beginning principal has to learn about not only the role but also the new school's culture and the meaning of that role within that context. At least three barriers prevent the principal from easily learning about a school's culture. The first barrier is access to information about the school, which is controlled in large part by both the teaching and the support staff. The beginning principal soon realizes that the new role restricts direct, unbiased access to knowledge of the culture resident in its members (Miskel & Cosgrove, 1985) and that the nature and accuracy of information can be determined only through observation and trial and error. The second barrier is the influence of the office on the nature of the interactions among staff members. Although the principal is a major influence in determining how teachers interact, the power and authority of the principal's role restricts and alters access to and knowledge of those interactions. The third barrier is the boundary placed between the personal and professional life of principals. Creating personal ties with specific staff members has micropolitical implications for the new principal and is discouraged by superiors for reasons associated with the evaluative nature of the role.

As argued elsewhere (Macmillan, 1992), these barriers are even more evident in school systems that practice the systematic rotation of principals. Staffs in these systems often view the principal as an interloper to be tolerated or marginalized. For beginning principals in these schools, once progress has been made toward breaching the above mentioned barriers, the thought of leaving their first school and of starting over again elsewhere becomes discouraging. Learning the role is still ongoing, excitement over possibilities for change continues, and initiatives begun are likely not at the stage of institutionalization. In the second year of her tenure, for example, Beth showed unguarded dismay when asked for her projections about the survival of her innovations beyond her tenure. Although the school district's rotation policy required her to be transferred within three years of this second interview, she had not considered that she would soon be appointed to another school and not be present to see the outcome of her efforts.

Not experiencing the satisfaction of watching projects become fully instituted may influence principals' perception of their role and of schools. Jim stated that principals may require more time in each school to experience the benefits of their efforts as these efforts come to fruition. For him, "people move too fast through the system for people to gather the seasoning" they need. This lack of seasoning in one institution may, in fact, cause principals to become socialized into viewing schools generically and not individually and into believing that their skills can be easily transferred from one institution to another. The long-term effect on principals may be the limiting of the amount of energy they invest in an innovation and the perceptual alteration of their role to one of facilitator. If the latter occurs, the responsibility for the implementation and final institutionalization of innovations may fall to those who have the opportunity to remain in the school longer than the soon-to-be-transferred principal (Macmillan, 1993).

CONCLUSIONS: DOES A CULTURAL SEPARATION BETWEEN PRINCIPALS AND TEACHERS EXIST?

In consideration of the data of this study, Marshall's (1991) micropolitical hypothesis seems to be an appropriate description of beginning principals' experiences. Unlike Marshall's participants, both Beth and Jim described internal conflict as they worked through their understanding of their school's culture and their preconceptions of the principal's role. External conflict also existed as both principals and teachers negotiated a new reality based on the culture of their schools, principals' understanding of that culture, and their role within it.

Both Beth and Jim discussed their sense of isolation arising from no longer being considered as equal partners with teachers in the formation and maintenance of their school's culture. Although they understood and recognized the influence that their practices had on their schools, they felt that teachers viewed them as adjuncts to and not equal participants in forming and maintaining the culture (Macmillan, 1992). For these individuals, school board policies denied them a definite sense of identification with one school, a situation compounded by teachers who believed that principals were extensions of central office administration and by central office administration who treated principals as integral members of their schools.

Principals in these situations are faced with the dilemma of serving the school or serving the system (Cuban, 1994). Like managers who have been excluded from close identification with and intimate involvement in the culture of their organizations (Kanter, 1977), these principals developed ties with other colleagues who had themselves been excluded from full and intimate participation in their schools. Both Beth and Jim talked of discussions they had with other new administrators and professional connections that they established with experienced principals in their school district. These ties served to legitimize their experience and to provide a sympathetic ear when problems arose. By virtue of their common experience of exclusion, these principals formed their own informal group based on common problems, common understanding of the role, and common view of how schools function in general. Because membership meant mutual support as each faced different and often conflicting demands placed on them by staffs and the central office, this group served to provide a sense of identity when Beth and Jim felt displaced by the nature of their role. Further, the ability to discuss issues or problems without micropolitical overtones or career-altering judgments became an essential component of this support (Parkay & Currie, 1992).

To answer the question posed at the beginning of this section — Does a cultural separation between principals and teachers exist? — a qualified yes would appear to be the response. The nature of schools and the nature of the role require exclusion of principals from participating equally in the life of their institutions. This may cause them to derive identification at least in part from the wider professional group of their peers who provide support and a sense of identity during periods of difficulty. Context, culture, and personalities seem to be influential to some extent and need to be investigated further to determine their actual impact.

12

The Dilemmas of Exercising Political Leadership in Educational Policy Change

Hanne B. Mawhinney

One of the persistent puzzles in the study of educational administration and governance is how to account for significant educational policy changes. Observers note that such changes are not common; instead most policies are viewed as incremental adjustments to the status quo (Chubb & Moe, 1988; Mazzoni, 1991a, 1991b). Despite the incremental bias of much policy making, it is also evident that significant changes are undertaken by governments. A number of American states and Canadian provinces have adopted and implemented redistributive educational policies that represent substantial change, innovation, and restructuring. Between 1985 and 1988, the province of Ontario enacted redistributive legislation that has "redrawn the structure of Ontario education" by extending public funding to all levels of the Roman Catholic school system in the province (Lawton & Leithwood, 1991). Given the pervasive bias toward incremental decision making in most educational subsystems, such shifts are a puzzle that have led researchers to examine the forces generating change.

Dynamic socioeconomic forces in the external environment are commonly identified as giving impetus to shifts in policy (Sabatier, 1988). Following this line of thinking, some researchers suggest that sudden revenue windfalls can provide an impetus for officials to take new policy initiatives (Orloff & Skocpol, 1984). Other researchers point to the forces generated by interest groups and issue networks outside the policy subsystem as being most influential in initiating policy shifts (Heclo, 1978; Kirst, Meister, & Rowley, 1984). Interest group activity does appear to have an impact on policy change, however, researchers taking a pluralist orientation often discount the influence of politicians, depicting them as "reactive puppets dancing on the strings of an incentive structure manipulated by others" (Mazzoni, 1991a: 32). More recent studies have found that, although elected officials often do a calculus of matching revenue surplus with interest group demand for innovation, many are also proactive in setting the agenda for change. Mazzoni (1991a) proposes a model that takes into account the influence of the proactive leader's policy calculus based on "personal concerns, policy standards . . . and political advantage" (p. 32). Although useful, this, and other models of policy change, leave much unclear about the role of political leadership and the exercise of power in policy change, and the decision criteria brought to bear in its exercise. There is a need to examine the complex dilemmas that arise when political leadership is exercised in adopting significant educational policy changes.

The purpose of this chapter is to examine such dilemmas of political leadership in redistributive educational policy changes. The chapter will:

describe the context of the adoption of a policy change by the government of Ontario that extended public funding for separate Roman Catholic secondary education in the province;

analyze the dilemmas evident in the exercise of political leadership in adopting this ideological policy change; and

discuss the theoretical, political, and ethical implications of these dilemmas of political leadership.

DATA SOURCES AND METHODOLOGY

This chapter draws from a larger study that developed an interpretive framework for understanding of the politics of educational policy change (Mawhinney, 1993). Guided by an interpretive research paradigm (Gregware & Kelly, 1990) and based on the need to adopt multicase designs (Strauss & Corbin, 1990), this qualitative study of two policy changes gathered data from interviews with 70 policy actors identified through a network sampling technique (Marshall & Rossman, 1989). The interviews, which lasted from 20 minutes to 2 hours, were taped and transcribed. Documents and newspaper coverage of the policy changes were used to confirm and extend the observations of the policy actors. The descriptive accounts, personal documents, field notes, transcriptions of interviews, official documents, and records obtained through a theoretical sampling process (Strauss & Corbin, 1990) were interpreted to discover underlying patterns and conceptual categories. Using methods of data reduction outlined by Miles and Huberman (1984), the study developed conceptual frameworks of dimensions of policy change. This chapter reports on the analysis of the political leadership dimension evident in one of the policy changes studied.

CONCEPTUALIZING POLICY ADOPTION

Understanding policy change requires that the influences shaping the alternatives chosen by decision makers be considered. The question of interest is: "What reduces the agenda to a manageable size, and what principles or forces serve to limit the range of alternatives considered?" (Simeon, 1976: 555). Answering this question requires identifying the assumptions that policy makers make and the actions they take. A number of approaches to answering this question have been developed. Hall, Land, Parker, and Webb (1975), for example, adopted a political systems framework in analyzing case studies of agenda change in British public policy. They argue that a policy change occurs when an issue is perceived by policy makers as legitimate, feasible, and having significant support. More recently, Egri and Stanbury (1989) have also focused on exogenous factors in assessing how Ontario adopted pay equity legislation. They argue that changing environmental variables, shifts in political power, and shifts in the balance of power of pressure groups influence the adoption of a new policy. Similarly, Smith (1989) focuses on the changing agenda in his study of British agricultural policy in the 1930s and the 1980s. He presents a critique of the pluralist assumption that interest groups have a major influence on agenda change implied in Egri and Stanbury's study. In his critique, the pluralist explanation of agenda change is inadequate in the case of the relatively closed policy community determining British agricultural policy. Instead, Smith (1989) proposes that agendas change when "new situations are created through the development of either new constraints or new perceptions" (p. 163). The emerging view of the agenda-setting process is that it is at the least "untidy" (Doern & Phidd, 1983: 102).

The untidiness of the agenda-setting process has not been acknowledged by the policy analytic models that have dominated the study of educational change until recently. Classical models assume that the boundaries of policy problems are well defined. Policy problems, from this perspective, are seen as structured decision issues "about which enough is known so that problems can be formulated in ways that are susceptible to precise analytic methods of attack" (Mitroff, 1983: 224). Confirmation of systematic alternative identification and search processes can be found in the policy-making procedures developed in many Canadian provincial government systems.

Some policies may indeed be developed through systematic alternative search procedures as implied in the theoretical literature on policy making. More common is the much less systematic, defined, and orderly process of policy adoption. The failure of rational decision models to capture this untidiness has led contemporary policy scholars, such as Kingdon (1984), to draw guidance in explaining the processes involved from alternative postrational conceptualizations, such as the "organized anarchy model" of decision making (Cohen, March, & Olsen, 1972).[1] Drawing from this theoretical perspective, Kingdon (1984) argues that it is futile to try to find the single origin of a policy change. Instead, he conceptualizes policy making as three largely unrelated and meandering "streams;" a problem stream consisting of information about policy problems and the effects of past policy interventions; a solution stream floating around in a policy community, composed of various advocates and specialists who analyze problems; and a political stream, consisting of the legislative contests, elections, and other aspects of politics.[2] Kingdon argues that policy change occurs when a "window of opportunity" joins these three streams. Such a window opens in response to a particular problem when "a policy community develops a proposal that is financially and technically feasible, and politicians find it advantageous to approve it" (Sabatier, 1991: 151).

Part of the impetus for opening a window of opportunity is that a problem is recognized. This commonly occurs through three mechanisms. First, problems may be recognized because of a change in some generally accepted indicators, such as a sharp rise in unemployment. Second, an unpredictable "focusing event," may draw attention to a problem. Third, normal feedback from programs may identify some problem. Kingdon characterizes solutions as floating around in a policy community, as if in a "primeval soup" of ideas (p. 123). Kingdon (1984) depicts the soup thus:

Ideas become prominent and then fade. There is a long process of "softening up": ideas are floated, bills introduced, speeches made; proposals are drafted, then amended in response to reaction and floated again. Ideas confront one another . . . and combine in various ways. The "soup" changes not only through the appearance of wholly new elements, but even more by the recombination of previously existing elements. While many ideas float around in this policy primeval soup, the ones that last, as in a natural selection system, meet some criteria. Some ideas survive and prosper; some proposals are taken more seriously than others. (p. 123)

The policy change examined in this chapter is consistent with this view of agenda setting as untidy, and best characterized by meandering problem, solution, and choice opportunity streams (Kingdon, 1984). In this "organized anarchy," when a stream of political events overlaps with the problem and solutions stream, a policy window is opened that can be exploited by a policy entrepreneur. When, however, the policy entrepreneur is a politician exercising leadership in adopting a change, a number of dilemmas can arise. Some of these dilemmas are discussed in the following sections of this chapter.

CONFLICTING INTERPRETATIONS — THE IMPETUS FOR POLICY CHANGE

The organization of Canadian education reflects the fact that the country is a federation of ten provinces and two territories governed by the Constitution Act of 1982. The precursor to the 1982 act, the country's founding Constitution Act of 1867, was significant in setting the framework of provincial control over education that exists in Canada today. In this framework the federal government does not play a direct role in K–12 education, rather, the provinces determine the direction of policy changes in their jurisdiction. The provinces are governed as parliamentary democracies led by a premier and a cabinet of members of the legislature who are held accountable by an official opposition and by members of other political parties. As in other provinces, citizens in Ontario, for example, are represented by members of three parties: the Conservative, the Liberal, and the New Democratic. Prior to the events described in this chapter, Ontarians had, for over 40 years, given the Conservative Party the mandate to govern the province.

Despite ideological differences, Ontario's political parties have all been guided by a liberal democratic tradition that attempts to ensure equality of access to various social benefits. Policy changes have had to take into account the rights and freedoms guaranteed through legislation such as the Constitution Act of 1867, and the Canadian Charter of Rights and Freedoms. Educational benefits have been particularly influenced by the religious and linguistic accommodations made in 1867 to negotiate the country's first Constitution Act. The act was negotiated by a coalition of individuals from all of the colonies of the day, who agreed to guarantee the continuation of existing privileges for Catholics in the region that has become Ontario, and for the Protestant minority of Quebec. This accommodation was an important foundation for the current educational benefits accorded Ontario's Catholic community. It is likely that the provision of separate schools for Catholics in the largely Protestant region of Ontario would never have been recognized had it not been for the desire of the powerful Protestants in the predominantly Catholic Quebec to control their own schools. As a result of these negotiations, with Confederation in 1867, education became a provincial matter, subject to the generally accepted practices of the day. In Ontario, these practices were codified in the Common School Act (1841), which contained a separate school clause to protect the rights of Catholic minorities. As the legal expression of the educational practice of funding only elementary schools at the time of Confederation, the act became the foundation for the refusal of successive Ontario governments to extend full funding for Catholic education beyond the elementary level for the next 140 years.

Despite a long history of advocacy for extended funding by the Catholic community of the province, it was not until William Davis made his surprise announcement that public support for secondary education was accorded the Catholic community. Indeed, the decision to extend full funding for Catholic secondary schools in Ontario has been consistently described by policy actors as a nonrational, arbitrary, and unilateral decision by the premier of the day. On June 12, 1984, William Davis, the Conservative premier of Ontario, announced to the surprised members of the province's legislature that: "It is the government's intention to permit the Roman Catholic school boards to establish a full range of elementary and secondary education, and as part of the public system to be funded accordingly" (Ontario Legislative Assembly, Debates, 12 June 1984, p. 2416).

Prior to that announcement, government support for Roman Catholic education was restricted to their elementary level only separate school system that operated in Ontario at the time of the Confederation of Canadian provinces in 1867. Although the province had funded elementary education for its Catholic minority from the time of Confederation in 1867, and had, through incremental changes during the 1970s, extended this elementary level of funding to grade ten, the concept of full funding had historically been vigorously resisted by the predominantly Protestant population of Ontario. Catholics had gained concessions during the 1960s and 1970s because an equalized grant plan increased funding for the elementary education and because grades nine and ten were funded as part of the elementary system. The announcement of full funding, therefore, represented a substantial policy change and reflected a fundamental shift toward recognition of the collective right of the Catholic community to "instill its values and beliefs" in its own school system (Lawton & Leithwood, 1991).

For Davis, the announcement represented the logical conclusion to an issue that had "been debated almost since the beginning of educational debate in the province," and that "had been front and center on the back burner, [and] had never really left the thinking of the government or even of the Ministry."[3] The policy change, in the former premier's view, flowed inevitably from policy decisions made 20 years previously. To many members of the province's educational community, however, the announcement represented a sudden and unexpected policy reversal. Unlike the Liberal and the New Democratic parties who had, since the early 1970s, formally supported the concept of full funding for a complete Roman Catholic educational system in Ontario, the Conservative Party had steadfastly rejected the concept. The shock of the announcement was such that, when interviewed almost ten years later, politicians, bureaucrats, and both separate and public school supporters commonly recalled their initial surprise. One separate school trustee commented, "It surprised everyone. There probably weren't eight people in the province who knew about it before it was done. It was a dictatorial decree."[4]

The announcement caused such furor in the province that some have blamed it for the defeat of the Conservative Party, which had governed the province for more than 40 years, in the subsequent provincial election of 1984. The Liberal Party, which signed an accord with the New Democratic Party to form a minority government, adopted the policy change as one of its first mandates in office. Despite the official support of all three political parties, the debate between supporters and opponents of the policy change grew so heated during the next few years that some observers have called it a "religious war" (Hickcox & Li, 1992).

Bill 30: An Act to Amend the Education Act, Chapter 21 (Statutes of Ontario, 1986) permitted separate school boards to perform the duties of a secondary school board with ministerial permission. In electing to undertake these duties, separate boards became eligible to share in legislative grants to secondary schools. Bill 30 included provisions for the transfer of staff and real property. Although the policy change did not designate facilities for allocation, it did require public school boards to transfer high schools, identified through negotiations, to their coterminous separate school boards, a factor that caused substantial conflict in some communities. The implementation of Bill 30, given Royal Assent in the Ontario Legislature in 1986, was complicated by the resistance of nondenominational public school boards and private schools, who launched a Supreme Court challenge to the legislation. Although the legislation was upheld, implementing full funding of Roman Catholic secondary schools became a complex and expensive process, complicated by the ongoing debate over the legitimacy of policy decision and of the political leadership that made the decision.

PERCEPTIONS OF THE IMPETUS FOR A POLICY DECISION

To say that the announcement by Davis that the province intended to extend funding for Roman Catholic secondary education was a surprise is to understate the shock it caused to public and separate school supporters in the province. Although there was "a rumor that the government was considering increasing the amounts of government funding to the separate system for grades nine and ten, there certainly was no warning . . . no prior consultations."[5]

A cabinet minister at the time indicates that there was no cabinet submission paper, "no policy, it never went through the normal channels of our policy committees of Cabinet."[6] In fact, Davis has acknowledged: "I

don't think that one would say that the policy statement I made in June
... was the creature of a lot of updated research and the normal process
that you might go through in a decision of that kind. I think it is fair to
state, and I will assume responsibility that this was done primarily
because I felt we should do it."[7]

The Ministry of Education, which normally would have been involved
in consultation on such a significant issue, had not been involved in the
decision. Betti Stephenson, the minister of education at the time, indicates
that the ministry had concluded that extension "should never happen ...
because it would be opening reasonable requests, on the basis of the
Charter, from all other groups of religious establishments, who wanted to
have their own schools."[8]

In fact, the minister and ministry officials had been working "for about
a year on the unification of a system within the province" that she felt
would have resulted in a "quality unified system which would make sure
that everybody had the opportunity to have their religious education, not
within a school program, but added to the school program."[9]

QUESTIONING THE LEGITIMACY
OF POLITICAL LEADERSHIP

In addition to the widespread debate generated by the substantive
change created by the Davis announcement of full funding, the breach in
the institutionalized procedures for consultation and debate of proposals
that characterized the decision raised concerns from diverse groups about
the legitimacy of the unilateral exercise of political leadership to promote
a distributive policy change (Hickcox & Li, 1992). Newspaper editorials
criticized the "Father Knows Best attitude" of Davis (*The Spectator*, June,
14, 1984). Even now the announcement is described by former politicians
as a process that "began totally illogically, because it was a unique and
significant, unilateral decision on the part of the Premier."[10]

Perhaps the most contentious criticism in this vein came from the Most
Reverend Lewis Garnesworthy, Anglican archbishop of Toronto, who
became an outspoken critic of the decision to extend funding and is "cred-
ited with coalescing opposition to the plan when, shortly before the May
1985 election, Garnesworthy compared the decision to extend funding to
a rule by decree in Nazi Germany" (*The Toronto Star*, February 20, 1986:
A4). An argument made by critics like Garnesworthy was that the Davis
decision was an "about-face," or as one newspaper suggested: "a squeal-
ing U-turn on the very stand he took against full financing of Catholic
high schools in his successful 1971 provincial election" (*The Toronto Star*,
July 2, 1984: A1).

One of the outcomes of the perception that the announcement was a
unilateral act of the premier was a widespread speculation about the

decision that was made. Critics, such as Malcolm Buchanan, the president of the Ontario Secondary School Teachers Federation, charged that "political expediency and vote-catching had more to do with (the announcement) than what will serve Ontario education" (*The Globe and Mail*, June, 13, 1984: 7). This charge was elaborated with suggestions that the move would bolster the chances of the Conservative Party led by Davis in the election that was soon expected to be called. Demographic changes in Ontario during the previous decades had increased the Roman Catholic proportion of the population to more than one-third of the province's population.[11] The charge was that the Conservatives wished to tap that support in crucial areas of the province, such as Toronto, where more than 40 percent of the population was Roman Catholic.

Some even charged that Davis had been influenced by G. Emmett Cardinal Carter, archbishop of the Roman Catholic Archdiocese of Toronto.[12] Critics suggested that timing of the announcement of the policy change just before the visit to Ontario of Pope John Paul, would heighten "the pre-election publicity points the Tories would glean from the visit of the Pope" (*Brantford Expositor*, June 15, 1984: 13). One columnist explained why Davis shifted from opposition to full funding in 1971 to support for it by noting: "What has changed is the demographic face of Ontario. There are 2.6 million Catholics in Ontario today, many of them having recently arrived, or, more-importantly, gained citizenship and voting rights in the past 13 years. The largest concentration of Catholic students is in Metro Toronto, where the toughest scramble for seats will erupt in the next provincial election" (*The Globe and Mail*, June 13, 1984: 7).

Others speculated that the announcement of an appeal on the legality of an earlier decision rejecting Catholic claims for public support earlier in the month by a Catholic student group called "Ontario Students For Fair Funding" had influenced Davis to make the decision. Still other observers believed that Davis had responded to the needs of a growing population of Catholic students. During the 1980s, there was a perception that the separate school system was growing and that its schools were overcrowded. Some critics took a different view and charged that Davis had not taken the real economic conditions in the province into account in making a decision that carried high costs. These critics suggested that Davis ignored the sense within the educational community that the province had just come out of a period of scarce resources and was heading into another one.[13]

INSIDE THE DECISION DOMAIN
OF POLITICAL LEADERSHIP

Part of the reason for these speculations was that many were not satisfied with the explanation that Davis gave of his decision. Davis indicated to reporters following the announcement that the decision "had nothing to do with the Pope and it has nothing to do with any pressure from Cardinal Carter . . . thirteen years ago, it just didn't seem right, but since then, there is no question the commitment of the separate school system has improved, and I can no longer, in all conscience, continue with funding grades nine and 10, but not grades 11 through 13" (*The Toronto Star*, June 13, 1984: A18).

Reflecting on the decision recently, Davis reiterated the logic and consistency of the policy change. Although acknowledging that the announcement was a surprise, E. Stewart, Secretary to the Davis Cabinet at the time, points out that it should not have been unexpected because "the thing never went away."[14] Davis echoes this analysis by indicating that "this issue was discussed off and on at many of our Cabinet meetings, or certainly at those Cabinet meetings we had once a year where we had some outsiders in."[15]

From the perspective of the former premier, the policy change was an entirely logical step, consistent with the incremental policy changes that had begun with the introduction of the Ontario Foundation Tax Plan. As Davis comments, "I think there are periods in history where you make certain choices, [that] lead to the inevitability of what happens next."[16]

The possibility that Ontario could have moved toward a single school system started to diminish with the introduction of a Foundation Tax Plan that "reaffirmed the legal and economic position of the public separate school system."[17] The requests of the separate school boards to become part of a plan to consolidate small school boards in the 1960s was "another step that made the ultimate decision more likely."[18] The next logical step toward full funding, according to Davis, came about as the result of "the conscious decision on the part of the government" to move toward total equity for grades nine and ten in Catholic school boards by equalizing the grants for those grades.[19]

Stewart notes that the government responded to the efforts of the "leaders of the separate schools and the church" to consolidate their position "to take maximum advantage of the rules that existed."[20] Davis comments that following the 1981 Conservative majority election there was no formal public request from the bishops such as had been made in 1970. At the same time he suggests: "The desire on the part of the separate school community and the church to have a reconsideration and at least a redefinition of this before the next election was there. And while there was no formal public pronouncement, I did indicate to the leaders of the church and through them the school system, that prior to another provincial general election, that I would either alter or restate or re-affirm the existing policy."[21]

The timing of the announcement was not, however, predicated on external events such as the Pope's visit. Rather, Davis indicates that "there was no plot to do it at that precise moment . . . [but] I wanted to do it while the House was in session."[22] Davis emphasizes that he had discussed the decision in the past with individual members of the cabinet extensively, and, when it was finally presented, only one minister was in opposition. Davis notes that "it was a government decision to support it."[23] The actual decision, was, however, his own, and was one that he felt "in conscience and equity, was the right thing to do, . . . [the decision] was not predicated on whether a large percentage of the population would now support it, oppose it or whatever. It was really a case of making a decision that what was presently the situation could not be maintained and something had to be done [and] it was just as much a decision predicated on what the right thing to do for the people very directly involved was, the teachers, the students."[24]

For Davis, then, the decision was one made on the basis of his logical and rational assessment of previous separate school policies, gained from his long experience, first as minister of education, and subsequently as premier and his conscience and judgment of the need for equity and fairness in a situation that he believed had to be dealt with. Davis recounts the kind of practical basis of judgment he relied on in making the decision:

I have to say that it was really just as much a decision predicated on what was the right thing to do for the people very directly involved . . . I think I had made up my mind prior to that [decision], but I was cutting my lawn, I used to cut my own lawn. These kids came across from Cardinal Léger [the local separate secondary school]. I don't think I said before the standing committee, so I cannot use the fact that they were Portuguese children, children of Portuguese parents, they knew who I was, they were very respectful and they had not been sent to see me. They had to cut across our front lawn on their way home, and it was at that time of year when the plans for grade 11 were to be made. And they were very polite, and they just asked me, they didn't know, no one at the school had been blaming anyone, but they had just been asked . . . to start paying fees that coming September, very large fees. And you know, I didn't have an answer for them. There was no point in my explaining to them the history, the tradition, how much we had done for grades 9, 10, etc. because the bulk of the kids were going to stay there and the bulk of the parents were going to put up money. They were just not going to transfer. Some might have out of economic necessity, and this would be true in most of the combined public and private high schools. And you know, I just reached a point where I just felt that there wasn't any logical alternative but to do this.[25]

In contrast, speculations by critics suggest a more political, self-interested set of motivations. As the following discussions suggest, these contrasting perspectives have a number of implications for understanding the politics of policy change.

CONCEPTUAL REFLECTIONS ON THE
EXERCISE OF POLITICAL LEADERSHIP

The processes by which Davis reached his decision to promote this policy change are less reflective of the parameters of the rational decision models commonly adopted as heuristics in policy literature. The policy change is, instead, more consistent with Kingdon's (1984) conceptualization of agenda setting as occurring when a window of opportunity links a problem and solution stream. Policy entrepreneurs like Davis who are able to identify a choice opportunity are seen as crucial to this process.

The agenda-setting process described here raises a number of conceptual issues not accounted for by either of these depictions. The role of political leadership, the exercise of power in policy change, and the decision criteria brought to bear in its exercise are key. The notion of policy entrepreneur recognizes the role of proactive actors in a policy change but does not really capture the kind of political leadership exercised by William Davis deciding to fully fund Catholic secondary schools.

In pluralist models, politicians are often depicted as "reactive puppets dancing on the strings of an incentives structure manipulated by others" (Mazzoni, 1991a: 32). Recognizing that pluralist models underestimate their impact, Mazzoni revised his "arena" model of policy change to differentiate the influence of organized elites, proactive leaders, and idea champions. The analysis reported here confirms an influence of political leadership akin to Mazzoni's depiction of the proactive leader's policy calculus based on "personal concerns, policy standards . . . and political advantage" (p. 32).

THE NORMATIVE DIMENSIONS
OF POLITICAL JUDGMENT

The perspective Davis appears to have brought to his decision making, is, however, also reflective of what Vickers (1965) calls the "appreciative dimension" of political judgment. Fischer (1980) suggests that this normative dimension of political judgment confirms the interpretive character of policy determinations. Political decisions, such as Davis made when he announced full funding, are rarely free from opposition nor are they the outcome of rational discussion only. Davis comments, for example, "I don't minimize the formal structure that is necessary to develop policy or policy change, there's a little more to it than that. . . . I think it's fair to state that some of it is instinctive."[26]

Political judgments are based on instinctive assessments of the normative conflicts among a range of groups. The capacity to exercise power and authority in political decision making is required to limit the potential for immobilization because of the disagreement and conflict in a polity. Pluralist systems "grant authority and power to those who coordinate and direct the activities of political deliberation" (Fischer, 1980: 76).

In Ontario's political culture, there is the expectation that consultation and debate will be used to generate normative consensus in a process of political deliberation. At the same time, there is a recognition that, "sometimes governments just have to bite the bullet and do things that they feel should be done, whether they're going to create shorter term difficulties or not."[27]

Evident in these views is the "dialectical conflict between normative consensus and the exercise of political power" that can be viewed as the capacity to make and enforce decisions in the face of major or minor opposition (Fischer, 1980: 76). In this process of facilitating decisions, political power also generates conflicts ranging from opposition to revolution. Conflicts arise because of the alienation of those who feel that they have been excluded from the decision-making structure.

Such alienation and ensuing conflict developed in Ontario's educational policy community following the Davis announcement. In their analysis of the extension of funding, Hickcox and Li (1992) conclude that the policy change "was not brought about by the exercise of democratic procedures, by consensus or collaboration. Rather it was the result of the exercise of power by a leader who believed in the move and who had the power to make it come about" (p.30). From the perspective of many critics and some supporters of the policy change, the failure of Davis to follow commonly accepted agenda-setting procedures of consultation and debate was problematic. One public school director reflects on the opposition that emerged by noting: "We felt that to have one person with that kind of power to stand in the legislature and be able to announce the extension of full funding in separate school boards, that now has a price tag of over a billion dollars, that's too much power in one person."[28]

The perception by many alienated critics was, therefore, that the decision had been a unilateral exercise of power from which their input had been excluded. The dilemma for political decision makers is "how to increase the capacity to act without generating counter-currents so that the very movement forward will not reduce the capacity to move on this and future occasions" (Etzioni, 1968: 352). Although the exercise of any kind of political power requires continual effort to minimize opposition, resistance, and alienation, the exercise of legitimate power is acknowledged to generate less resistance and, thus, requires less effort. Power is legitimated, according to Fischer (1980) when "those who exercise it seek to justify their decisions and actions in the context of commonly accepted beliefs and values internalized by society's members" (p. 77). In cases where value conflicts are fundamental and ideological, efforts to reach legitimate consensus require the ongoing involvement of political leaders.

In the view of a senior policy advisor, instances of ideological conflict require concerted efforts to manage the policy issues that emerge.[29]

In the case of the extension of full funding, Davis was not around to manage the issue. Davis has indicated that, when he made the decision on the separate school extension, he did it "without knowing at that stage whether [he] would be running again or not."[30] Nevertheless, within six months he had resigned as leader of the Conservative Party and was replaced by Frank Miller, who was to lead the party into a provincial election a few months later in May 1985. The already limited legitimacy accorded the policy change by critics was further eroded by the retirement of Davis.

One critic comments that "the Bill Davis announcement just prior to his resignation . . . was the epitome of a disaster."[31] Management of political deliberation through ongoing discourse by the political leadership of a polity is required to move toward normative consensus. Such management requires that political leaders make valid judgments about norms and values in conflict, a fact recognized by Davis himself when he comments that, as a political leader, "you're never going to be on the right side of every issue, [but] if you are doing what you think is the right thing, but not necessarily perceived as being politically acceptable, how you deal with it in terms of explanations, discussions with the public, really is every bit as relevant as the position itself."[32]

ISSUES IN LEGITIMATING THE EXERCISE OF THE POWER OF POLITICAL LEADERSHIP

The issues discussed here have particular relevance for understanding policy change. Rational models of policy based on traditional behavioral science discount the value judgments upon which such management must proceed. The assumption is that there is no logical way of resolving value conflicts because values are not objective, and, therefore, not measurable, being based on opinion, belief, and intention. Postpositivist critics take issue with this discounting of the reasoned, value-based discourse that does take place in politics. To facilitate analysis and generate understanding of the nature of the normative discourse, the role of ideas in policy debate and argument must be undertaken.[33]

The issues of power and legitimacy in policy change suggested in this chapter also have relevance to understanding the processes involved. One of the purposes of an agenda-setting process that incorporates widespread consultation is to legitimate the policy change. Legitimation is particularly crucial in policy changes perceived as ideological shifts. The failure to legitimate an adoption may be a factor in ensuring that the kind of political debate often assumed to occur in agenda setting continues throughout a policy process. Rather than being a functional characteristic of agenda setting as proposed by stage models, political bargaining and maneuvering will continue through the development and implementation of a policy. It may lead, as it did in the case of the extension of full funding, to challenges to the legitimacy of the policy in public, political, and legal arenas during the development and implementation of the policy change. The source, nature, and impact of the challenges to the policy are described by one observer who notes that the policy change:

Caught so many people unaware and unsuspecting and a lot of those people became immediately opposed to it. They became emotionally, ideologically, administratively opposed to it, right from the very first moment. And a lot of those people were people whose cooperation and assistance would have made implementation of it an awful lot easier. Instead of that, it got their backs up and they opposed it right along the line and as you know it ended up in the Supreme Court of Canada, which is just a symptom in a sense of the kind of opposition that policy had.[34]

The political leadership described in this chapter must be recognized as influenced by several broad forces including such structural pressures as those that arise from the "historical, institutional, economic and social characteristics" of a political community (Pal, 1992: 123). The preceding discussion also confirms that agenda setting is influenced by recurring institutional processes, such as the requirements that elections, party policy, and leadership conferences be held at certain times. As one long-time senior policy advisor to the Ontario government commented, "governments are only in power for four and five year cycles at the most, so that tends to dominate the thinking, it tends to take over on the planning process."[35]

Similarly, the timing of budgets and the demands created by parliamentary sessions influence agenda setting. Inevitably, agendas are also influenced by unpredictable events that may interrupt or replace a policy development process in progress, as was the case with the proposal for unified school boards that Stephenson's Ministry of Education staff were working on at the time of the Davis announcement.[36]

CHALLENGES IN GENERATING LEGITIMACY AND SUPPORT THROUGH POLITICAL LEADERSHIP

The analysis outlined in this chapter confirms that agenda setting is at least an untidy process, characterized by multiple influences and interpretations of problematic conditions. These conditions create many of the dilemmas encountered by political leaders. The challenge for political leaders is to overcome the problems posed by these conditions and to generate support and legitimacy from the public in doing so.

Governments must be seen to be developing public policies to enhance the public good, at the same time the interest that all governments have in "maintaining popularity, getting re-elected, and rewarding friends may at times eclipse, even if only partly, the stated goals of a policy" (Pal, 1992: 180). Thus, although the direct goals of a policy may not be met, the policy may be valued by politicians for the public support it generates for the government. This phenomenon is evident in Ontario politics, according to one senior government advisor, who suggests that: "If you ask the current government what their priorities are, what their plans are, what their objectives are . . . they will all be very high-sounding. But at the top of the list, unstated, the first objective of any government is, 'we want to be re-elected.'"[37]

Political impact may also be viewed in broader terms than popularity. It may be viewed as the impact a policy has on the legitimacy or stability of a political system and not just the party that happens to be in power. For example, a policy such as Bill 30 may achieve its direct goal of extending full funding for separate school secondary education but may fail in generating support for the political system. Observers commented that the way in which the extension of full funding was announced undermined support for not only the Conservative Party but also the political system as a whole.

Support and legitimacy are generated from the ideological and symbolic beliefs that members of the political community have. As the reactions to the Davis announcement confirm, governments that fail to acknowledge the deeply held ideological beliefs related to a policy change can generate a legitimacy crisis. A former government official observed this phenomenon when, following the full funding announcement, politicians who tried to explain the legislation away, calm the waters, or rationalize the change as simply the addition of another three years to the system, were challenged by a public that did not see it that way. They saw the policy as "a major ideological change, because, up to that point, the government had steadfastly refused to extend the separate school system any further than grade 10."[38] Legitimate consensus does not involve complete agreement; it does require some attempt to reconcile the conflicting assessments of the goals of a policy change. Failure to undertake such reconciliation can be disastrous for a political party. An observer suggests, for example, that: "many of the [Conservative] members of the House were aghast and feel to this day that that's what lost the election for them. There was no legislation at that point, it was only a policy announcement. But many, if not most of them, at that time felt that's what lost the election for them."[39]

The implication is that the political impact of such a legitimacy crisis may extend beyond the initiating event, particularly if stakeholders in a policy change and segments of the public continue to feel that their concerns are being overlooked. This phenomenon was evident following the defeat of the Conservatives, when, despite calls for a referendum on full funding, the new Liberal government began to speed up the implementation of full funding. Despite the attempts of the new government to generate legitimacy for the policy process by referring draft legislation to the Standing Committee for consideration through public hearings, a number of groups demanded a referendum on the issue. The Coalition for Public Education, a coalition of public school supporters, argued, for example, that the parties had not "heard what the people of Ontario were saying" during the election that defeated the Conservatives.[40] At the time, the response of Sean Conway, the minister of education, was negative. He argued that Ontario was a "parliamentarian, not a plebiscitarian democracy"(*Kitchener-Waterloo Record*, July 24, 1985: 1).

Upon reflection, Conway acknowledges that, in the face of a legitimacy crisis, political responses based on such "rational, legal and constitutional criteria were all irrelevant."[41] According to Conway, "The shocks to the Conservative party in Ontario are still reverberating from a premier making so important a decision without any consultation among his supporters. It fractured the Conservative party and that fracture is still there to some extent."

It is evident, however, that the legitimacy crisis extended beyond the Conservative regime. According to Conway, "*Bill 30* had a profound impact on that kind of top-down policy."[42] It left a residual distrust of political decision making that was, in Conway's view, a forerunner to public reaction to the politics of the Meech Lake Accord, the failed attempt to resolve Quebec's involvement in the Canadian Confederation. The rejection of policy making by political maneuvering by the public in that case affirms the importance of government actions being perceived as legitimate.

IMPLICATIONS FOR UNDERSTANDING THE ROLE OF POLITICAL LEADERSHIP IN POLICY CHANGE

There are a number of implications for understanding the role of political leadership in policy change that flow from the political impacts of the decision processes discussed in this chapter. These implications call into question the models of policy that have focused on instrumental actions of government. Unlike the instrumental actions embodied in concerns over resource allocation that have been the focus of the extensive research on policy outcomes, symbolic actions have either been ignored or seen as "part of manipulative efforts to control outcomes" (March & Olsen, 1989: 47). Yet the symbolic dimensions of policy, which relate to fundamental, core ideas defining a polity, are central to the policy process. The legitimacy of governmental policy making is established when it supports core ideas and values, such as distributional fairness, equity, and equality. The effect is not simple. One of the key implications of the analysis given here is that a policy change that is perceived by segments of the polity as lacking legitimacy can generate a paradigm shift in public perception of the proper mandate for political decision making.

There are significant implications for our understanding of the nature of political leadership as it is exercised in generating policy change of the phenomenon discussed in this chapter. This analysis contradicts the view taken by rational models of policy based on traditional behavioral science that political leadership can be exercised without value judgments. The chapter fulfills a small part of the postpositivist policy research agenda by outlining some of the dilemmas of educational policy making in the liberal democratic state that arise because value-based judgment is central to political leadership. The chapter is also significant in that it examines ethical dimensions of political leadership, found in decision criteria based on "honesty, integrity, fairness, and caring" (Jackson, 1993: 41) that have been ignored by dominant policy models. In this way the chapter contributes to understanding the unique ethical dilemmas that pervade our social life (Ignatieff, 1984: 138–142).

NOTES

1. The organized anarchy model, developed by Cohen, March, and Olsen (1972), focuses on decision making as a process that is loosely connected with organizational goals or intentions. Decision making can occur through oversight, with little focused attention to the problem; as flight, where a problem moves on to a more attractive choice opportunity; or as resolution, which occurs when a choice resolves the problems attached.

2. For a recent use of the Kingdon model in education policy see Holderness (1992).

3. W. G. Davis, personal communication, February 17, 1992.

4. R. Anderson, personal communication, December 13, 1991.

5. M. Buchanan, personal communication, December 19, 1991.

6. N. Sterling, personal communication, February 29, 1992.

7. W. G. Davis, personal communication, February 17, 1992.

8. B. Stephenson, personal communication, January 6, 1992.

9. Ibid.

10. Ibid.

11. In 1984, approximately 2.4 million of Ontario's 8.6 million residents were Roman Catholic.

12. One journalistic account by Claire Hoy (1987), a conservative *Toronto Sun* columnist, claimed that Davis had promised Carter to sponsor full funding by the time he left office.

13. W. Mitchell, personal communication, January 17, 1992.

14. E. Stewart, personal communication, February 17, 1992.

15. W. G. Davis, personal communication, February 17, 1992.

16. Ibid.
17. Ibid.
18. Ibid.
19. Ibid.
20. E. Stewart, personal communication, February 17, 1992.
21. W. G. Davis, personal communication, February 17, 1992.
22. Ibid.
23. Ibid.
24. Ibid.
25. W. G. Davis, personal communication, February 19, 1992.
26. Ibid.
27. W. Mitchell, personal communication, January 7, 1992.
28. D. Dodds, personal communication, February 19, 1992.
29. E. Stewart, personal communication, February 17, 1992.
30. W. G. Davis, personal communication, February 17, 1992.
31. D. Dodds, personal communication, February 19, 1992.
32. W. G. Davis, personal communication, February 17, 1992.
33. Scholars of practical discourse such as Toulon (1958), and more recently Townsend (1991), have attempted to explicate the "informal logic" of normative reasoning.
34. W. Mitchell, personal communication, January 7, 1992.
35. E. Stewart, personal communication, February 17, 1992.
36. A former senior government policy advisor reflects on this process by noting:

If I were sitting with a group of civil servants looking back on some of the policy development projects I was involved in, it would be fairly characteristic that there would be a whole lot of stuff going on that would have been of no particular interest to anybody except the people who were doing them. So I think you have to exercise a fairly close judgment before you know exactly what significance to attach to [it]. What do you say, if for example, the Minister says 'I want you to do a policy paper on the extension of funding to separate schools'? So now it goes over to the civil service side, and they do 15 drafts of the policy papers. They say we have five basic policy options and they are a, b, c, d, e. And what may happen in real life is that they work on that for six months. They are basically not talking to anybody. They boil that down to three. It goes to the Minister and the Minister in two minutes says well, a, b. & e and f are stupid so we are not going to do those. And work it up again just looking at c and e. Now if at that point a Minister then goes to some stakeholders and says 'Look, we are looking at these two options, now renumbered a and b, what do you think?' That may be a significant encounter in the development of the process, but it may be a lot shorter than the seven agonizing months the civil servant did something that nobody was interested in" (personal communication, January 9, 1992).

37. E. Stewart, personal communication, February 17, 1992.
38. W. Mitchell, personal communication, January 7, 1992.
39. Ibid.
40. The Coalition for Public Education was formed of five church groups, a provincial school trustees association, and the Ontario Secondary School Teachers Federation.
41. S. Conway, personal communication, January 16, 1992.
42. Ibid.

V

DILEMMAS IN THE PROFESSIONAL DEVELOPMENT OF SCHOOL ADMINISTRATORS

13

Problem-based Learning as an Approach to the Professional Development of School Leaders: A Case Study

Brigid Limerick and Frank Crowther

This chapter reports on the initial stages of a two-year project, Project Queensland Leader Development (Project QLD), which uses problem-based learning (P-bL) as the theoretical base to assist the professional development of practicing and aspiring principals in public schools in the state of Queensland, Australia.

A critical issue that the directors of the project encountered when the program commenced in early 1994 pertained to the ways in which participants defined (or had difficulty in defining) a problem. We, therefore, examine in this chapter, after describing the background to the project, the ways in which we tried to assist participants to conceptualize problems as dilemmas, our analysis of their dilemmas, and our attempts to understand progress in moving toward what both participants and directors might regard as truly useful professional development strategies. We conclude the chapter with an attempt at rigorous self-criticism in asking ourselves, as university-based consultants, about the reality we are creating through professional development, when our own perceptions of leadership problems impose structure on principals' perceptions of "the way we do things around here."

BACKGROUND OF THE PROJECT

Project QLD developed as a response to an expressed concern regarding approaches conventionally taken to leader development in schools. University courses, we were told, are often perceived as unable to assist principals with their day-to-day practices, while state-run principals' conferences are sometimes regarded as expensive sessions in which outside experts are contracted to talk to participants in on-off presentations. Both approaches are increasingly unsatisfactory. Time is at a premium, principals are being questioned by their communities for time spent out of school, many do not want to take on the extra commitment of formal study; yet, their personal needs for professional growth and renewal mean that they remain dependent upon outside assistance. The challenge presented to us was to work collaboratively with a group of innovative and entrepreneurial principals to create a program that was genuinely focused upon the workplace rather than upon our own expertise and preconceived notions of school-based leadership.

At the end of 1993, two significant Australian documents were released, signifying a concrete interest from Australian governments in an expanded role in developing teacher professionalism and particularly leader development. It may also be argued that the documents in question reflected an economic rationalist trend that emphasizes the importance of school leaders in the implementation of complex economic and political platforms. The first document, *Leaders and their Learning* (Department of Employment, Education and Training, 1993) emanated from a Project of National Significance on Leadership and Management Training for Principals that was funded by the Australian government's Department of Employment, Education and Training. At about the same time, the Queensland Department of Education produced *The Professional Development Framework for Principalship*, based on executive competencies required of all senior managers by the Queensland State Public Service. Relatedly, the Department of Education introduced a Performance Planning and Review scheme in which principals were required to plan their own professional development, incorporating consideration of system, school-based, and personal priorities. The project directors decided to use all three documents as guides but to focus primarily on the Queensland framework because this was of most direct applicability in planning a collaborative professional development program. Thus, when we responded to a request from principals attached to two Queensland School Support Centers in late 1993 to work with them to design a long-term strategy for their professional growth, we believed that the policy framework for such a strategy was available.

Our interest in P-bL had originated as a result of a course conducted by Phil Hallinger at the University of Western Australia in August 1993, which one of the project directors (Crowther) had attended. The experience of the second director (Limerick) in setting up and running Women in Management programs that used an action learning model, was also important in the developmental stage of the project (Limerick & Heywood, 1993).

The emergence of P-bL from the field of medical education has been well documented elsewhere (Barrows, 1985; Barrows & Tamblyn, 1980; Blunden, 1991; Hallinger & Bridges, 1994; Margetson, 1991, 1994; Ross, 1991). Each of these authors influenced our thinking in planning Project QLD. Blunden's (1991: 115) definition in particular provided us with a helpful orientation: "Problem-based learning uses a situation or experience which students might face in practice, as the starting point for learning. It is an educational method which is learner-centered and in which the instructor is the facilitator of the process rather than the source of knowledge imparted to the students, problems are the tools of learning and students are participants rather than passive recipients of their learning."

Hallinger and Bridges (1994: 16–19) outline six underlying principles that are the key to differentiating P-bL from other methods of leader development. These are: identification of a problem, the collaborative nature of the teaching, the emphasis on student learning being largely self-directed, the encouraging of cooperative group learning, the focus on implementation, and the use of formative evaluation. Our development of Project QLD was guided largely by Hallinger and Bridges' principles.

OVERVIEW OF THE PROJECT

Project QLD began officially in February (the beginning of the school year in Australia) 1994 with 110 participants (36 females and 74 males) attached to seven School Support Centers in disparate geographical locations across Queensland. The participants ranged from newly appointed principals (often female in the "outback") to very experienced principals (usually male in large city schools).

The project was conceptualized as a four-semester skills development course for both practicing and aspiring principals. Each semester was to be organized around a specific theme from *The Professional Development Framework for Principalship*. The first theme was corporate leadership. It is the development of problems within this theme that provides the focus of this chapter. The Department of Education provided the following definition of "corporate leadership":

All principals within the Queensland Department of Education have leadership functions that extend beyond their individual schools, to include responsibility for the formulation, implementation and review of departmental policies, goals and programs. Within the school itself key elements of this priority include creating and articulating a shared vision, team building, managing change, establishing participative processes, devising mechanisms for curriculum development, enhancing teaching and learning, and creating and maintaining a supportive learning environment. (Department of Education, Queensland, 1993: 2)

Thus, our first semester's work in Project QLD focused upon problems that principals expected to encounter and felt they needed to address, in responding to their employer's definition of their corporate leadership roles and responsibilities. Building on Bridges and Hallinger's P-bL framework, the course was based on five strategies:

interactive dialogue through three 3-hour structured seminars spaced across a semester;

school-based action research into their problems;

high quality multimedia resources, relevant to the semester's theme and the participants' problem areas, were provided by the project directors to support their action research inquiries;

networking, not only with those in their own local cohort but with colleagues from other centers working on similar problems; and

presentation of their outcomes at an end-of-semester seminar.

Figure 13.1 illustrates the significant role that it was envisioned networking would play in the overall P-bL process.

The course structure we devised for Project QLD was, we believed, theoretically sound. For example, it appeared to us to acknowledge characteristics of successful leader development programs of the type identified by Roland Barth (1986), founder of the Harvard Principals' Centre (including personal and professional recognition; voluntary attendance; a neutral and protected setting; participant diversity; participant involvement in program content development; and a variety of delivery formats). The structure was also consistent with the view of researchers like Daresh and LaPlant (1984) that effective leader development incorporates a concern for long-term growth, is directed at local school needs, and involves participants in all phases of planning and implementation. This type of conclusion, combined with a growing preoccupation in the literature about the limitations of conventional university courses (Thurston & Lotto, 1990) and of deficit or remediation approaches (Barth, 1986) convinced us that P-bL had much to offer as the starting point in the development of our own course.

FIGURE 13.1
Networking in the P-bL Process

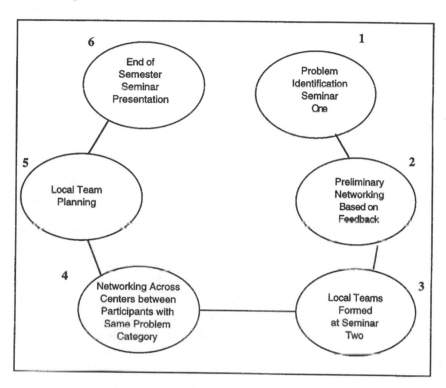

CONCEPTUALIZING PARTICIPANTS'
LEADERSHIP PROBLEMS

After the first seminar, participants were requested to send to us, as project directors, a description of their proposed problems and plans of action. Using these individual descriptions, the problems were categorized by the project directors into five themes:

Working in Leadership Teams,

Managing Change,

Vision Building,

Working with Parents, and

Empowering Others.

Of significance is the range of ways in which problems were described by participants. Some problems encompassed one or more pages of description, some were stated simply as topics, some as questions, and some as goals. The range was surprising; we had assumed that a precise statement involving a value conflict would characterize each response. In our first session together, participants had analyzed real-life case studies where serious value conflicts had to be resolved. The concept of "dilemma" had been defined at that time as "an issue characterized by a seemingly unresolvable conflict of values."

In the ensuing month, participants were expected to review readings and audiotapes on the topic of corporate leadership that were provided to them. At the same time, the directors completed a proposal feedback form in which they commented upon the proposed plans of action and identified individuals working on similar problems who could be contacted as a starting point in the P-bL process. Each participant was provided with further readings, selected because of specific relevance to individual topics.

At the second three-hour seminar, held at each of the seven centers in mid-semester, a balance was struck between provision of resources relevant to the five topics and sharing of ideas among participants working on the same theme. By the completion of seminar two, participants had reconceptualized their problem statements, had in some cases reformulated teams, and had identified specific procedures for action research within their school situations. About one-third of the total cohort had located themselves in teams focusing on an identical problem statement. Approximately another one-third were located in looser team arrangements, with a range of individual problem statements. A further one-third comprised individuals pursuing individual topics. Participants' restatements of their problems were again collected. As previously, a wide range of formats had been used to describe problems, some of which involved an explicit value conflict but many of which did not. Because our definition of problem included the notion of value dilemmas, we reanalyzed participants' statements and generated a revised categorization of themes, together with a list of value dilemmas that we could identify in the statements. Our revised conceptualization, as outlined in Table 13.1, was then fed back to participants through a Project QLD newsletter. Participants were asked to use this synthesis to help them focus on the inherent value dilemma in their action research and in their seminar three presentations.

The themes and dilemmas in Table 13.1 represent the project director's conceptualizations of participants' problems. Our intervention in the problem-solving process raises several important questions. Does such an intrusion facilitate practical problem solving by imposing conceptualizations that are recognizable to external consultants or does it divert

TABLE 13.1

Thematic Problems and Value Dilemmas in Corporate Leadership

Theme One: Leading the New Organization.
- Democratic Leadership/Directive Leadership: When should I use which style?
- Corporate Leadership/Pedagogical Leadership: How can I be both a manager and an instructional leader?

Theme Two: Implementing Corporate Directions.
- Professional Loyalty/Personal Integrity: To what extent should personal values be a component of a principal's professionalism?
- Empowering Staff Through Involvement/Creating Burnout Through Involvement: Can we have the one without the other?

Theme Three: Forging Vision.
- Inclusive Values/Particular Values: Does social justice supersede the well-being of particular groups and individuals?
- Individual Identity/Collective Identity: Does a collective vision compromise individualism?

Theme Four: Parent Involvement.
- Lay Involvement/Professional Identity: How can I encourage parent involvement without inhibiting the work of teachers?
- Participatory Democracy/Interest Group Influence: Do interest group abuses of the democratic process suggest its limited appropriateness for school governance?

Theme Five: Professional Development of the Teacher and Administrator.
- Corporate Leadership/Pedagogical Leadership: Should teachers' development be managed by administrators?
- Positional Authority/Collegiality: Is it possible to implement Ministry requirements for teacher appraisal while remaining "collegial"?

attention from "real" problems by presupposing that academic-type conceptualizations are of prior importance? We return to this issue in the final section of the chapter.

Only upon completion and analysis of seminar three presentations was it possible to gauge whether participants had internalized P-bL as an appropriate response to the challenges of modern school leadership. Seminar three involved participants in presentation of the outcomes of their semester's inquiries: a restatement of their problem with its inherent dilemma, a description of P-bL strategies used, and a reflective discussion of outcomes. Presentations were done verbally — some in teams and some individually — using a variety of media and with a written accompanying description. Examination of the content of these oral and written presentations indicated that participants had adopted a range of positions relating to P-bL. Table 13.2 summarizes these positions.

TABLE 13.2
Principals' Responses to Problem-based Learning after One Semester

Category	Sample Explanations	N
No progress with P-bL	• Job interferences (e.g. transfer) • Personal interferences (e.g. health)	11
Attempted implementation, no outcomes	• Very limited networking • Theoretical solutions to problems not understood till "after the fact" • Problem intensified under examination	9
Attempted implementation, created a technical solution	• "Solution" tended to be identified early and adhered to even when complex exigencies arose • No authentic collaboration with staff or community	9
Comprehensive implementation, created a solution of personal relevance	• Emphasis on own site in P-bL process • Extensive action research	31
Comprehensive implementation, created a solution endorsed by peers for application elsewhere	• Extensive networking • Extensive use of external resources • Extensive action research	21
Moderate implementation, reinforced positional authority	• P-bL processes conceptualized around the principal as problem solver	29
TOTAL		110

From these findings, several conclusions have been drawn in relation to principals' preliminary involvement with P-bL:

1. *Problem-based learning does not suit all educational administrators as an approach to professional development.* Some participants had difficulty identifying problems in their workplace, while others would willingly do so only when the time, resources, and assistance in addressing them were

readily available. For others, P-bL may pose threats to their traditional conceptions of leadership and may, therefore, be subverted.

2. *Where authentic problem-solving processes are established, problems diminished in significance.* "Comprehensive implementers" frequently asserted that they had not, in fact, created definitive solutions to their problems. Rather, they had created *processes* that seemed to inspire confidence in stakeholders that a serious problem was being addressed. Thus, what appeared at the outset to be a significant educational concern frequently turned out to be relatively unimportant once an authentic problem-solving process was set in place.

3. *Problem identification should be regarded as a broad process that encompasses all relevant viewpoints.* Rational approaches to problem solving frequently identify problem identification as the first step in a sequence of strategies. Project QLD participants tended to contest this proposition, asserting that, where problems had been defined narrowly or too soon, some stakeholders had tended to become alienated and the principal may have been perceived as part of the problem rather than part of the solution. In several instances, principals chose to leave problems open-ended rather than declare closure and risk such difficulties. Generally speaking, however, it was found that, by broadening problem statements to encompass diverse viewpoints, agreement about the nature of the problem could be reached.

4. *School-based administrators frequently lack appreciation of the value of networking in problem solving.* To the extent that networking was successful in Project QLD, it tended to be facilitated mainly by female participants. An analysis of actual networking dynamics suggests two possible explanations for this phenomenon. First, female principals tended to be younger, less experienced, and, perhaps, more in need of advice. Second, female principals tended to view time more flexibly than did male counterparts, with less need to declare closure on tasks. Overall, however, systematic networking was undertaken by only one-fifth of the total group of participants, with time, cost of long distance communications, and reluctance to contact peers not personally known cited most frequently as encumbrances.

CONSTRUCTING WHOSE REALITY?

The use of the word "problem" in P-bL raises some interesting questions. Some principals denied they had problems within their definition of the word, or felt that they could not afford to admit they had problems (again within their definition of the word). Some felt that, by their very nature, problems should be easily solvable; others felt that it was their responsibility to address problems on site rather than through their professional development. In other cases, as we have described, principals either intuitively, or as a result of the type of experiences we provided, came to view problems as both manageable events and opportunities for interpersonal development and fulfilment. Overall, it is clear that, as project directors, we were coming into direct confrontation with commonly accepted practices in the "way we do things around here" and that P-bL requires a degree of consciousness-raising that is a painful process for participants.

There is no dearth of evidence to support the claim that, in the past decade, school principals have been set adrift in a veritable ocean of change and that many are battling to stay afloat (Leithwood, 1990; Leithwood & Steinbach, 1993a; Mulkeen & Tetenbaum, 1990; Newton & Tarrant, 1992; Sergiovanni, 1991). Into this climate, then, comes a problem-based professional development course that, rather than providing answers or life rafts, asks them to problematize their working lives. Given this context, the findings that we have outlined are, perhaps, not surprising.

As directors of Project QLD our goal has been, and continues to be, to empower principals to lead effectively and meet the challenges of their positions in a climate of rapid change. The immediate challenge for us is to be wary of constructing their reality artificially through imposing our own structures on their work. Rather, we must constantly strive to use our theoretical understandings and facilitation skills to enhance the processes by which they can better understand their everyday work and willingly share and learn from each other. We believe we have made some progress in achieving this goal.

14

Boundary Mentoring: A Solution to the Persistent Dilemma of How to Educate School Administrators

Angela Thody and Lee Crystal

This chapter examines the relationships resulting from, and the possible effects of, boundary mentoring as a means of preparation for educative leadership. The research had its empirical genesis in two unusual[1] and contrasting schemes of mentorship. The first was an intraprofessional mentoring program in which experienced school principals mentored newly appointed principals. The second was an extraprofessional comentoring scheme in which academic faculty were partnered with business executives at similar levels of seniority. Both programs involved outsider mentoring, hence the adoption of the term "boundary mentoring."

The intraprofessional principalship mentoring was organized by a consortium of local education authorities[2] in northeast England and is part of a national mentoring program financially supported by central and local governments. The extraprofessional comentoring program was organized by the University of Luton, was original to Luton, and was financially supported by the employment department of the British government. The focus of the research was to consider types of socialization arising from mentoring by seeking evidence to demonstrate its effects in reinforcing the cultural norms of a profession or in destabilizing that culture, a topic not previously researched as far as could be ascertained. These two pilot projects were ideal for comparison of these socialization aspects because one is contained within a profession and the other is cross-professional. The research sought to explore the possibilities for assessing reinforcement and destabilization within each.

The term "reinforcement" was adopted to describe the likely outcome of the school mentoring program. The pairs of experienced and inexperienced principals were working within commonalities of professional and organizational expectations and with, therefore, apparently minimal likelihood of role-conflict expectations. It was assumed that the sharing of common role values and mandates would facilitate receptiveness to the professional norms and of accepted ways to behave within them. This cloning possibility was emphasized by the configuration of the partners' relationship in which "age" or "experience," leads unpracticed "youth" who may feel under an obligation to their elders and, hence, more ready to accept their ideas (Wright, 1991). Intraprofessional mentoring may, therefore, result in the rapid learning of effective established practices or of the repetition of possible outdated systems and ideas.

Destabilization was felt to be the appropriate term for the possible outcome of the comentoring scheme in which junior-senior relationships were replaced by those of equivalence of status and extraprofessional elements were incorporated. This brought the possibility of dissonance between the professional expectations, organizational parameters, objectives, and contexts of the mentoring partners. This may cause the participants to perceive inapplicable learning and so negate the effects of incorporating a fresh perspective on administrator development. The injection of business management norms into education may deflect from the faculty role in instructional leadership while educational administrators' attitudes may engender questioning of business norms. Both partners in the extraprofessional scheme appeared likely to acquire new ideas from each other and in this sense destabilization must be viewed as having more positive connotations than the word is commonly assumed to imply. The contrasting outcomes of reinforcement and destabilization are illustrated in Figure 14.1.

This project is a pilot for these concepts and for the methodology of assessing their impact. The findings from the small sample are included and it is hoped thereby to stimulate dialogue on how to develop this aspect of mentoring evaluation. This chapter discusses perspectives on program design, including national and international monitoring developments, program formalization, and participants and pairing; methodology; propositions and findings; and summation and future research.

FIGURE 14.1
Mentoring Outcomes' Continuum

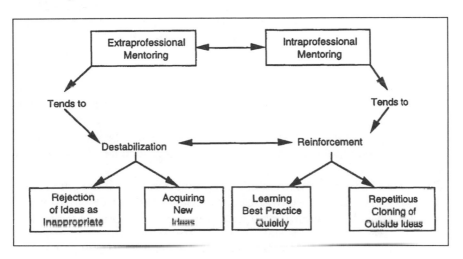

PERSPECTIVES ON PROGRAM DESIGN

National and International Mentoring Developments

Mentorship in English and Welsh education was given national support through government endorsement of this scheme for the mentoring of newly appointed school principals for whom it was deemed so significant that it was the only government-supported training that is part of a national scheme (although organized by 11 regional consortia) from 1992 to 1995. School principals in England are not required to have qualifications in educational administration so this mentoring could have been the only job training they received. It is part of a general movement to school-based, school-focused, and school-managed training in England, which began to emerge in the late 1980s and is extending as site-based management becomes a reality for all aspects of education (Thody, 1993b). Within this movement, the value of off-site training provision (usually in universities) for educational administrators is being questioned and the benefit of the alternative, work-based, mentor-led, individualized learning is being stressed (Bolam et al., 1993).[3]

In devising the comentorship, the University of Luton built on its existing links with local companies. The University of Luton has always been vocationally oriented, with close employer liaison for curriculum development, student career preparation, and academic staff development through, for example, industrial placements. The genesis for this program lies in those contacts and from the recognition of the needs of academic faculty for wider management experiences as their roles have become increasingly managerial. Parallel with this practical recognition of the value of sharing ideas with another profession has come the academic acceptance of the similarities of management whether public or private sector (Ackroyd, Hughes, & Soothill, 1989; Stewart & Ranson, 1988). There is, however, questioning of the appropriateness of in-company mentoring models to the public sector (Ritchie & Connolly, 1993) and a general acceptance that professional expectations and moves remain significantly different. The comentorship scheme was supported by the government department with responsibility for trade and industry because there is national concern about the relevance of education to the needs of the national economy and mentorship is seen as a way to meet those concerns.

The most common pattern in all mentoring programs is that of experienced people leading those who are inexperienced (Baird, 1993; Walker & Stott, 1993), which was the arrangement in the school principal mentorship discussed here. This seems to replicate normally what is reported as being the most helpful informal assistance to beginning principals, that is, experienced principals as "buddies" or "critical friends" (Lyons, 1993: 197). In contrast, the comentorship was by those equal in status, a much rarer form of mentorship comparable to, for example, the Tasmanian Teaching and Learning Project (McCann & Radford, 1993), the Peer Assisted Leadership Program from North West Laboratories (Barnett & Mueller, 1989) and the Illinois mid-career project mentoring (Ashby, 1991). It differed from these in its central feature of comentoring across different professions.

The value of mentoring is often assessed in terms of its contribution to career advancement or to induction socialization (Boettinger 1975; Caruso, 1992: 46–52; Kram, 1985; Roche, 1979; Williams, 1993). The "pursuit of a career dream . . . is a fundamental of all mentoring" (Caruso, 1992: 88) and career advancement has been described as a major motivation for entering a mentoring program (Zey, 1984). In contrast, the possibilities of career advancement in these two schemes had to be seen mainly in terms of career enhancement (enrichment of the current job or a sideways move) or career contentment (satisfaction at doing the current job to the best of one's abilities and finding ways to enjoy it more) (Thody, 1993c: 2–5). None of the participants could be said to have had, therefore, a "vested interest" in agreeing with their partners or in accepting each other's views. Neither partner could influence directly the other's career advancement. Related to this issue is the question of why these participants entered mentorship when there was no career ladder with which the mentor could help. This was one of the topics about which participants were questioned. Their answers may have significance, not only for the issues relating to potential reinforcement but also for mentoring in general. Previous research has used career progression as a measure of mentoring success; this cannot be applied here, but is it possible to find other measures of value for mentoring?

Program Formalization

There is an underlying tension or dilemma in much of the writing about mentoring that often points out that both good personal relationships and formalized structure are needed for successful mentoring, yet the chemistry identified as being so important to successful mentoring is, it is claimed, more likely to be positive in a spontaneously occurring relationship (Caruso, 1992; Chao & Gardner, 1992).

Both of these programs had to be formalized in the following ways:

Instead of being established by the spontaneous actions of the partners, the school principal mentorship was devised by the School Management Task Force while the comentorship arose from the initiative of the Enterprise Department of Luton University.

The training was devised by the organizers. Both programs used the same mentor trainer. The training included discussions of the roles of mentors and introduced possible elements including observation, counseling, active listening, touring, ideas exchanges, project mentoring, and frameworks for management learning. The comentors were trained together and received one-half day of training. The principal mentors had five days of training and the principals who were mentees had none. All the school principals attended the training; three of the comentors could not attend, although they were briefed later.

A structure was suggested that the mentors might adopt. The comentors agreed to join the project for six months during which time they would meet about six times. The principals' scheme operated over a similar period during the newly appointed principals' first year in office. The principal pairs had five days allotted and funded for mentorship activities.

The pairing was selected by the organizers.

The time allowance was determined by the scheme (although participants could chose to extend it).

There was an expectation of some evaluative activity.

The mentors in the principalship program received financial compensation for their schools for the time they spent mentoring and for any travel expenses incurred.

The programs were informal in that no one was compelled to participate. Mentors, mentees, and comentors were all volunteers and all had the option of leaving the scheme or asking for another partner if the first relationship proved unsatisfactory. Neither of the programs was part of a structured management development scheme. The training emphasized a choice of activities that might be included in mentoring but was not prescriptive. Partners determined when, where, and how often their meetings might occur.

In what ways might the level of program formalization reflect on the possibilities of creating reinforcement or destabilization? Formalization is considered to decrease mentoring effectiveness because of the possibilities of dissonance between the views of the partners. The voluntary nature of participation might mitigate this, however. Those joining the programs were likely to have very positive attitudes to mentoring and to management learning (Noe, 1988). In allowing self-selection for involvement in these programs, it was intended to ensure that participants were likely to have these positive attitudes and so benefit from the study.

Mentoring Participants and Pairing

It was assumed that possibilities of destabilization or reinforcement might be related to the extent to which there were similarities among mentoring participants and the extent to which it was possible to produce dyads with commonalities. In both programs, the mentors, mentees, and comentors shared few similarities among themselves or with their partners; the one common characteristic was that of participating voluntarily, a factor that research indicates is the most important correspondence in mentoring. Beyond this factor, the possibility of more than the most crude matching was precluded because the group was small (12 pairs) and because the partners needed to work in reasonably close proximity to facilitate meetings.

From those in the principalship scheme, six pairs were selected for the research, the six being those currently active in mentoring partnerships. Their pairings had been arranged by the local organizing committee that consisted of experienced school principals deemed to have knowledge of their colleagues who would be the mentors. Matching to mentees' personalities was difficult, however, because the mentees were newly appointed and were not known to the committee. Mentors and mentees (six male, six female) were all leaders of schools for Year 6 and below.

In the comentorship program there were six male and six female participants in six pairs. The academic faculty were all from the same university but from different departments, and were at Head of School level (a school being a grouping of between 15 and 20 academic staff). Organizations (for example, National Westminster Bank, Vauxhall Motors, Statoil Health) that had links with the university were approached and employees asked to volunteer for the project. All employee participants were in middle management roles, two from manufacturing, two from the public sector, and two from the service sector. Although all participants shared management responsibilities, no matching of personal characteristics was attempted.

Both programs used the common mentoring pattern of one-on-one, with the partners formally assigned to each other. The partners, however, were not working physically closely and were in separate organizations in different environments. Openness to other informal mentors could offer the possibility of partners escaping from any destablization arising in the original schemes and a good mentoring experience in these programs might direct them to seek additional informal mentorship. The school principals spontaneously reported having used additional mentors and this is discussed further in the findings section of the chapter.

METHODOLOGY

All participants in the program, the six comentoring pairs and the six currently active principalship pairs, were surveyed. The small size of the mentoring group (not unusual in mentoring research, for example, Ashby, 1991) enabled in-depth interviewing and open-ended answers to questionnaire items. Both partners in each pair were reviewed because the destablization and reinforcement rationale for this research required information from both perspectives (in contrast, for example, Williams, 1993, reported solely mentor perceptions; and of 24 research reports on mentoring analyzed by Caruso [1992] none reported both perspectives). The size of the group also enabled the researchers to track partners individually and, thus, avoid degradation of data.

Both researchers were semiparticipants in the programs. (Thody conducted the mentor training for both programs; Crystal organized and administered the comentorship.) This personal involvement had the disadvantage of potentially biasing the results (Thody, 1989, 1991), hence, the choice of a hypothesis that was not linked directly to the supposed success or lack of success of either program but more to whether it picked up on outcomes that were not within the control of the researchers. In addition, the researchers differed in their personal views on the value of mentoring (Crystal, 1993; Thody, 1993a) and were, therefore, likely to treat each other's results rigorously. The personal involvement had the advantage of giving access to data that would not otherwise have been possible and of encouraging participant responsiveness.

Establishing a Definition of Mentoring

In assessing destabilization and reinforcement, it was important to ascertain how far the partners' views on definitions of mentoring were in accord at the beginning and end of the process. The challenge to be met was to select a generally accepted role model for mentoring against which the views of the participants could be measured.

Many readers will be familiar with the continuum along which definitions of mentoring are strung out beginning with the seminal work of Levinson and others (1978) with their father, friend, teacher, sponsor, guide, exemplar, and counselor dimensions. Kram (1985; 1988: Chap. 2) added the idea of context specific mentorship, which is useful in this research because of its distinction between mentoring for personal growth and mentoring for growth within the institution. Kram's distinctions arose, however, from an assessment of in-company schemes in which institutional career growth is an option, but the career dimension was not appropriate here. Equally, given the cross-professional nature of the comentoring program and the established experience of all the participants (even the new school principals had managerial responsibilities as deputy principals), definitions that included skills transfer as an essential element seemed inappropriate (Caruso, 1992: 44), as did those that included advocacy and resource referral (Geiger, 1992: 66). There also is a need to indicate differing levels of intensity in a mentoring relationship (Shapiro, Haseltine, & Rowe, 1978; Phillips-Jones, 1982) and to take account of the less precise meanings of mentoring used in education in comparison with business (Restine, 1993).

To meet these requirements, and to facilitate program comparison with other national schemes, it was decided to adopt the definitions of mentoring developed from the evaluation of the English principals' national mentoring scheme (Bolam et al., 1993). This definition was the summation of the views of 542 school principals to create mentorship categorizations. These were considered adaptable for the comentorship scheme because they included academic faculty. Participants were, therefore, asked to prioritize their views of mentoring among the categories: catalyst (role model, confidante, sounding board); linkage broker for contacts (networker, door opener, sponsor); solutions guide (counselor, adviser, facilitator, listener); problem solver (tutor, teacher, coach, protector, trainer); buddy (friend); and other.

Initial Questionnaire

The initial questionnaire required respondees to provide their definitions of mentoring and their expectations of gains from participation in the programs. It was administered to all participants at the beginning of the program. The questions were open ended and the data that emerged were compared with the categories selected for the mentor definition during the interviews. All participants completed this questionnaire.

Group Interview

The group interview was held after the first three months but was only possible for the comentorship participants. It was a pilot to test the method, and it was not originally intended to include the results. The meeting was chaired by one of the researchers and enabled participants to review progress and to exchange experiences. This produced valuable material that was incorporated in the findings. The meeting was recorded virtually verbatim onto a word processor and printed as instant transcriptions.

Structured Interviews

In-depth, structured interviews of all participants were selected as the main source because they help "make the subject feel comfortable reflecting on the mentor-protégé relationship" (Ashby, 1991: 220). Five participants were interviewed face to face to pilot the structured questions (two comentors, two mentors, one mentee). The other school principals were interviewed by telephone for practical reasons of time, distance, and cost. Comentors were all interviewed personally. The interview schedules contained 20 questions (31 were piloted). A repetition technique was used, the same question being posed in different formats and at different times in the interview to verify participants' responses.

Questions were asked to ascertain the degrees of actual and perceived similarities between and among partners on the assumption that similarities lead to reinforcement. The areas investigated were those of personal and professional characteristics, of definitions of mentoring, and of the preferred characteristics of mentors. Questions also aimed to discover the extent to which participants' organizations supported their involvement to establish how far it would be possible for participants to introduce new ideas should destablization occur. Partners' management aims and styles were explored to discover whether similarities or differences indicated possibilities of reinforcement or destablization. Partners' choices of elements for their mentoring programs were also discussed in the interviews because it was thought that tendencies to choose formal elements indicated a greater likelihood of reinforcement.

Evaluation Questionnaire

All participants in both programs were asked to record the meetings and other activities that had taken place and their views on the outcomes and processes of mentoring. These were posted with free post services for return and there was a 50 percent return from principals and 100 percent return from the active comentors.

This questionnaire was designed for a further research project and did not specifically address the destablization or reforcement issues. The responses outlined what had occurred in the mentoring processes and these are described in the introduction to the findings below to illustrate the context within which the research took place.

FINDINGS

Program Summary

Ten of the 12 pairs completed the program (all the principals and 4 of the 6 comentoring pairs). One of the comentors failed to start because of illness and one pair failed to meet, ostensibly because of "pressure of work." It is noteworthy, however, that in each of these pairs, one mentor was unable to attend the initial training, which may have indicated a lack of commitment. Could this have been because of expected destablization?

Each pair met for a median five times (for between one and three hours each meeting) and telephoned each other a median six times. The training was felt to be very useful by all the principals and one of the comentors and of some use by the other seven comentors. This may reflect differences in the extent of training; the principals had five days and the comentors had three hours. All but one of the school principal mentors and mentees rated their mentoring experience as very useful professionally and personally. Only one of the comentors rated the program as very useful professionally and personally although the other seven rated it as of some use. These differing evaluations could indicate the extent of reinforcement and destablization that resulted.

Reinforcement and Destabilization: Propositions and Findings

Proposition I

The greater the similarities between partners, the greater is the likelihood of reinforcement.

Status. In the principals' program, all shared the obvious similarity of status. All comentors likewise defined their status as broadly similar. All were from middle management, although there was considerable difference in what this meant in relation to the number of subordinates for whom each was responsible.

Management education. Mentees in the principals' program had received more formal management education at a higher level and were more likely to have had induction courses than had their mentors. Comentors were much more similar. All had undertaken induction and, with one exception, short courses; only one pair was not similar with respect to possession or absence of a management degree.

Organizations. The principals were all leaders of schools for pre Year 7 children, but there were variations in age ranges and types. Although these may not appear significant to an outsider, several mentees spontaneously stressed the point that their mentors did not have the required experience for some specifics. When asked directly if they thought it important for mentors to have the same responsibilities as themselves, the general opinion was that it was not necessary, yet, earlier comments belied this view. The comentors had widely differing responsibilities and areas of technical expertise.

Length of experience. In the principalship program, the pairs were meant to have very differing experience. The gap between partners was, however, much greater than that envisaged by the School Management Task Force that initiated this mentorship program. The task force had decided that five years was the minimum experience if principals were to make an effective mentor (presumably because such experience would produce a didactic approach to advice that was likely, therefore, to lead to destabilization). None of the participants in this program made any comment to indicate support for this view. In the comentorship program, two of the pairs had identical lengths of experience, one pair was at almost the same point, and one had a six-year difference.

Gender. Gender matching of school principal partnerships differed from the national pattern. Two pairs (33 percent) were partnered with the same gender (63 percent nationally, Bolam et al., 1993: 3, 6). One of the female principals was particularly pleased to be matched with a male mentor because "there are so few men in infants' schools" so a male perspective was valued. Two of the comentoring pairs were of the same sex and two were mixed.

When asked directly if gender were important in mentoring, all except one were adamant that it did not matter. Spontaneous comments indicated otherwise. For example, there was the comment that, "We hit it off straight away — we have a common interest in football." One couple from each of the programs remarked on the embarrassment of meeting an unrelated member of the opposite sex away from their organizations. One mentor mentioned that, "We had the same upbringing, school, and social interests so it helped" (two males).

Age. All participants were close in their middle years; the only two in their twenties were paired (by chance) with each other.

In summary, the expectations were that the chances of reinforcement would be greater in the intraprofessional program. In practice, reinforcement similarities were present in both programs, as were possibilities for destablization. Status and age similarities were evident in both schemes.

Destabilization possibilities arose in both programs from either actual or perceived organizational differences and from covert attitudes to gender. There were greater differences in the management education of the principals than in the comentoring pairs.

Proposition II

The greater the perceived need for similarities between partners, the greater is the likelihood of reinforcement.

The majority perceived a need for professional, status, and organizational matching but not for gender, age, and experience matching.

Half the principals' group rated intraprofessional partnering as essential, as did two of the comentors (one from business and one from the university although they were not partners). The belief in the uniqueness of professions was very strong and apparently quite enough to cause destablization where cross-professional mentoring was tried. The mentees were more adamant about the need for intraprofessional mentoring than were the mentors. It was inferred that this was because the mentees wanted solutions to immediate problems; mentors from outside education could give general management advice but could not offer specific knowledge of the type needed by those new to their principalships. Such attitudes appear to support the reinforcement theory. Three of the school principals who were not opposed to extraprofessional mentoring had themselves been in business or had a secondment therein.

In reflecting on potential gains from extraprofessional mentoring, school principals suggested:

Very valuable — I have been in business myself and there are the same problems of management. Teaching can be too blinkered. (mentee)

Management is the same anywhere — I could advise in any sphere — education is too parochial. (mentor)

It would give insights into other areas of management — especially financial and different styles of personnel management. (mentor)

In-depth management skills (from a mentee who said intraprofessional mentoring was essential)

Reducing the insularity of education; different management strategies (mentee who had taken a business management course and who ran a business)

Business comentors did not perceive that they would learn from extraprofessional partnering with educational peers, although they were interested in outsiders' "friendly view of how they worked" and the possibilities of new ideas. They felt they gained most from learning about the mentoring process and how this might be adapted for their own organizations. Had they been able to partner within their own professions, they felt they would have gained from sharing the same "vocabulary and background" and from more easily being able to make contact and share technical knowledge.

The losses perceived by school principals when offered the option of extraprofessional mentoring featured this same technical knowledge and contextual understanding. One school principal encapsulated these in stating that "You have to have done this job to know what the difficulties are" (mentee). Another expressed it as, "You can lose sight of the children with an emphasis on business management." Staff management was conceived of as different in schools compared to business (mentee who is involved with an education-business partnership scheme). One school principal considered that businesspeople would find educational problems "quite abhorrent" and the "demands and confusions" overwhelming. One school principal felt he would only be confident to mentor a person running a small business.

Extraprofessional mentoring would result in a loss of trust because managerial credibility would be absent, and school principals thought it would take longer to establish a relationship with a mentor from another profession. The latter appears to have been true in these two programs. The comentors intended continuing their relationships after the mentoring program ended more than did the principals. This difference between the two programs seemed to arise because the comentors felt they had only just begun their friendships as the program ended.

Principals in the mentoring program were also asked what they thought they might gain or lose through being partnered with someone of the same experience as themselves. Three envisaged it as valuable (all three had tried it in addition to this program). Most could see no gain because there would be insufficient difference in experience to exchange and considered that it would be more difficult to settle into a relationship. The comentors were asked to consider the possibilities of working with someone at a different level of seniority than themselves. Similarly, the majority were not in favor, fearing difficulties of settling into the relationship and a learning loss because one of the partners would be inexperienced.

Five of the 12 principals considered that personality matching was essential, although none wanted to select their own partners and none had been matched on personality grounds. Five of the comentors thought personality matching would be helpful; three thought it was not essential.

In summary, there was a strongly perceived need for professional, organizational, status, and personality matching that indicates desire for reinforcement. The school principals and the academic comentors seemed, however, to be more willing to gain from the potential destablization of unmatched partnerships than did the business comentors. Both groups preferred the type of program in which they participated to the alternative scheme — which may indicate only that we rationalize support for whatever we know and dismiss that which we have not experienced.

Proposition III

The closer the similarities between partners' definitions of mentoring, the greater is the likelihood of reinforcement.

Catalyst was the definition most often selected by participants in both programs with *solutions guide* as the second option. This contrasts with the majority choice before the program began when most selected solutions guide. This change may indicate a movement from a desire for reinforcement to an acceptance of the value of destablization. Among the comentors, there were a few who liked the *problem solver role*, but only one of the principals selected this role.

Principals were least happy with the idea of mentors as *buddies* (and few of them rated friendliness or sociability as important characteristics in a mentoring partnership). "It's better than a buddy system," said one mentee. "You can be assured the mentors will listen to your problems without you having to listen to theirs." One mentee, however, stressed the important of friendship: "Friendship definitely comes into it — it has to because this is a reciprocal relationship." Four of the eight comentors favored a buddy role, which appears to lean more to reinforcement than to destablization.

Eight of the ten pairs had matched expectations of the main role a mentor might adopt, reinforcement possibilities in both programs. There was, however, no perceptible relationship between matched (or mismatched) suggesting expectations and similarity (or lack of similarity) of other characteristics or perceived need for similarities. The pair who had the most related views of mentoring were both male but differed in all the other descriptors. Both of them had stressed the importance of matched personalities and friendship in the mentoring relationship. The pair who had least agreement were both female and of the same age group but differed in other descriptors. The lack of relationship between views of mentoring and of other characteristics emphasizes the conclusions from most mentoring research — effectiveness depends upon attitudes rather than upon any innate characteristics.

In their ratings of the importance of possible characteristics for mentoring, the comentors exhibited greater similarities, both within and among pairs, than did the school principals. Comentors rated all the characteristics as essential or helpful, whereas the principals classified some as nonessential. Perhaps the reinforcement of intraprofessionalism makes other similarities less important. (The characteristics to be rated were positive attitudes to mentorship, openness, ability to listen, friendliness, willingness to respect confidentiality, and respect for each other's views.)

Proposition IV

The more supportive a participant's organization, the more knowledge an organization has of a participant's involvement in the program and the greater the gains perceived for the organization, the greater is the likelihood of destabilization.

Organizational Support

These mentorship schemes could best be described as "non events" for all of the organizations in that both programs and participants assumed support rather than formally requesting it. "Since I have used more time on this than is actually funded, I suppose I have had governors' support," remarked one mentor. Those of the participants' colleagues who were aware of the programs' existence registered acceptance rather than support or opposition. A few asked interested questions. Some school staff made light jokes. One deputy head made disparaging remarks (the person concerned had been passed over for the principalship held by the mentee concerned). One of the comentor's companies was described as "very supportive" and had offered cover for the time spent on the program. This company holds a national award for its investment in training.

Organizational Knowledge

Durham and Gateshead Local Education Authorities[4] (who are the legal employers of all the principals researched) financially supported the principals' program and played a small part in selecting some of the participants. Hence, they were aware of participation.

The de facto employers and the principals' "line managers" are the schools' governors and the principals' relations with them are more significant for the incorporation of any new ideas into their schools. All the mentors, but only four of the six mentees, informed their governors of their participation in the program. There was disparity in their attitudes to the need to inform governors. Some were adamant that the governors did not have to be informed; others were equally adamant that they did. Some felt that they needed to request permission from governors, others that it was no concern of the governors. In some cases, it was formally reported (each principal submits a report to their governors at the end of each term) as just part of staff development. The mentees' governors were rarely informed directly. "I am sure that the chair and vice chair of governors know, but it didn't arise at governor's meetings. The agendas are long enough already so I didn't want to bring it up," commented one mentee. In contrast, two mentors implied that "permission" was needed, as did one mentee. "As this involves my being out of school, I had to have the chair's permission" (mentee).

All the school principals had informed their deputies and most had also informed the rest of their staff as well. This would appear to be unavoidable because primary schools are so small and adult visitors noticeable, but visitors are common and a visiting mentor or mentee could arrive and leave unobserved because all other staff would be teaching. Deputies and colleagues were casually informed. In four cases (three mentees, one mentor) the principal stated that, "It's nothing to do with them."

All of the comentors had informed their line managers and senior managers of their participation. Other colleagues may have been aware of the program's existence but only by chance. None of the comentors had requested permission to participate, and none had made a formal report about involvement. The idea of joining the scheme had been suggested by the organizations of six of the eight comentors.

Organizational Gains

School principals, both mentors and mentees, assumed organizational gain would arise from their personal development gains. Comentors assumed there would be personal rather than organizational gain, with the exception of their companies acquiring knowledge of mentoring. The general assumption from participants in both programs was that the gains lay in the absorption of new ideas — or destabilization (14 of the 20 responses). However, in the principals' program, there was a strong expectation of reinforcement through reassurance and a reduction in the loneliness that is associated with principalship. This supports Kram and Hall's conclusion that mentoring "may offer an antidote to stress" (1991: 503). Those anticipating new ideas were mainly mentors; those anticipating reassurance were mainly mentees. Prior to the program's commencement, all thought the main gain would be in new ideas.

Proposition V

The extent to which partners perceive they have similar aims and management styles indicates the likely extent of reinforcement (similar ideas are likely to be suggested).

Proposition VI

The extent to which partners understand each other's aims and styles indicates likelihood of reinforcement (inappropriate ideas are unlikely to be suggested).

There were insignificant differences among the principals in their reported aims and styles. The comentors, predictably, differed in their aims. For example, the academics did not talk about customer need or profit. All participants were similar in perceived management styles. There was a predominance of "people" cultures, flexibility, and collaborative styles, although two of the principals indicated that they could be autocratic. Partners were also asked how they perceived each other's aims. The similarities were marked with only one person misconceiving the partner's aims. When being questioned about these aspects, respondents in the principals' program emphasized the similarities, often prefacing their remarks with, "Oh, his ideas just replicate mine," or "We're just the same — we see eye to eye." It was unexpected to find such congruence between partners who had been randomly matched. Possible explanations could be that extensive reinforcement occured in both programs or that all were quoting what is generally accepted as "good management."

Proposition VII

The more informal the program design and participation, the greater is the likelihood of reinforcement.

All participants were volunteers, thereby creating a basis for informality. The degree of informality was then measured by ascertaining which elements of mentoring were most often selected. (The informal elements were judged to be those of general or specific discussions; the formal elements were the establishment of initial contracts, tours of each other's organizations, observation of each other at work, exchanging documents about each other's organizations, setting an agenda for each meeting, and keeping records of meetings.) Informality was also gauged through asking participants if they felt that mentoring required training — those who answered negatively were deemed "informal." It was also assumed that those who anticipated continuing the relationship after the program was completed had developed a degree of informality.

Elements of Mentoring Selected

Agreements on which elements of mentoring were essential varied considerably and no pattern was discernible. There was a slight preponderance for the informal discussions being essential, but the comentors rated as essential more of the formal elements than did the school principals. Four of the 8 comentors rated observation highly compared with only 2 (a pair of mentor and mentee) of the 12 principals. Whichever elements had been selected, however, there were answers that also stressed that whatever was done would be in accordance with the needs of the partners rather than according to any format for mentoring: "We did set an agenda but it usually changed as something else cropped up." "It's always left that he will contact me when I'm needed."

Continuing Contacts

All the comentors definitely thought the relationship would continue. The school principals were more equivocal. Those principals who thought they would not continue to meet included comments such as "Time will preclude our meeting" or "I would prefer it not to continue — there are issues of confidentiality to consider." One pair stated that they would continue "informal mentoring — we both enjoy it and our interests are very close." Another pair were very clear about future intentions — the mentor had promised to phone each half-term; both partners intended to keep in touch.

It is surmised from this that the school principals were ready to move out of a reinforcing relationship as the mentees matured. In contrast, the comentors, having taken longer to get to know each other, were gradually becoming aware of similarities and of their value to each other. This could be described as readiness to move out of destabilization.

Proposition VIII

The greater the use of unofficial mentors from outside the program, the greater is the degree of perceived destabilization.

No attempt was made to ascertain if partners used other mentoring-type relationships during the program, but comments during interviews indicated that partners were using alternative, additional, mentoring relationships. Explanations for contacting other mentors included, "He's in the same type of school as myself" (although the differences with his mentor's school were slight), "She's just nearby" (but the "official" mentor could have been contacted by phone), "Only another new head would appreciate this issue" (from a mentee who had stated that experience was essential in a mentor). "I use the headteachers' networks," explained another principal. One might surmise from this that reinforcement was being sought and that, even within the intraprofessional program, some destabilization was occurring.

No comentors mentioned other mentoring contacts. Two were planning to encourage in-company mentoring programs as a result of their participation in this one.

The programs did not preclude the use of other mentors and, perhaps, it was an indication of the success of the program that additional mentors were used. It is suggested that, in choosing additional mentors, the mentees were expressing some resistance to ideas or approaches suggested by their mentors. This does not necessarily imply criticism but can be taken as a sign of maturity of a mentee who has learned the value of consultation or who is ready to manage without the original mentor's guidance. Mentoring has been defined as "more valuable when it allows an escape hatch from the formal system" (Caruso, 1992: 39), so, perhaps, this informal mentoring development is the escape hatch.

CONCLUSION

It is accepted that the size of these mentoring programs inhibits generalizations, but the findings give leads to future areas for investigation. The expectations were that reinforcement would be greater in the intraprofessional program, but, in practice, there were possibilities for both reinforcement and destabilization in both programs. Status, age, gender, and experience matches existed in both programs to create reinforcement. Professional and organizational matching was, however, considered to be very important by participants in both programs, and most felt they would learn less from an intraprofessional program than from an extraprofessional one. This would seem to indicate an assumption of destabilization. This was reflected in the gains registered from participation that centered around the acquisition of new ideas. In contrast, the belief that mentoring reduced stress indicated more of a reinforcement outcome. The matching of personalities, management aims, and styles (and perceptions that a match existed) were all deemed important to reinforcement possibilities by the program participants (and by the researchers). The pairings could not be designed to match those who were similar in these respects, yet, the partners emerged as perceiving themselves to be remarkably similar — much more so than chance matching would lead one to expect. Is this because reinforcement is a natural concomitant of volunteer mentoring?

Finding a way to assess reinforcement, destabilization, and other impacts of this type of administrator preparation was problematical. The "feel good" factor would not address organizational effectiveness (Wilson & Elman, 1990). Career achievement measures would be inappropriate for these programs and require longitudinal data (Chao & Gardner, 1992). Specific project outcomes were not planned (Ashby, 1991), so no simple measure of output was apparent. The difficulty of separating effects of mentoring from effects arising from other initiatives is well known (Caruso, 1992: 128) and is compounded in these programs by participants being employed in different organizations such that competing influences are more diverse than those within a single organizational culture. Private sector mentoring controls are deemed inappropriate for the public sector (Ritchie & Connolly, 1993). Assessing value added through inspection and review may be essential (Carter, 1993: 170), but practicalities impede it. Pre- and post-mentoring observation of participants at work would be time-consuming, intrusive, and likely to prejudice subjects to make visible change deliberately (Thody, 1991). The possibility of interviewing colleagues and employers of participants would provide outsider perception, but such interviews are difficult to arrange. In the principals' program, not all of the participants had informed their governors or colleagues of their participation and some did not wish to do so. In the comentorship program, all line managers were aware of participants being in the program. Some participants felt strongly that the confidential nature of mentoring relationships would be breached by including outsiders in the research. Without some development of the means of assessing mentoring there is too much reliance on the participants' estimate of the feel good factor.

Destabilization and reinforcement appear to be new criteria for assessing mentoring outcomes. The terms chosen have the disadvantage of having common meanings, both of which imply negative outcomes. Both words, however, are intended as neutral descriptors, either of which can indicate bad or good outcomes (see Figure 14.1). A first need, therefore, may be to find alternative terminology. Second, the propositions adopted in this study for the discovery of outcomes need extended study to check both validity and to test as outcomes from other methods of principalship preparation. Such comparisons might help mentoring to prove itself as more than "a pleasant time sharing stories" (Greiger, 1992: 65) or simply a re-creation of an apprenticeship model of learning (Thody, 1993a).

ACKNOWLEDGMENTS

The assistance of Christine Chadney and Anne Punter of the University of Luton as research assistants on this project is gratefully acknowledged.

NOTES

1.   No replica schemes have been found in the literature, but the extensiveness of mentoring programs makes it possible that somebody, somewhere is trying the same approaches.

2.   England and Wales are divided into 117 administrative areas for education, each managed by an elected council and executive officers. They run the majority of schools.

3.   Beginning in April 1995 schools with newly appointed principals have a government grant of £2,500 to spend on principalship training through government-approved training. This is to be provided by universities, colleges, d.e.a. consortia, or private providers. It is not yet clear what form of training will be approved, or whether mentoring will be retained.

4.   Each English and Welsh school has a board of governors who are elected or appointed people from the community. The governors select, promote, and dismiss staff and can decide their salaries. They are, therefore, in the position of employers.

15

The Need for Mentoring in a Developing Country

Morkel Erasmus and
Philip C. Van der Westhuizen

Over the past century, the task of the principal has changed drastically. Initially, the principal was responsible for the teaching-learning activity and was concerned primarily with the instruction of pupils. As schools expanded and more teachers joined the staff, the principal's task gained an ever greater management dimension. Yet, in both the literature and in practice, the professional development of school principals has long been neglected. Although trained as teachers, many principals have not been well-trained for management tasks (Hallinger & McCary, 1990), and continued professional support is often not addressed in traditional training programs. The successful transition from the classroom to the principalship is no simple matter. Research in developed nations, such as England (Weindling & Earley, 1987) and the United States (Daresh 1987), indicates that newly appointed principals experience problems regarding role clarification, management skills, and ability to adapt to the social environment of their new schools. If beginning principals are to succeed, alternative training methods need to emerge, especially in developing countries where principals often perform in isolated environments.

The question examined in this chapter is how best to prepare school principals in developing countries for the demands of the twenty-first century. Specifically, we look at the potential role of mentoring in the professional development of principals. As Thody and Crystal note in a previous chapter, various programs for the in-service training and professional development of principals already exist in England and Wales, the United States, and other nations. In some U.S. states, the successful completion of an internship is compulsory for appointment as a principal, and an experienced mentor often plays an integral part in these programs. Ohio, for example, legally requires beginning principals to work under the guidance of experienced principals to prepare them for the transition from the classroom to the principalship (Daresh & Playko, 1990a). The research indicates that, when experienced principals mentor less experienced colleagues, the mentoring relationship is seen by both as the most important aspect of their professional development (Daresh, 1988a; Healy & Welchert, 1990; McHale, 1987).

Paradoxically, in developing countries, such as the Republic of South Africa (RSA), where principals tend to function in relative isolation, the professional development of beginning principals has been neglected (Van der Westhuizen, 1990). Moreover, principals are not obliged to improve their qualifications in educational management over the course of their careers. Van der Westhuizen points out that principals in the RSA are trained teachers, but many have not received managerial training. This situation contributes to the fact that beginning principals experience problems with integration into administration (Van der Westhuizen & Janson, 1990). Although some departments of education present short orientation courses for newly appointed principals, further training is undertaken only of one's own free will. In most developing nations there is no fixed policy in this regard, and structures for formal mentorships simply do not exist. The isolation within which most principals operate in these countries allows, at best, for the maintenance of skills and, at worst, causes the manifestation and continuation of poor managerial behavior.

To promote the professional development of school principals in developing countries, we argue that experienced principals serve as mentors to their beginning colleagues. Mentoring provides participants with ongoing feedback — feedback typically unavailable in the absence of such systems (Cohn & Sweeney, 1992; Gibble & Lawrence, 1987). For the purpose of our discussion, mentoring is defined as that phenomenon that takes place during the induction phase of the newly appointed principal, where experienced principals and their protégés commit themselves within a work relationship to enhance the professional development of both. In this chapter we examine the aims and characteristics of a good mentoring relationship, the responsibilities of a mentor, identification of mentors and protégés, and, finally, the potential advantages and disadvantages of a mentoring system.

THE AIMS AND CHARACTERISTICS
OF A GOOD MENTORING SYSTEM

While the immediate aim of mentoring is "on-board assistance" for beginning principals, the ultimate aim is to promote continuous professional development as these principals' careers progress. Hamilton and Hamilton (1992) claim that the single most functional aspect of a mentoring system is the promotion of principals' self-confidence. To accomplish this, the relationship between the mentor and protégé must be of a two-way, interactive nature in a risk-free environment. The parties must feel free to share problems and feelings concerning their professional roles. The voluntary participation of both the mentor and protégé is an important aspect of a successful mentorship, because a forced relationship can only give rise to unnatural work conditions that would impede meaningful growth and development (Barnett, 1990a). Activities must be jointly set and directed at developmental areas of the protégé, as well as practical management challenges the protégé will confront.

Daresh (1988b) points out that beginning principals need opportunities to form their educational philosophies, professional convictions, and values and to share them with other colleagues. They also need to develop an understanding of different management and leadership styles and how these different styles can be integrated to suit their own situations. Finally, within a mentoring relationship, a beginner can articulate career objectives, identify strengths and weaknesses, and consider how weaknesses can be bridged and strengths expanded.

Calabrese and Tucker-Ladd (1991) believe that successful mentorships manifest coinvolvement, inclusiveness, directiveness, reciprocity of activities, development, and role-modeling. To these characteristics Daresh (1988b) adds the following four:

beginning principals must accept responsibility for their own professional development;

fraternal behavior and mutual trust is vital;

individual plans of action and objectives must be determined; and

a wide range of alternative instructional activities must be made available.

Daresh and Playko (1992b) further recommend remediation, orientation, and socialization; specifically, remediation in respect to specialized aspects of the principal's appointment, an orientation to the new role, and socialization to the principal's place and role within the school as a social environment.

Daresh (1988b) points out that individuals confront predictable age- and career-specific needs at each phase of a career. A successful mentoring system, therefore, will manifest continuous growth and development as a central characteristic throughout preservice training, induction, ongoing in-service training, and whenever developmental needs change (Daresh & Playko, 1988). As many mentoring contact sessions as possible are essential to success, and, during these sessions, attention should be given to the acquisition of technical management skills and to personal and professional needs.

RESPONSIBILITIES OF THE MENTOR

A mentor must accept responsibility for the teaching-learning activities within the relationship. The mentor must be capable of recognizing and developing the protégé's talents and skills and must create opportunities for professional development. These responsibilities can be classified into two main roles: providing guidance and support and orienting the beginner and initiating a network with other colleagues into which the new principal can integrate.

These two roles can be best achieved through:

Advising: Respond to the protégé's needs concerning acquisition of new insights, skills, and information. The mentor must be available to react to questions and problems.

Communicating: Ensure that communication channels are always open.

Consulting: The mentor must give emotional support throughout.

Guiding: The mentor must orient the protégé to the norms and values of the school community.

Providing a role model: The mentor must serve as a role model by consistently demonstrating expertise and professionalism.

Protecting: When necessary, the mentor must serve as a buffer between the beginner and other people in the school who could have an adverse influence on the protégé's achievements.

Developing skills: The mentor must be attuned to supporting the beginner in the acquisition of the required skills for the post. (Daresh, 1988b; Daresh & Playko, 1989a, 1989b).

According to Daresh and Playko (1992b), an ideal mentoring relationship should be based on analyses of the professional objectives, interpersonal management styles, and learning needs of the two parties.

IDENTIFICATION OF MENTORS AND PROTÉGÉS

There is a strong possibility of a mentoring relationship failing if the right partners are not placed together. However, the identification of two people who will adapt within such a relationship is by no means an easy task. The ideal is to place a beginning principal with a mentor who is truly concerned about the professional development of inexperienced colleagues and who sincerely wishes to establish a mentoring relationship. It is also sensible to allow a protégé to choose his or her own mentor.

Mertz, Welch, and Henderson (1989) and Barnett (1990a) are of the opinion that gender plays an important part in the success of a mentoring relationship because research indicates that women experience feelings of overprotection, stress, and social distancing in the presence of male mentors. It is also important that age differences between mentors and protégés not be too great. If the difference is greater than, perhaps, eight years, the protégé may experience too much dependence on the mentor.

Although experience is an important characteristic, not all experienced principals make good mentors (Calabrese & Bartz, 1990). In fact, a mentor need not be a principal while mentoring. Daresh and Playko (1990a) are of the opinion that a person's ability to act as a mentor has less to do with his or her effectiveness as a principal than having certain key personal characteristics, the most important of which is the desire to help colleagues in their professional development.

A mentor should also demonstrate the following:

outstanding knowledge, skills, and expertise: A protégé needs to learn from a mentor who not only knows what to do but also how to do it correctly (Playko, 1990);

infectious enthusiasm for both the role of mentor and principal;

the ability to generate the right questions, as well as provide the right answers;

acceptance of alternative ways to act: A mentor must refrain from being highly prescriptive and not insist on only one way to handle a matter. Protégés must be given the opportunity to work out their own modus operandi. A mentor must create a climate wherein a protégé can discover things and make decisions without being protected from failure (Playko, 1990).

a desire to see protégés achieve at a higher level than they do themselves: Meaningful relationships require mentors to accept that others may do things better than they do and not only accept but also encourage these higher levels of achievement; and

promote the principles of continuous reflection and purposeful learning. (For additional characteristics see Schein, 1978; Daresh & Playko, 1988; Daresh & Playko, 1989a; Daresh & Playko, 1990b; Daresh & Playko, 1992c.)

Levine (1989) says that it is precisely these complex skills that mentors must possess that makes it difficult to find suitable mentors. The following types of individuals are not likely to become good mentors:

those who pursue positions of power within the school where they are to act as mentors;

those who are occupying new posts, because they also have much to learn and will not have sufficient time to do both;

those who have a reputation for large-scale staff turnover because of work dissatisfaction; and

those who appear to be omniscient, because this can have an adverse effect on an
    open work relationship.

And, just as certain characteristics distinguish effective mentors, so,
too, must a protégé exhibit certain characteristics as preconditional for
successful mentoring activities (Daresh & Playko, 1989b), including:

enthusiasm for work and for involvement in the study of the work sphere;

initiative and a conscientious involvement in the development of one's own
    potential;

commitment to envisaged plans and activities;

an open and objective attitude;

insight into one's self and others; and

a sense of humour.

Protégés must also be receptive to all learning opportunities that may
occur in a school. They must realize that their mentor is not the only
person from whom they can learn. In addition to the mentor, colleagues,
parents, and the community can also provide abundant learning experiences upon which to draw. Nevertheless, protégés must remain receptive
to suggestions made by their mentors, or the mentor may lose interest in
the relationship.

Having provided listings of mentor and protégé characteristics most
likely to produce a successful mentoring relationship, it would be naive to
suggest that just because the right partners are placed together, mentoring systems are immune to other problems. In the next section we examine the potential disadvantages of mentoring systems and conclude with
a discussion of the benefits these relationships provide both protégés and
mentors.

POTENTIAL ADVANTAGES AND
DISADVANTAGES OF A MENTORING SYSTEM

Daresh and Playko (1992a) contend that the full potential of mentoring
has yet to be truly achieved. Reasons for this include focusing only on
specific spheres where beginning principals experience a need and of
attention being devoted only to the acquisition of technical skills. A
further obstacle occurs when a protégé becomes too dependent on the
mentor. Daresh and Playko (1992b) believe that this is the result of
protégés relying too heavily on mentors providing answers to all their
questions. As a result, the protégé loses opportunities to derive benefits
from his or her own experiences.

Research by Mertz, Welch, and Henderson (1989), Barnett (1990b), Lemberger (1992), and Daresh and Playko (1992b) suggests other potential disadvantages or obstacles to mentoring:

Mentors become overprotective and prescriptive.

Mentors pursue hidden agendas.

Protégés acquire a limited perspective from the mentor.

Some mentors are unable to recognize or accept the limitations of their protégés.

Mentors can be excessively idealized by their protégés.

Protégés sometimes try to become replicas of their mentors.

Some mentoring systems are too structured.

Some mentors set unattainable standards for their protégés.

Some mentors find the status associated with the position uncomfortable.

Some mentors find the hierarchical relationship between themselves and their protégés unnatural.

Some mentors tend to keep the process confidential and do not share their findings and results.

Some mentors experience problems when observing a protégé in that they give too much direction and support instead of simply observing the protégé's behavior.

Moving from the participants to the organization, Lemberger (1992) suggests that a climate prevalent in many schools, specifically, that each person do his or her own thing, solve his or her own problems, and not seek help from others, must first be eliminated before mentoring can come into its own. Another factor noted by Irvine (1985) was that mentoring can be extremely time-intensive and, thus, a major impediment. Nevertheless, the mentors in Irvine's sample indicated that the advantages of mentoring clearly outweigh its disadvantages.

Among these reported advantages are that mentoring contributes to the acquisition of self-confidence, the cultivation of management expertise, and even improved communication skills in beginning school principals (Barnett, 1990a). As they learn the so-called tricks of the trade (Playko, 1990), beginning principals who participate in a mentorship manifest a more purposeful approach in their management tasks, a more serious approach to finer detail, and a greater awareness of what educational leadership entails (Daresh & Playko, 1990a). In fact, the value of the relationship is only truly realized when the protégé moves away from the mentor and is accepted and respected as an equal colleague during what Healy and Welchert (1990) refer to as the qualitative development phase.

From the perspective of the veteran principal, Daresh and Playko (1992a) are of the opinion that mentors derive as much from mentoring systems as do their protégés. Veterans experience mentoring as a challenging and highly stimulating activity, particularly if they have reached a stage in their careers where new challenges and the excitement of the principalship have diminished. For example, mentors are influenced positively by their protégé's energy and enthusiasm (Healy & Welchert, 1990; Mertz, Welch, & Henderson, 1989), and, with respect to personal convictions and values, mentors' skills are often improved through the opportunity to serve as a source of help for others' personal reflections (McCullough, 1987).

CONCLUSIONS

The school principalship has an extensive management component, and it is important how well principals are prepared for these tasks. Although mentoring has been a success in such countries as the United States, England, the Netherlands, and Israel a well-developed and structured mentoring system does not, as yet, exist for principals in the RSA or in many other developing nations.

From this chapter, the conclusion can be drawn that mentoring is an interactive and dynamic process that is an essential instrument for preparing both present and future school principals. At the outset, we noted that the need for mentoring in developing nations is not without problems. For example, the time required for supervision and interaction competes with the time needed for regular management tasks. For mentors in developing countries, who are unlikely to have assistants to cover for them, this is time they can ill afford. Nevertheless, this loss of time is more than offset by the fact that both beginning and experienced principals report the mentoring relationship as central to their professional development. Perhaps most importantly, when fully realized, mentoring systems will create networks that provide present and future school principals with opportunities to liaise with other principals. These liaisons can enable them to keep abreast of the latest management practices and research findings and, thus, overcome professional isolation, one of the major obstacles to the successful preparation and functioning of school leaders in a developing country.

VI

DILEMMAS OF SHARED LEADERSHIP IN DECENTRALIZED SCHOOLS

16

Reframing Educational Leadership in the Perspective of Dilemmas

Jorunn Møller

Major reforms on almost all levels in education are now taking place in Norway, as in most of the Western industrialized countries. In the public debate, a key word in these reforms is decentralization. However, parts of the reforms can be identified as centralization (Karlsen, 1993); it depends on which changes you are focusing, from which perspective you analyze the changes, and how you understand the sum of efforts toward restructuring. Decentralization is also defined as a state steering strategy, which also emphasizes the paradox of the twin tendencies of decentralization and centralization.

In Parliamentary Report No. 37 (1990–91) "On Organization and Guidance in the Educational Sector," the policy statements toward restructuring[1] of schools are outlined. Management by objectives, adjusted to the school as an organization, is said to be a central principle of governance. Thus, the ministry will continue decentralizing the regulation of education by rules and by giving the local authorities more autonomy and better possibilities to plan their economy. At the same time, they will centralize the control of goals by means of a new national curriculum where the goals are more clearly articulated and tied to a national evaluation program. The principal is given increased formal power and is placed in a key role in implementing the curriculum and evaluation program. The new role demands a more active participation on issues concerning classroom practices, demands more supervisory activities, and puts more emphasis on the employer role.

From my earlier experiences as a supervisor at the county level with responsibility for leadership development and in-service training, I had learned that the new role "mandated" from above caused a lot of concern and uncertainty for superintendents, principals, and teachers. "Answers" to educational challenges were given or advocated. In policy documents, "building a learning organization" had become the new "magic concept." More professional and reflective practice among educators was given as the answer to increasing the quality of teaching and learning. However, it was more difficult to uncover the meaning of everyday practice because, at the same time, more attention was given to accountability and control of teaching.

Given this situation, I chose to develop more specific research questions in collaboration with people in leadership positions at different levels in the school system. Although leadership is not necessarily connected with formal position, I wanted to examine how principals and superintendents experienced and conceptualized their leadership role in a specific political and cultural context. As a result of discussions with principals and superintendents from three municipalities, ongoing peer review through critical inquiry became a central issue in the research questions addressed in the study. Such a practice is definitely not characteristic of the school culture in Norway. To study it, one would have to create an alternative in the everyday practice. Because the research question required the construction of a new practice, an action research approach (Kalleberg, 1990) was chosen, although the choice was also inspired by Schön's (1984) advocacy of an alternative approach to research on educational administration.

The action research approach also offered the possibility of contributing to the practical concerns of principals and superintendents in a situation where new role prescripts demanded more active participation in issues concerning classroom practices. These administrators saw action research as a means both to develop their own competence and to improve practice (Carr & Kemmis, 1986; Elliott, 1991). At the same time, the action research approach could contribute to a better understanding of educational leadership: how principals and superintendents described educational leadership, how they explained their actions in specific situations, and how these descriptions could be related to the historical and cultural context.

HOW THE STUDY WAS INITIATED AND CONDUCTED

In preparing the study, I cooperated with the school director of the county of Oslo and Akershus and constructed a three-step negotiation with municipalities and schools to ensure clear agreement that the ideas were promising and that the participants were willing to commit themselves to a collaborative project over a two-year period.

In the first step, I wrote about my ideas for a collaborative project, focusing on educational leadership and the context of restructuring, in a letter sent to all 23 superintendents in the county, inviting them to a meeting if they were interested. The second step was a meeting where further details of the project were discussed with superintendents who had declared interest; potential gains and strains were emphasized and the terms of participation were elaborated further. The terms included both time-release commitment from the superintendent and the schools and financial considerations. Participation was limited to three municipalities, so I asked the superintendents to apply for participation after the meeting. Five superintendents applied to participate in the project.

After having selected three municipalities based on the superintendent's commitment to the project in the application, as far as it was possible to understand and interpret it in a written statement, a third step required the principals and vice principals to confirm the agreement to participate. A meeting was organized in each of the three municipalities, and each of the participants was asked why he or she had chosen to participate. Again we discussed the terms of participation and possible benefits and tensions in participating in such a project, stressing that there was still time to withdraw. I tried to be clear about what I thought would be the required time but emphasized that it was very difficult to anticipate this in advance. This was a collaborative project where they would have a voice. I also included my own interest in the project as a part of my career as an academic and as part of a doctoral thesis.

Their decision to participate was a combination of an interest in exploring promising new ideas, expectations of professional growth, and getting a chance to work closely with peers from other schools and school levels. Some also saw the project as important because of the political situation in Norway, with growing skepticism toward schools and plans for national evaluation. The project could represent a proactive instead of a reactive response to this situation. However, it also became clear that some were not sure what they had committed themselves to, and some of the principals had even felt forced into the project by their superintendents. After having had an opportunity to discuss their own interest in the project, they were willing to give it a try.

We negotiated what was of practical concern to the principals and superintendents and tried to sort out our shared and separate interests, as far as it was possible to say in advance. We also agreed upon procedures for my publication of data from the study. One important principle was to include their response and critique to a preliminary interpretation of the data. I also saw reciprocal critique as a guard against the imposition of an idealized abstraction on the part of the researcher (Lather, 1986). The meaning should be constructed through negotiation with the participants, and the release of data should also be negotiated (Simons, 1987).

The negotiation procedure that took place before the project started was perceived and articulated as important to prevent misunderstanding that otherwise could emerge later. However, throughout the project I learned this was not just a question of establishing the right technical procedures (Jenkins, 1978); it also became a moral issue (Møller, 1994).

OBSERVATION, PEER REVIEW, AND JOURNAL WRITING

The main features of the project were connected to observation, counselling, peer review, journal writing, and reflection among colleagues and facilitators. In the project we emphasized observing everyday situations. Therefore, the principals and superintendents were asked not to stage special situations when an observer was present. This is, of course, difficult because an observer will always have an impact on a situation. We wished to investigate what kind of learning opportunities arose in daily activity when one made use of systematic observation and reflection. We agreed upon eight observation days at each school and each office of superintendent. In addition, seminars and group meetings were organized where the participants reflected on their experiences with observation, journal writing, and peer review.

The criteria for observation emerged out of a shared discussion of theory and practice and were agreed upon in advance. The principals and superintendents were asked to explicate the "theory" of leadership implicit in their own practices. Together with two consultants from the school director's office, I worked as an external facilitator. As facilitators, we tried to help them reflect on their practices in the light of theories they articulated. The discussion often centered around the questions: What does it mean to exercise good leadership practice in this context? What did you do in this context that serves as an example of your theory of leadership? How can you explain it? Argyris and Schön's (1978) distinction between "espoused theory" and "theory-in-use" functioned as an analytical framework. We also tried to combine experiences with theory by providing analytic concepts that could be helpful in analyzing the practice.

DATA COLLECTION

The research was qualitative in design and comprised several methods for collecting data. Throughout the project I tried to secure solid documentation of what was happening and how the leaders interpreted different events. Data are based on field notes from observations, peer review, and group meetings. In addition, the participants' journal writings served as important documentation. Before group meetings the leaders were asked to reflect on certain issues in a journal. I conducted interviews and kept a personal journal, reporting and reflecting on what I was doing and how and why the research process developed. Meetings with the other two facilitators and with the school director, where we examined our facilitation strategies, were also recorded.

The analyses that were given back to the participants were treated as hypothetical, and the participants were encouraged to respond. However, the participants also emphasized the limitations on their time to reflect on practices and issues, given the different working conditions of a researcher, principal, or superintendent. Therefore, the relationship could very easily turn out to be asymmetrical, where they accepted the analysis because they did not have time to look at it critically. Thus, it became important to establish trust by building a shared history of predictable, nonexploitative behavior on these issues.

REFRAMING EDUCATIONAL LEADERSHIP
IN THE PERSPECTIVE OF DILEMMAS

When we started our collaborative research project, each principal and superintendent was asked to register management-leadership actions and reflect on his or her own leadership on four different days during a week. An alternative was to describe a critical incident where he or she did not know how to handle a situation or felt uneasy with the solution. The purpose for journal writing was to become aware of the kinds of situations one pays attention to and the thinking attached to it.

The principals' journal writings show a day with constant interruptions where they continually have to respond to emergencies. Housekeeping and maintaining order are given significant weight, and all problems are seen as important. It seems difficult to give priorities to different situations. The superintendent, staff, and parents must be satisfied; the school must be supplied with adequate materials; and, in addition, they have to take care of teaching duties as part of their job. They are strongly action oriented and have very little time for reflection on actions taken. They seem to be constantly responding to the needs of the moment. Time pressure was mentioned as a frustrating aspect of their job.

The superintendents' journal writings show a similar pattern. This pattern is consistent with findings reported in Fullan's (1982, 1991) summary of research on principals and district administrators and in research on leadership conducted in Sweden (Lundgren, 1986; Stålhammar, 1985). Leaders are strongly oriented to action and they seldom give reflective activities priority.

Among those who focused on critical incidents, the journal writings were dominated by the managing of conflict on an ad hoc basis. The ambiguity in the nature of demands is a significant element in the job of being a principal or a superintendent. In a way, they are squeezed between the intentions of the state and policy makers, what parents require, what teachers expect, and what students need. Their journals describe their complaints about teachers not doing their jobs, their feelings of depression while managing conflicts among staff and parents, and the difficulties attached to implementing a national curriculum that they believe in.

The combination of being a teacher and a principal was stated as particularly difficult at the school level. It resulted in an even more fragmented day where one often had to leave activities unfinished. This description was confirmed throughout the two years I followed principals and superintendents in their jobs. Some of them stated that the time they had planned for the project, designed for reflecting on their action, was conceived of as a luxury activity. A few principals also felt guilty because they were not available to their staff during these hours of reflective work.

TOWARD A DILEMMA LANGUAGE
OF EDUCATIONAL LEADERSHIP

Administrators are, to some degree, caught in a constant struggle "pulled at the same time upwards toward state mandates and downwards toward collegial/parental expectations" (Hannaway & Crowson 1989: 3). The contradictory expectations of principals and superintendents result in situations that require choices where competing values cannot be fully satisfied. Which expectations are most important? To whom does one's loyalty lie in a conflict situation? Sometimes one has time to reflect on what is desirable, and it is possible to take both moral values and practical consequences into account. However, often the decisions are made spontaneously and intuitively. Decisions can only be analyzed, understood, and given meaning in retrospect.

The action research project offered an opportunity to systematically reflect on action with colleagues and an external facilitator. Together we were engaged in developing an analytical framework that could help us analyze, understand, and give meaning to what had happened in specific situations that called for leadership. Often leaders described their actions in everyday practice as a choice between different sets of dilemmas. The dilemma was a concept that captured the contradictory orientations they experienced and where there were no right answers. Each course of action carried its cost and benefit. The challenge was to find adequate compromises (Berlak & Berlak, 1981; Cuban, 1992). By organizing and stimulating reflection on action among peers, it became possible to discover how different factors were interrelated. This gave leaders an opportunity to become aware of internal and external forces that bear on their own solutions and to clarify alternative courses of action.

In other words, thinking in terms of dilemmas was part of the principals' and superintendents' own conceptualizations. Dilemmas were also presented within a theoretical framework at seminars and meetings later in the project. Berlak and Berlak (1981) and Ball (1987) were important references. Based upon data that comprised observations in schools and district offices, discussions and interviews with the people participating in the project, and their journal writings, two general areas of dilemmas emerged: dilemmas related to loyalty and dilemmas related to control and steering issues. Although overlapping and complex, they can, nevertheless, be divided this way for analytical purposes. One will find moral and ethical dimensions interwoven, particularly within dilemmas related to loyalty. Often the moral dimension is more implicit than acknowledged. Sometimes it is mobilized and made explicit through reflection with peers.

The specific "dilemma-language" for leadership reported in this chapter was my construction based on the leaders' description of and reflection on their everyday practice. However, when I presented the analysis, they confirmed that I had captured important aspects of their work as they understood it.

The dilemmas of steering were expressed in actions where there was a tension between administrative control versus professional autonomy, challenge versus support, and change versus stability.

In addition, a dilemma of ad hoc problem solving versus reflection and long-term planning emerged, probably as a result of participating in action research. It is not exactly related to dilemmas of steering, but it deals with leaders' apirations to be considered as professionals.

The dilemmas of loyalty were expressed in actions where the principals found it difficult to decide to whom their loyalty should be in a conflict situation: students and parents, teachers, superiors, common curriculum, or personal pedagogical values? Which groups were most important? Was it possible to discover a pattern of decisions?

What I have chosen to describe as dilemmas of loyalty are related to significant moral and ethical issues. At the heart of educational practice is the making of moral decisions (Cuban, 1992: 7). When I, nevertheless, do not choose to use the concept of moral or ethical dilemmas in this context, it has to do with the way these dilemmas were perceived by the practioners. Moral imperatives are not necessarily part of the leaders' pattern of resolution, although the same dilemmas can be reframed in a moral perspective. The data from the project show several situations where principals and superintendents discuss and have to decide to whom and to what their loyalty is attached. The superintendents participating in the project were very much engaged in the implementation of the national curriculum. Their loyalty to this curriculum was clearly expressed, and they initiated courses for teachers and principals related to central issues in the curriculum. Their loyalty in this respect was also reflected in cases presented for the school board. On the school level the same pattern was found when espoused theories were expressed. When it came to theories in use it was far more difficult, and the principals were sandwiched between contradictory expectations. Some were also unaware of having a practice contradictory to central values in the national curriculum.

The dilemmas of steering have become even more problematic because of the paradox of the twin tendencies of decentralization and centralization. The ministry and politicians expect principals to be the most important change agents for school development in a culture where individual autonomy has been a central value for a long time. The "zones of influence" (Berg, 1990: 83; Shedd & Bacharach, 1991: 59) are being disturbed by mandates from the state. However, it will still be a question of how much it is possible for the principal to influence classroom practice and whether the principal has anything to offer to improve practice. Without a common language for analyzing teaching and limited traditions for reflecting on teaching, both teachers and principals must now learn very quickly to communicate in ways that match their subtle sense of teaching (Little, 1988). Will the teachers accept the principal as a supervisor? The answer is probably, but it depends on what he or she has to offer.

Dilemmas of loyalty and steering can both be analyzed in the perspective of legality and legitimacy (Berg, 1990: 28–29, 1993: 170–171). These key concepts relate to the tension between formal and informal steering of schools: "Generally speaking the term state legality pertains to the formal steering of schools codified and manifested in the form of curricula, rule systems, and so on. Social legitimacy for its part stands for those informal control mechanisms that are rooted in such things as traditions, rituals, school code/culture, trends in public opinion and/or other unwritten rules" (Berg, 1993: 1).

These concepts highlight a perspective of leadership as relational and dialectic (Ljunggren, 1991; Wadel, 1992) and encourage identification of power relations and conflicts of interests in schools. A basis of relational conception of power can be found in Giddens' (1984: 93) definition: "Power within social systems can thus be treated as involving reproduced relations of autonomy and dependence in social interaction. Power relations therefore are always two-way, even if the power of one actor or party in a social relation is minimal compared to another."

To see power as a relationship means, in other words, that the actions of both subordinates and superordinates influence the structures of domination. All actors both constitute and are constituted by the structures in which they find themselves. A similar approach to understanding leadership has been offered by Foster (1989), Bates (1989), and Smyth (1989). The legitimacy of leadership cannot be commanded, it can only be granted. The same way teachers may limit a principal's actions, the principals may limit a superintendent's actions, and vice versa (Cuban, 1988: 194–195). Micropolitical actions will be mobilized when there is a threat of losing obtained autonomy (Blase; 1989; Hoyle, 1986; Ljunggren, 1991). This is a phenomenon traditional theories of leadership based on a structural or human-resource perspective (Bolman & Deal, 1991) do not take into account, thereby losing an important aspect of understanding the process of educational leadership.

THE DILEMMA-ORIENTATION USED TO
ANALYZE EVERYDAY EXPERIENCES

The dilemma-language, when applied to specific situations of leadership, shows how interwoven different dilemmas are. Everyday practice is complex, and the same situation can comprise several dilemmas. The immediate interpretation of a situation in terms of a dilemma is seldom the only way of understanding what is happening. As you unravel the patterns of resolution, a different kind of dilemma often turns out to be involved as well (Groundwater-Smith, 1993). Understanding educational leadership from the perspective of dilemmas should, therefore, include considering the same situations through the perspective of different dilemmas. In the following text, I give examples of some of these dilemmas and highlight a specific dilemma by referring to specific actions of leadership. To some degree, however, I try to show how the different dilemmas are connected to each other and can be analyzed from the perspective of state legality versus social legitimacy.

ADMINISTRATIVE CONTROL VERSUS
PROFESSIONAL AUTONOMY

Teacher autonomy is often seen as the symbol of professional status; it is a positively value-laden concept, and it is taken for granted that it will also limit the power of the principal. I will, however, distinguish between individual autonomy, concerning the autonomy of each teacher in his or her classroom, and collective autonomy, concerning the school as a whole (Berg, 1993: 58; Hoyle, 1986: 120). As I show later, collective autonomy is synonymous with professional autonomy, not individual autonomy. In the Norwegian context, neither external nor internal accountability issues have emerged on the agenda until recently. There has been a strong norm of noninterference in the teacher's classroom activities.

Change in society's economy has, however, accentuated the opposition between control and autonomy in schools. Established zones of control are challenged. In the media there are complaints about the quality of education and the lack of necessary academic and social qualifications obtained by students by the time they enter university or employment. Teachers are depicted as antagonistic to change. The ministry responds by placing the principal in a key role in change efforts and school improvement. Their increased formal power may also mobilize the micropolitics between principals and superintendents.

The following situation[2] highlights the dilemma of administrative control versus professional autonomy.

The staff at Hillside, a primary school, has, through a long process, developed a shared vision and formulated a shared policy. Glasser's "School without Failure" has inspired teachers to organize their relationship with students in specific ways, involving students in curriculum planning and problem solving. They are trying to break down the boundaries between the different classes, having a shared responsibility for all students at the school. When new teachers are employed, both the principal and the teachers are engaged in sharing their vision and motivating the new teacher for commitment.

When Hansen got tenure at this school, he received a lot of information about how the school worked, what goals they had set, and how they tried to accomplish them. In conversations with the principal, Hansen says he will be committed to the school's vision. There is, however, often a gap between espoused theories and theories in use. The principal very soon understands that Hansen is not able to differentiate the curriculum in class. He is also unwilling to accept shared responsibility for all the students. His concern is his own classroom and his own students. He does not care about other students.

The principal decides that he has to do something and initiates several conversations with Hansen. He gives him pedagogical literature to read, and he ensures that experienced teachers are willing to share their knowledge with Hansen. However, nothing seems to have any effect. Now Hansen insists on teaching in his own way. To the principal, a dilemma emerges, and he frames the dilemma with the following questions: Can I accept that a teacher refuses to follow the school policy? For how long shall I accept this when this teacher declared that he would be loyal to the school's vision when he started working at the school? When is the time for support, and when is the time for confrontation and demands? When do I use sanctions? What kind of sanctions do I have? The principal also fears that noninterference will have a negative effect on the rest of the staff. Is it a good idea to try to persuade this teacher to move on to another school where individual autonomy is still accepted?

The dilemma concerns what it means to be a professional and when the principal has the right to intervene. It can be analyzed through the lens of legality versus legitimacy. No doubt, seen from the perspective of legality, the principal has the right to intervene in classroom activities in this situation. The question is whether this will be of any help to the students. The principal can, to a very small degree, influence employment policy.[3] Hiring is done by the school board at the municipal level where the teacher unions also have an important voice. There is even less opportunity to influence firing. Thus, in reality, the principal lacks sanctions to apply and is left to rely on argumentative authority. The principal's many conversations with the teacher have the purpose of convincing the teacher that changing practice is to the benefit of the students. We do not know whether this teacher is a bad teacher for the students. We only have the principal's perception and description of the situation.

The importance of developing a vision has been emphasized in recent years (Hoyle, 1986). Research on leadership has dealt with strategies used by school administrators to foster a more collaborative culture in schools (Leithwood & Jantzi, 1990; Leithwood & Steinbach, 1993b). A shared vision and commitment building among staff are perceived to be crucial to school improvement. The rationale behind shared vision building has to do with the creation of meaning, ownership, and mutual trust. As Fullan and Hargreaves (1991: 94) point out, "While commitment to collaboration is important, over commitment or compulsion can be damaging." Vision without voice very easily results in bureaucratic control. However, the opposite makes it impossible to validate education.

As the situation at Hillside School illustrates, building a shared vision does not solve the dilemma of steering. The stability of staff members may change. New people come in without the same ownership of and committment to the vision. The principal and the teachers are left with the challenge of including new staff members in the established culture without disempowering them. How can one create a balance between mandates and menus? Maybe the established culture needs critical voices.

The situation also highlights what it means to be a professional teacher, and who is going to define standards for good teaching. This can explain why the dilemma is difficult to manage. Neither the principal nor anyone else can prescribe what is going to happen in classrooms. One needs to maintain a balance between individuality and collaboration and recognize that there must be room for individual ways of teaching. However, teachers have a lot more collective tasks now compared to earlier days. Thus, the need for developing a collective knowledge base and to reflect on teaching among peers has increased. In addition, the system is only partially independent. As a profession, teachers have freedom of movement within the limits defined by what society expects of its schools. However, these boundaries for action are abstract, indistinct, and often contradictory. The reason is to be found in the conflict-permeated structure of the state school system (Berg, 1993; Lundgren, 1986). It is not correct to interpret the autonomy given by the society as an individual freedom. The autonomy is given to the profession. It means that the teaching profession has the right to construct and uphold standards of good teaching. However, teacher autonomy has long been interpreted as the right of each individual teacher to make independent judgments about classroom practice (Little, 1988).

The standards of good teaching are to a great extent implicit, and critical reflection, which could serve as a protection against arbitrariness in teaching and also guard against the power of the profession, is not taken care of. Both principals and teachers need to examine closely their own and others' professional judgments (Handal, 1989).

From the arguments above, it should follow that individual autonomy is difficult to accept. However, the principal's dilemma does not disappear with that. To change a culture of privacy in teaching requires a long-term strategy where in-service training is combined with support, challenge, and patience. In addition, structural frames must be changed.

Dilemmas related to issues of loyalty also were evident in the situation at Hillside School. As a middle manager, the principal has the responsibility to implement the common curriculum. In this case, the principal found that the teacher did not differentiate his teaching in proper ways, although he had a mixed ability group in the class. Consequently, one could say that the principal should intervene. He will find support in the school law, but, nevertheless, the possibility to act seems a lot more limited. At the same time, as an employer, the principal has a caring responsibility for his staff. What is the best way of caring in this situation?

Similar steering dilemmas can be found in the relationship between the principal and the superintendent. In this relationship, the principal is subordinate to the superintendent, and the superintendent is subordinate to the regional authority. They are, at the same time, bosses and subordinates. They are expected to lead and direct others while obeying orders. In fact, teachers, principals, and superintendents have a lot in common. Although the settings vary, they perform the same roles — instructional, managerial, and political — share the same commitment to a common purpose anchored in student growth, and work within bureaucratic organizations where members are simultaneously subordinates and superiors. How they define their limit of what can or cannot be done will differ and permit a whole range of practices (Cuban, 1988: 179).

CHANGE VERSUS STABILITY

The principal as a change agent is focused on the debate of restructuring in Norway. However, at both the school level and the district level leaders experience the internal pressure of stability rather than change. Although Norway has a state education policy embodied in legislation, curricula, and regulations, it is passed through various kinds of filters from the central government to the regional, the municipal, and the school levels. Furthermore, state directives, often being highly contradictory, are interpreted by different people at different levels. Sometimes it is considered, at the school level, to be good leadership to create resistance to state reforms because significant values are at risk in the context of budget cutting. All changes are not necessarily worth fighting for.

How and from where does the principal or the superintendent get their legitimacy to lead? Lortie (1987) is rather pessimistic about the the principal's potential to be a change agent. There is a strong pressure toward conservativism and stability within the system. In his study of principals in Chicago, Lortie found that there were four powerful tendencies toward stability relating to recruitment, role constraints and psychic rewards, constraint of system standardization, and career contingencies. Ståhlhammar's (1985) study shows similar tendencies. Very few principals initiated changes at the school level. Pressure toward stability was far more important.

My study reveals that principals' approach to change is very cautious, even when they have strong pressure from superiors to act as change agents. It seems best to be on the safe side, not disturbing everyday practice too much. Yet there is an acknowledgment of the need for changes in schools. One situation that happened at Village School illuminates the dilemma of change versus stability.[4]

The principal and vice principal at Village School asked a peer for consultation and observation concerning a staff meeting they were planning. The topic was new role expectations toward teachers. The leaders found some teachers' attitudes toward caring problematic. By putting this topic on the agenda of a staff meeting and following up later with in-service training, they hoped for fewer complaints about students. According to the principal's opinion, the teachers were complaining too much instead of asking what was the best way of helping the children who need caring. Empathy and priorities could be a better solution. However, at the same time, the principal knew he could very easily be perceived as increasing the teachers' workload, stress, and guilt instead of giving necessary support. He wanted to initiate change in the staff culture without increasing stress.

In the staff meeting they chose to focus on what they should do with students who were impolite and did not show respect for teachers, thereby causing much trouble and stress. The teachers wanted to focus on this because they felt insecure; they did not know how to manage the students. In the meeting teachers shared ideas about their own experiences and gave each other advice concerning classroom management. If anybody started to complain, the principal or the vice principal tried to turn the perspective to focus on positive aspects of the situation. The leaders expressed satisfaction with the meeting.

Will processes like this result in changes in the relationship between teachers and students? Are the leaders too cautious in their approach to change? Shifting perspective, this situation can also give an example of the dilemma of challenge versus support. The teachers at Village School have worked there for many years. Most of them are women, apparently eager to rush home when their teaching duties are finished. The principal identifies the school as traditional, and there is low motivation for experimenting with new approaches to teaching. They do not have pressure from parents. In fact, according to the principal, most parents are satisfied with the work done by the teachers. Experimenting with new approaches will increase teachers' insecurity at work. Teaching is already perceived as difficult and overloaded. Seen from a cultural perspective, it is probably a good idea to take very small steps toward change at this school. The principal believes that support is the most important leadership strategy to use, although he tries to be loyal to the superintendent's expectations of stimulating a more collaborative culture in the school.

The vice principal at Village School is, however, more impatient. This is revealed in her journal writings:

At this school, the teachers feel so insecure when they have to do things other than being classroom-focused. The insecurity increases even more when we try to stimulate school-based evaluation and planning and ask them to evaluate their work systematically. To my surprise, a lot of teachers have neither confidence and faith in themselves nor a professional attitude toward their job. I wish I could make them change, give them new perspectives on their job, new challenges, make them feel they are developing. Extended professionalism is necessary today. That is what the common curriculum requires. I really get depressed, when a 15-minute increase in collective planning time creates a huge discussion within the staff. Sometimes I wonder, is it possible to initiate change at this school? I get so frustrated at the lack of enthusiasm, involvement, and commitment among my colleagues. How is it possible to change them?

The vice principal had been inspired by reading Stenhouse's statements about the teacher as a researcher; she wanted to initiate action research at the school but found few interested. According to her, there should be a limit for how much support teachers get. A reflection from a principal at Oakridge School, a lower secondary school with 350 students, shows similar frustration. Initiating change seems to be a difficult and almost impossible task:

I really want to be a visible and assertive principal, but very often I do not succeed. . . . The staff is used to having a voice in every decision-making, and I can recognize this as important for raising enthusiasm and commitment. But there is a limit. This whole year I have been thinking about how to initiate peer review and a more collaborative culture when it comes to teaching at this school. But the staff wants to give other things priority. I have chosen not to insist on my proposition, but I am not satisfied with it. How can people give something priority if they don't know what it means? I have tried to use an implicit strategy, starting to talk about this more informally, and I can see interest is awakened in some. Everything would have been so much easier if only the superintendent could say: "You must implement peer review!" Then I could use my time on the motivation phase instead of this very slow process. The district office should be more demanding! (Or is this another excuse for me not being able to do what I want?)

In her journal writing the principal at Oakridge School wishes for more support from the superintendent. However, the question still remains: Will it be of any help? Looking at schools from a micropolitical perspective, there are a lot of ways to resist steering. The principal has to convince staff that change is necessary, good for the students, and good for the school. At the same time, it is important to emphasize that our choices are not always based on altruistic behavior. Many may have private privileges and interests to defend.

LOYALTY TO STUDENTS AND PARENTS
VERSUS LOYALTY TO TEACHERS

Most leaders say they will place emphasis on the interests of students if there is a conflict between students and teachers. In everyday practice it is far more difficult. The principal is responsible for care for the employees, and the teachers expect their boss to support them in conflicts. Sometimes, it is also difficult to judge what is to the benefit of students. The principal often chooses to compromise between different interests. A situation from Village School illustrates a percieved need for compromise:[5]

Two students in grade six have, according to a teacher, been very impolite. The teacher insists on their making a formal apology in front of their classmates. The students, understanding what happened differently, refuse. This makes the conflict even worse, and both the students and the teacher get into an awful wrangle. The teacher complains to the principal, and so do the students and their parents. After listening to both parties, the principal and the vice principal think that the teacher has behaved unwisely in this situation. The conflict was probably caused by her way of talking to the students. Nevertheless, they have to find a compromise, and, although the teacher can be criticized, so can the students. They have also behaved badly. The principal and the vice principal are afraid what will happen to the teacher's reputation in the neighborhood if they do not give her support. As employers, they feel an obligation to be supportive of both teachers and students. While the students will leave for another school next year, the teacher will go on teaching at this school, and they have to take care of a good relationship. The challenge is to get both the students and the teacher to understand that the same incident can be understood from different perspectives. Will they succeed?

In one way, this example shows that the long-term consequences are important when choosing what to do. Although both the principal and the vice principal agree with the students, they choose not to show it. They fear a deep conflict with the teacher. This observation gives support to Campbell's (1993) conclusion concerning the way principals cope with ethical conflicts in schools. According to her study, principals are reported to justify administrative decisions based on consequentialist arguments. By doing this, they reflect a decision-making framework within which moral and ethical values are largely suspended. "Suspended morality implies that while individuals may not 'buy into' organizational values completely on a moral or ethical level, they behave, nevertheless, in accordance with institutional demands. . . . In a sense, individuals are able to 'suspend' their own sense of morality to suit their personal situations, needs, and choices" (Campbell, 1993: 9).

However, when talking to the principal and the vice principal about this incident, it becomes clear that their decision is not based entirely on a desire to avoid conflicts with the teacher; it is felt as an ethical dilemma concerning right or wrong. An ethic of caring was visible in their reflection, and they wanted to be caring both to students and to teachers. However, conflict and guilt are inescapable risks of caring: "Conflict arises when our engrossment is divided, and several cared-fors demand incompatible decisions from us. Another sort of conflict occurs when what the cared-for wants is not what we think would be best for him, and still another sort arises when we become overburdened and our caring turns into 'cares and burdens.' Any of these conflicts may induce guilt" (Noddings, 1984: 18).

What happened at Village School can also be understood as a dilemma of challenge versus support. Which strategy will be perceived by whom as a caring strategy? The teacher has a problematic relationship with these students, and she expects the principal to support her when she gets into trouble. That is part of the school culture. What kind of leadership is needed in the long run? As both Huberman (1989) and Sikes, Measor, and Woods (1985) have pointed out in their research on career cycles of teachers, human development is a far more discontinuous, fluid, dialectical, and sometimes random business when one begins to look at individual lives. Having formal responsibility for teachers' development, it may be difficult for a principal to know when support is the right strategy for growth and when challenge is a better alternative. To confront this teacher will probably be very unpleasant for the principal. Maybe, after all, this is a case of suspended morality.

AD HOC PROBLEM SOLVING VERSUS
REFLECTION AND LONG-TERM PLANNING

The principals and superintendents participating in the project were all concerned about how they could develop their competency. Their decision to participate in the project had partly to do with expectations of professional growth. Their espoused theory of leadership emphasized the importance of reflection and long-term planning, but their theory in use was more characterized by brevity, discontinuity, and ad hoc problem solving. There was always something else that needed their attention, and they had to respond to emergencies daily, as journal writings, interviews, and field notes from peer review reveal.

I have become more and more aware of how important reflective activities are. But to find time for systematic reflection in everyday practice is problematic. You can't be a supervisor to teachers without competency. However, we always have too little time. (Journal writing from the principal at Pioneer School.)

When you are engaged in daily work and routines, and a lot of things are happening, to find time for reflection becomes a burden. There are always tasks you *must* do. . . . In fact, I found writing in a journal very time-consuming. It is a burden. However, I have experienced some benefit out of it. Participating in this project has stimulated more reflection. Usually I never write down my reflection, but I do reflect on what is happening. (From the interview with the principal at Village School.)

I give priority to be available for my staff. My door is always open. This means other tasks have to wait if teachers need to talk with me. Maybe that is a wrong priority? Maybe I should sometimes close my door in order to do some paperwork and more long-term planning? I always have to do paper work at home. I know I haven't managed to be an initiator of pedagogical change, even though I know the staff expect me to do it. I don't have enough time to do all of the tasks. In addition, I am not a very good ideological leader. Maybe I haven't realized how important it is. By participating in this project, I have discovered new aspects of leadership, and I think I have developed both my thinking and my skills. I am now motivated to take more education; I think I need it to become a real educator. But time is a problem. I am so dissatisfied by having so little time for administration and leadership. (Field notes from the vice principal at Pioneer School.)

My question here is how real this dilemma is, when the patterns of resolution reveal that ad hoc problem solving is always given priority.

Are the leaders' descriptions a way of defending why they have not met expectations of being more reflective? The principals know the right answers. They have participated in several courses for leaders, and they have learned that long-term planning, having a vision for their school, and reflection on action are important in calling oneself a professional.

Their reflections on action and sharing of experiences also reveal that involvement in action research is not merely stimulating. Systematically evaluating one's own practice with peers can also be a painful process, resulting in an intensification of one's work.

It was easier to be a principal before. All this discussion has resulted in a feeling of frustration and discouragement. There are so many expectations, and I experience a lack of competency, which is not a good feeling. So much ought to be done, and time is a very critical factor. (Principal at Village School.)

Participating in the project has given me a kick. I recognize new demands which can stimulate growth. I am more competent now, I think differently, and I have become more analytical. However, the more you are conscious about the work you are doing, the more difficult it is to be a leader. My days have become even more demanding, and I am more demanding towards other colleagues. I think it is important to know that everyone doesn't follow the same path and speed as oneself. (Principal at Country School.)

What was earlier taken for granted is now questioned. Sometimes it feels very frustrating. Maybe faith in reflective activities is given too much weight in the discussion about professionalism in schools. Both principals and superintendents will, nevertheless, be involved in a struggle for negotiating, maintaining, and renegotiating their legitimacy to influence the change process in schools. In this process, analytical competency and reflection on action among peers may become crucial.

CONCLUSION

In this chapter I have looked at educational leadership from a perspective of dilemmas. The dilemmas experienced by principals and superintendents constitute an analytic language for looking at leadership in action. Examples of dilemmas of loyalty and steering were analyzed in the perspective of state legality and social legitimacy. This offered an opportunity to relate what was happening within a local context to more general political, social, and cultural issues and to examine how the hierarchical structure and the micropolitical activities within schools both steer and restrict our activities and perceptions.

To understand dilemmas as reflections of the contradictions in society does not remove the individual's responsibility to act. Individuals will interpret the dilemmas differently and have different capacities for managing dilemmas. Nevertheless, contradictions in society are an integral part of the explanation of the regularities explored. Individuals both shape and are shaped by structure and culture.

The immediate interpretation of a situation in terms of dilemmas is seldom the only way of understanding what is happening. As indicated in this chapter, the participants in the project found that, by clarifying one dilemma, another one may be revealed. Sometimes the process of clarifying and reflecting on what is going on causes more frustration than emancipatory feelings for the participants. Apparently, this may have a connection to leaders' aspirations to be considered as professionals in a job where they feel they continually have to respond to daily emergencies.

To initiate change in schools probably presupposes a combination of change in structural frames and a practical and theoretical education for principals and superintendents, as well as for teachers. This education should include an understanding of the type of control that state and society exercise on the school as well as an understanding of the micropolitics of schools.

NOTES

1. Restructuring is used as a term that embraces major changes to the organization of teaching and learning, to decision-making structures, to the conditions of teaching, to the patterns of roles and power relationships in schools, and to the content of education (Hargreaves, 1991).

2. The description from Hillside School is based on the principal's presentation of a case that was discussed with peers at a meeting. The principal needed advice about what to do in this specific situation. Hillside School is a primary school with 220 students and 19 teachers.

3. This is an issue that is under debate in the Norwegian context right now. Many politicians call for a change where principals can appoint teachers, but, so far, the teacher unions have succeeded in fighting against this change in law.

4. The description from Village School is based on field notes from peer consultation, observation in a staff meeting, and peer review. Village School is a primary school with 200 students and 18 teachers.

5. The description is based on separate interviews with the principal and the vice principal. They both mentioned the same conflict when interviewed, probably because they were trying to find a compromise during the week when the interviews took place.

17

Devolution and the Changing Role of the Principal: Dilemmas and a Research Agenda

Robert D. Conners and Fenton G. Sharpe

During the past decade a conspicuous contemporary feature of school system management in many countries around the world has been the process of devolution of decision making from central authorities to more self-managing schools. The process is aimed at achieving schools that are more responsive to local circumstances and needs and more flexible in dealing with rapidly changing environments. The ultimate aim of the process is to promote better teaching and learning.

Yet, widespread as devolution is and profound as its implications are for the roles of system and school administrators, the process remains little understood and its benefits and limitations have not been explored by cohesive research programs. In light of the paucity of research on devolution, this chapter has three major purposes. First, it explores the concept of devolution — its benefits and negative consequences — and briefly describes its emergence in Australia, with particular reference to the state of New South Wales. Second, it analyzes a role dilemma created by devolution for school principals. Data from a pilot research project are presented that focus on the issue of devolution creating increased managerial responsibilities for principals and at the same time impinging on the principal's role as an instructional leader. Third, it presents a framework for research on devolution that focuses on the role of the principal as an important mediating variable that links devolution with improved student outcomes.

DEFINING DEVOLUTION

Devolution is a process through which an agency of control, such as a government or a school system, deliberately relinquishes aspects of control over the organizations for which it is responsible, thus, moving them along a continuum in the direction of total self-management (Davies & Hentschke, 1994; Sharpe, 1994). In education, devolution is merely a management device that moves the discretion, authority, responsibility, and accountability for some decisions from a central agency to the individual school. In Australian circumstances, these new powers may formally be given to the principal or school council. The process, therefore, increases the amount and level of responsibility of the principal or school council and changes the principal's role in significant ways.

CLAIMED BENEFITS OF DEVOLUTION

Recent literature records many claims for the positive outcomes associated with greater school autonomy. Some of these claims are tentative and modest and are, at times, based on the findings of research; others are sweeping and largely unsubstantiated.

With regard to the quality of management, greater school autonomy is said to lead to more effective and efficient management; the alignment of responsibility, authority, and accountability; and a greater concern for people. It is more likely to be based on expert and referent power than legitimacy, rewards, and punishments, and the prime focus will be on cultural and symbolic rather than technical aspects of leadership (Caldwell, 1993; Cheng, 1993).

In relation to structures and processes, school self-management is said to transform the patterns of authority positively, and improve the processes of communication, planning, decision making, problem solving, resource allocation, staff relations, supervision, evaluation, feedback, and local and system-wide accountability (Cheng, 1993; Codding, 1993; Herman, 1991; Sawatski, 1992; White, 1991).

It is said to be associated with greater participation in key decisions by teachers, other staff, parents, the local community, and students; a greater sense of shared vision and mission; and improved parent confidence and support, based on greater knowledge and involvement. These factors are expected to lead to more collaborative, flexible, and responsive school cultures with a greater focus on real student needs, quality teaching, and better learning (Chapman, 1994; Cheng, 1993; Codding, 1993; David, 1989; Davies & Hentschke, 1994; Finn, 1986; Malen, Ogawa, & Kranz, 1990).

For school-based personnel it is claimed that greater school autonomy will be associated with an increased sense of understanding, ownership, commitment, empowerment, initiative, job satisfaction, professionalism, motivation, morale, and self-esteem. In turn these will result in better quality recruits being attracted to teaching and more collaborative, innovative, productive, and effective teaching (David, 1989; Herman, 1991; Malen, Ogawa, & Kranz, 1990; Sawatski, 1992).

Finally, greater school autonomy is said to lead to improved student behavior, less vandalism, more equitable outcomes for disadvantaged students, more productive students, better test results, and a focus on broader educational outcomes (Cheng, 1993; Chubb & Moe, 1989; Codding, 1993; Herman, 1991; Scott, 1990).

CLAIMED NEGATIVE CONSEQUENCES
OR DANGERS OF DEVOLUTION

Those who oppose or question the wisdom and effectiveness of devolution are no less outspoken about its perceived shortcomings and dangers. Several commentators have questioned the motivations behind the moves to greater self-management. They see devolution as a tool of economic rationalism, associated with funding cutbacks, with a prime focus on efficiency rather than educational effectiveness, and with an aim of cheaper rather than better schools. They fear the process is designed to weaken public education and lead to privatization. It is seen as a process of "devolving the blame and concealing the cheque-book" and "devolving responsibility without power" (Barcan, 1992; McCarty, 1993; Smyth, 1993; Watkins, 1991). Others are concerned with equity issues — that funding formulas in a devolved system will neglect students with special needs; that increased competition among schools will inevitably lead to winners and losers; that with local selection, inequities in staffing will develop for schools in unfavored locations; that local decision makers will favor dominant groups; and that for many students there would be even less choice than under centralized systems (Bell, 1993; Codd, 1993; Meyenn & Parker, 1993; Watt, 1989).

Role issues are also of concern. The most commonly expressed are that devolution transforms principals from educational leaders to site managers and that teachers' time is diverted from teaching to decision making on administrative matters. The literature suggests that many principals feel weighed down by an additional workload. There are concerns that principals lack expertise in key aspects of management and that teachers are ill-fitted to participate meaningfully in matters of budgeting and policy making. There is also a concern that, as the local community becomes more involved in school decision making, there will be a confusion of roles between professionals and lay participants. Despite these role issues, there is very little evidence from research anywhere that principals in devolved systems would prefer to return to the previous, more centralized model (Caldwell, Lawrence, Peck, &

Thomas, 1994; Chadbourne & Clarke, 1994; Murdock & Paton, 1993; Ribbins, 1993; Watkins, 1991).

Finally, there is significant unease among many commentators about the lack of a research base for such a wholesale transformation of school management in systems around the world and that the whole movement is an act of blind faith. In particular, there is little research so far that supports any direct or indirect link between devolution and student outcomes. What research there is appears to be equivocal about such matters as the empowerment of schools and teachers. (Chapman, 1994; Malen, Ogawa, & Kranz, 1990; Purkey, 1991; Sharpe, 1993).

DEVOLUTION IN AUSTRALIAN GOVERNMENT SCHOOL SYSTEMS

During the past six years devolution has taken place in all six Australian states and two territories, although the speed of change, the aspects of management chosen for devolution, and the change processes utilized have varied markedly from system to system. All school systems have experienced significant cuts in the size of out-of-school administrative and support staffs, ranging from about 25 percent to 50 percent, with the trend continuing in almost all states.

The primary areas of devolution have been utilities, buildings, staffing (including selection), the development and strengthening of school councils, and the establishment of school charters. Control over curriculum, however, has tended to become more centralized in most systems (Caldwell et al., 1994).

Overall in Australia, there has been a significant trend to school-based management of processes and a smaller shift in the same direction for structures and relations with the school's environment. The position in relation to inputs is less clear. The apparent increase in control by governments, systems, and curriculum authorities over policies, culture, outcomes, performance, curriculum design, assessment, and reporting has the power to modify the benefits many schools are sensing from greater freedom in other aspects of management.

NEW SOUTH WALES — A CASE STUDY

During the past five years in New South Wales (NSW), there have occurred large-scale structural, administrative, and curriculum changes that have taken place at what appears to be a breathtaking and often disconcerting pace for many participants involved in education. The majority of the reform proposals were initiated by a conservative government that took office in March 1988. Proposals for reform were presented in a White Paper on the curriculum, "Excellence and Equity" (November

1989); a report on restructuring the public school system, "Schools Renewal" by Scott (June 1989); a report by Carrick, "Report of the Committee to Review NSW Schools" (September 1989); and a major report by Scott, "School-Centred Education: Building a More Responsive State School System" (March 1990). The majority of the reforms proposed by Scott (1989, 1990), which focused primarily on the devolution of decision making to more self-managing schools, have been implemented in the public school system in the period 1990–94.

Now that a variety of reforms are firmly in place, it is appropriate to review the impact of the changes upon one group of key players in the NSW public school system, that is, the primary (elementary) and secondary school principals. In presenting and analyzing changes that have taken place, we will argue that a dilemma has been created for the school principal. That is, with increased and different demands created by devolution, is it still possible for a principal to be an educational leader as well as an effective manager?

The Scott reports of 1989 and 1990 found that the efficiency and effectiveness of the public education system in NSW were hindered by the existing structures of a highly centralized education system. The management review proposed a Schools Renewal Strategy that was designed to improve the responsiveness of the public school system to the variety of educational needs that were evident in a complex multicultural society with a changing socioeconomic context. The strategy was described as a "downside-up" approach that aimed to put the school at the center of the system, with it being supported by the system rather than supporting the system. This approach to educational administration has had far-reaching repercussions for the entire system and required a redefinition of the role of the central executive, the region, and the school in the provision of public schooling. An analysis of these changes at the macro level has been undertaken by Sharpe (1993, 1994).

It was recommended that the central executive should concentrate on policy development and coordination, department-wide general management oversight, and corporate planning and coordination. The ten educational regions in NSW were retained and were given considerably expanded management responsibilities with a consequent increase in the size of their administrations. The region has responsibility for planning and implementing educational programs, planning human resource allocation and development, supervising financial and administrative operations, and coordinating and supervising performance evaluation.

The grouping of schools into inspectorates and the role of inspector were abolished. The inspectorate has been replaced by a schools management unit based on a "cluster" of schools with a cluster director in charge of each cluster. The role was seen as a collegial one, with the cluster director helping to coordinate collaboration among schools and helping them to implement departmental policies as well as representing the interests and needs of the schools to the regions.

CHANGES AT THE SCHOOL LEVEL

Changes that have the potential to directly influence the operation of the school and the principal's role, include:

principals now have responsibility for school budgets;

schools are required to establish five-year plans and prepare yearly operational plans;

local selection of principals and all other administrative positions, including heads of departments, and a limited number of classroom teacher positions;

establishment of a system of performance appraisal, including drawing up yearly performance agreements, for the purpose of helping staff focus their teaching and administrative practices on activities determined by priority education outcomes;

conducting quality assurance reviews that are intended to assist school development by helping schools review and develop their programs to meet the needs of their students and to provide an accountability function that assures the public that schools are working effectively, are achieving high standards, and are making effective use of public funds;

voluntarily creating school councils (now in over 60 percent of schools across the state), with parents and community members in the majority, to assess needs, to develop and ratify policies to meet needs, and to determine budget priorities as a response to needs; and

de-zoning to provide schools with an opportunity to draw pupils from wider geographic areas and to compete for students, but that requires competition between both primary and secondary schools.

In addition to these changes, curriculum changes at both the state and national levels have a direct impact on schools. Extensive curriculum changes instituted by the State Board of Studies at both the primary and secondary levels have focused on the reorganization of the total curriculum around six new key learning areas in the primary school and eight areas in the secondary school. For example, a new primary K–6 English Syllabus was introduced into primary schools in 1994. There have been efforts to develop national goals and curriculum statements and profiles in eight key learning areas as a basis for assessing student outcomes at various stages of learning in years K–10. The eight areas are: the arts, English, health and physical education, technology, mathematics, science, studies of society and environment, and languages other than English. Each statement defines the area and outlines its essential knowledge, skills, and processes and describes the broad scope of the curriculum and the strands into which it is organized. Along with the eight statements are eight profiles, which are descriptions of the progression in learning outcomes typically achieved by students. Each profile contains eight levels of achievement establishing a framework for reporting student progress.

IMPLICATIONS FOR THE ROLE OF THE SCHOOL PRINCIPAL: SUMMARY STATEMENT

Devolution and other changes within education in NSW have had a dramatic impact on the role of both the primary and secondary school principal. The role of the principal has become more complex and demanding in terms of the additional knowledge, skills, and time required. Principals have had to acquire skills in financial planning and budgeting, marketing, working with external bodies, such as school councils and Quality Assurance Review panels, interviewing and selecting staff, curriculum vitae writing, long-range school planning, implementing new curricula, and external assessment requirements. In addition, the impacts of these changes have had to be assimilated in relatively short time intervals. School principal reactions to these changes and their impact upon the principal's role are discussed in a later section of this chapter.

THE ROLE OF THE SCHOOL PRINCIPAL UNDER DEVOLUTION: TRENDS IN THE LITERATURE

During the past five to ten years one key theme in the theoretical and research literature on school leadership has been the impact on the school principal of the devolution of authority and other changes within school systems in many industrialized countries in the world. A number of writers in Great Britain, such as Weindling (1992), Bell (1993), and Ribbins (1993), have discussed the increased financial and human resource responsibilities, marketing, and public relations tasks now required of the school and have pointed out the complexity of the situation where principals are subjected to many different pressures as they cope with an increased and different type of workload. Bell argues that headteachers find somewhat daunting the increased managerial demands made upon them as responsibilities are devolved to schools. He points out that "head teachers are required to carry out two different and sometimes conflicting sets of functions, professional and chief executive or managerial" (p. 6). He states that devolution has shifted the role of headteacher from leading professional to chief executive with a consequence that senior staff are spending less time on educational matters. This situation was not welcomed by many headteachers as they came to grips with an increased volume of work. Weindling cites results from a research study that indicated principals regretted moving away from being the leading professional to being more of a chief executive. The principals in Weindling's study, however, remain optimistic about the future of schooling in a devolved system but argue that "if this is to continue, heads must find a balance between their role as leading professional (educator) and their role as chief executive (administrator), and so avoid self-destructive conflict" (p. 75). Ribbins, in his discussion on the role of the principal also describes the impact of devolution on the two major dimensions of the principal's role, which he describes as administrative tasks versus curriculum duties. He queries the notion that if heads emphasize one aspect of their role, they are assumed to do so at the expense of the other. He considers the "professional-organizational dilemma in terms of the polar extremities of a single continuum" (p. 6) a naive view because one could argue that these orientations should be seen as independent rather than as antithetical. Ribbins draws upon some of his own research into the role of the principal that indicates the focus of some heads is predominantly on administrative duties while others deny they have had to give priority permanently to the administrative dimensions of their work because they have come to terms with their administrative responsibilities and can focus on new curriculum initiatives. Ribbins queries whether retreating into administrative trivia is a defense to protect some heads from the harder intellectual and personal effort required to fulfill the role of an instructional leader. Newton (1993), in his study of headteachers in Barbados, draws a similar conclusion when he discusses how headteachers are more prone to undertake tasks in the administrative area and claim that demands on their time and the pressure of work make it impossible for them to be effective educational leaders.

Murphy and Hallinger (1992) have described how structural decentralization and the devolution of authority in North America have dramatically changed the work environment in which principals operate over the past five years. Principals are now confronted by a more complex and fragmented environment and are being asked to change from transactional to transformational leaders (Murphy & Hallinger, 1992). Murphy and Hallinger also argue that "the trend towards an expanded educational leadership role for teachers creates a potentially confusing scenario with respect to the instructional role of the principal" (p. 82).

Goldring (1992) has described similar pressures upon and changes to the principal's role in Israel where the move to greater decentralization and diversity in the education system has made public schools increasingly complex and fragmented. Murdoch and Paton (1993), in describing reforms in New Zealand where education has moved from a highly centralized to a decentralized system, state that school principals have had to learn a whole new set of leadership and management skills. They point out that principals' reactions to changes have been mixed, with some principals coping well with the required dual role of educational manager as well as the school's professional leader. The authors point out that principals require prior and ongoing systematic training and support that is specifically developed to meet the challenges of devolution.

Blairs (1992) has argued that the principal's role as instructional leader is under threat and that administrative management will become the major part of the principal's role with little time left to devote to instructional leadership behaviors, such as defining the school's mission, managing curriculum and instruction, and promoting a positive school climate. Blairs views the administrative management role as important for instructional outcomes in that "many of the managerial activities are, in fact, closely linked with instructional leadership, especially with regard to resources and the effective implementation of programs. These activities must be part of the principal's role" (p. 31). However, she argues that the demands of the administrative management role should not be to the detriment of the instructional leadership role. And yet, she claims, there is an "air of immediacy and accountability" associated with many administrative requirements and that they are getting quality time and attention at the expense of instructional leadership.

According to Caldwell (1992), principals in Australia are often not adequately prepared to meet the challenges of a new role under devolution. He claims that "ongoing professional development and training are critically important but increasingly difficult to resource, given the economic circumstances which prevail" (p. 7).

Caldwell identifies four dimensions of leadership that emerge when one examines the impact on the principal of recent changes in education: cultural, symbolic, educational, and responsive. He describes cultural leadership as "the capacity to work with others in the school community to create and sustain a culture which reflects not only the core values which should underpin the provision of an excellent education, however defined, but also reflect 'the new ways we do things around here' in a self-managing school under market conditions" (p. 17).

Principal behavior in this dimension includes effective communication with parents and the wider community, marketing the school, and working within "frameworks of accountability." Symbolic leadership involves keeping abreast of trends and issues stemming from various sources, sharing knowledge, establishing appropriate structures and processes in the school, and monitoring the implementation of strategies for school effectiveness. Educational leadership focuses on the processes of learning and teaching and the support of learning and teaching. Responsive leadership "refers to the capacity of the principal to work with others to demonstrate that the school has indeed been responsive to the needs of the student, the local community and society at large within the particular framework of responsibility of self-management which applies to the school" (p. 18).

In one of the few studies in Australia investigating the effects of devolution upon the role of principals, Wildy and Dimmock (1993) investigated the extent of instructional leadership of primary and secondary school principals in western Australia and the degree to which they shared or delegated associated tasks. They found that instructional leadership appears to be a shared responsibility involving staff at all levels, with principals not assuming a great deal of the responsibility.

One explanation of this situation may be the increased workload reported as a concern of principals in Victoria implementing devolution in the Schools of the Future program (Caldwell et al., 1994). The principals also were concerned about a lack of timely information and a lack of time for effective implementation in a context of dwindling resources, but were confident that benefits, such as a capacity for self-management, improved curriculum, and better human and resource management, would be achieved and would outweigh the negative aspects.

SUMMARY STATEMENT

This brief overview of the literature and research on devolution in a variety of countries with different educational traditions has indicated that the school principal's role has changed dramatically. The principal has had to assume more and different managerial responsibilities and has had to acquire a wide range of skills to effectively and efficiently undertake the altered role. The literature indicates that, for some principals, there is tension and conflict associated with their current role as they perceive that their managerial responsibilities impinge upon their role as school educational leader. How to carry out both roles effectively and whether both roles can be carried out effectively is a dilemma that appears to be faced by school principals as a result of devolution and other major educational changes.

PRINCIPAL ROLE ANALYSIS: A PILOT PROJECT

A pilot project has been carried out by the authors to explore what impact devolution has had on the role of the school principal in the 1990s since the Schools Renewal Strategy was implemented. The project was initiated to answer the following questions:

1. What do school principals consider are the main advantages and disadvantages of devolution?

2. How do principals view their current and preferred roles?

3. What dimensions of the principal's educational leadership role receive the most emphasis?
4. What management functions receive the most emphasis from school principals?

Thirty eight principals completed a questionnaire that investigated the impact of devolution on how they undertook their role as school principal. The subjects included 26 primary principals (12 male and 14 female) and 12 secondary principals (8 male and 4 female) with differing demographic characteristics and representing different classifications of primary and secondary schools. Approximately two-thirds of the principals had completed graduate study in educational administration during the past five years. The primary principals had experience as a principal ranging from 1 to 21 years with a mean experience of 6.7 years. The 12 secondary principals had an experience range from 2 to 9 years with a mean of 5.2 years. Because of the small number of subjects involved in the project, the responses on primary and secondary principals have been aggregated for the analyses that were undertaken.

ADVANTAGES OF DEVOLUTION FOR THE PRINCIPAL

The 38 principals listed a wide range of benefits that had occurred as a result of devolution. Most of the benefits related to the principals considering that devolution had provided them with more control over a wider number of areas compared to pre-devolution. For example, 19 of the principals appreciated the increased financial control and flexibility; 16 principals considered there was an increase in their general autonomy and empowerment, which was evidenced in having more flexibility in selecting staff, organizing school structures, developing curricula to more readily meet the needs of the students, providing for staff development at the school, being freed from the slowness of some bureaucratic decision making, and being able to involve the school community more closely and meaningfully in the development of the school. Several respondents cited other advantages including increased job satisfaction, more control over the school's vision, being a leader rather than a manager, and growing personally through change and challenge.

DISADVANTAGES OF DEVOLUTION FOR THE PRINCIPAL

Thirty six of the 38 principals described how devolution had had a negative impact on their role as principals. Two principals believed devolution had not had a negative impact on the principal's role. The 36 principals who considered there were disadvantages associated with devolution all considered their workload had increased considerably, that they had insufficient time to carry out their responsibilities as required, and that they were experiencing greater stress and pressure levels. All these principals were concerned at the increased accountability that had developed as a result of devolution and the uncertainty over accountability mechanisms to regional and head offices. There was also general concern at the constant and significant changes and the inordinate amount of paperwork and administrative trivia. Specific concerns related to lack of adequate training for new dimensions of their role as principal under devolution (for example, financial management), an increased workload in noneducational areas, such as building maintenance, and the reduced time that could be directly allocated to teaching and learning in the school.

PRINCIPALS' VIEWS OF THEIR CURRENT AND PREFERRED ROLES

The principals were asked to rate to what degree they considered themselves a school manager or educational leader in their present role. The scale and principal responses are displayed in Table 17.1.

As Table 17.1 indicates, 13 principals (34.2 percent) considered they were currently predominantly a school manager while 22 principals (57.9 percent) considered they were currently partly a school manager and partly an educational leader. Only three principals, all secondary, described their current role as predominantly an educational leader. In describing their managerial role, 14 principals pointed out that they spent over 70 percent of their time on administrative duties. In the discussions

TABLE 17.1
Principals' Description of Their Current and Preferred Role

	Current Role		Preferred Role	
	N	Percent	N	Percent
Totally a school manager				
Predominantly a school manager	13	34.2		
Totally an educational leader			2	5.3
Predominantly an educational leader	3	7.9	21	55.3
Partly a school manager and partly an educational leader	22	57.9	15	39.5
Other (please describe)				
Total	38	100.0	38	100.1

of their current role, all 38 principals considered devolution had moved them into a more managerial role. Their major area of concern as educational managers was financial management, because of their lack of financial expertise (eight principals expressed the need for a bursar). Other major areas of increased administrative involvement included industrial relations, school councils, participating in regional activities as leaders of courses, and strategic planning. Principals pointed out that policies stemming from devolution had increased their managerial duties, and other policies from the Department of School Education had also added to their work load. They complained about time pressures, the amount of paperwork, and the speed of change, as the following comments describe:

There is pressure to perform in areas where little training has been provided. Areas have kept changing, speed of change has made the tasks more difficult.

Responsibilities for budgeting and developing strategic plans that are accountable. While having done this previously, the sophistication of management of a school now requires more time that has to be taken away from the real purpose of schooling, teaching and learning.

As Table 17.1 reveals, 21 principals (55.3 percent) indicated a preference to be "predominantly an educational leader," but only 3 considered they were currently fulfilling that role. Two principals preferred a role totally devoted to educational leadership while 15 principals indicated a preference for a role that was partly school manager and partly an education leader. These data suggest the principals in this project still wish to play an educational leadership role in the school and are currently frustrated and experiencing a role conflict as managerial responsibilities preclude their desired involvement as educational leaders.

DIMENSIONS OF PRINCIPALS' EDUCATIONAL
LEADERSHIP ROLE RECEIVING THE MOST EMPHASIS

The principals were asked to indicate the extent to which they were involved in defining the school mission, managing the curriculum, improving the quality of teaching, promoting a positive school climate, and evaluating and providing feedback to staff. Several interesting trends in principals' responses are indicated in Table 17.2. The indicated involvement of all 38 principals in all five areas parallels Caldwell's (1992) description of the four dimensions of leadership that emerge as a result of recent changes to the role of the principal. To some degree, the principals in this project are cultural, symbolic, educational, and responsive leaders.

Table 17.2 suggests that principals take a dominant leadership role in some areas and a shared or collaborative role in other areas. Principals

TABLE 17.2
Description of Principals' Educational Leadership Role

	Do Not Perform		To a Minor Extent		Equally with Others		To a Major Extent		Alone	
	N	Percent	N	Percent	N	Percent	N	Percent	N	Percent
Defining and communicating the school mission	0	0	1	2.6	11	28.9	25	65.8	1	2.6
Managing the curriculum	0	0	7	18.4	24	63.2	7	18.4	0	0.0
Improving the quality of teaching	0	0	9	23.7	22	57.9	7	18.4	0	0.0
Promoting a positive school climate	0	0	0	0.0	8	21.1	30	78.9	0	0.0
Evaluating and providing feedback to staff	0	0	3	7.9	21	55.3	13	34.2	1	2.6

indicated that they played a dominant role in defining and communicating the school mission and in promoting a positive school climate. They considered they played a shared role in managing the curriculum, improving the quality of teaching, and evaluating and providing feedback to staff. The data in this pilot project support the findings of Wildy and Dimmock (1993) that principals share instructional leadership responsibilities. However, the tentative results suggest that, unlike the subjects in the Wildy and Dimmock study, the principals in this study perceive themselves as assuming a greater deal of responsibility for educational leadership in their schools.

MANAGER FUNCTIONS RECEIVING THE MOST EMPHASIS

The principals were asked to what extent they performed alone or with others the management functions of marketing the school, managing finances, managing resources, and managing buildings and grounds. They reported that they had a major involvement in all four management areas (Table 17.3), with financial management being the most common area of major involvement. This involvement in financial management was one welcomed by principals, because they reported it gave them more financial control and flexibility, but it was also an involvement that was causing some anxiety because of time pressures to complete budgets and perceived deficiencies in financial management skills.

A majority of principals (68.4 percent) also reported that they took major responsibility for and were directly involved in managing buildings and grounds. Marketing the school and managing resources, while still having principal involvement, tended to be undertaken on a more shared or delegated basis.

The principals in this pilot project reported a major personal involvement in key management areas that have received emphasis as a result of devolution and, as a consequence, for many principals there appears to be a role dilemma that needs to be overcome or at least minimized. However, there is a need for further research to help us understand this dilemma. There is also a need for a more general research framework that moves us away from dichotomizing or viewing managerial and instructional leadership activities as diametrically opposing responsibilities and instead to address the dilemma by exploring the extent to which various approaches to the new management and leadership responsibilities of principals are directly or indirectly related to student outcomes in self-managing schools.

TABLE 17.3
Description of Principals' School Management Role

	Do Not Perform		To a Minor Extent		Equally with Others		To a Major Extent		Alone	
	N	Percent	N	Percent	N	Percent	N	Percent	N	Percent
Marketing the school	2	5.3	4	10.5	11	24.2	20	57.6	1	2.6
Managing finances	0	0.0	0	0.0	9	23.7	27	71.0	2	5.3
Managing resources	0	0.0	4	10.5	19	50.0	14	36.8	1	2.6
Managing buildings and grounds	0	0.0	6	15.8	6	15.8	19	50.0	7	18.4

TOWARD A FRAMEWORK FOR
RESEARCH ON DEVOLUTION

The framework presented in Figure 17.1 identifies the key variables and their relationships involved in the devolution process. The framework suggests that research on devolution should be carried out at the macro or system level as well as at the micro or school level. For this reason, the framework separates these two levels of focus. The variables can also be divided into three components representing the time element in the change process. These components are context, process, and effects. This is not a simple linear model, however, and the framework recognizes the constant interactive flow that takes place among all of these components at all stages of the change process. Context has been divided into contextual variables (the variables in the wider society beyond the school or system) and a description of the system or school prior to the change (the internal context).

The change process provides the intermediary variables between the status quo and the more devolved system or school. An analysis of that process is critical in determining to what degree observed outcomes (for example, those that do not match intended goals) may be attributed to the goals and context of the change as opposed to the events of the change process itself. Effects have been divided into direct effects, such as more autonomy at the school level in managing financial resources, and indirect effects, such as improved teaching and learning. Links between devolution and the quality of teaching and learning can only be established by a two-stage process, with the direct effects as intermediate variables. In this framework, the contextual variables include such matters as the historical, political, economic, social, geographical, cultural, educational, industrial, and theoretical-philosophical contexts; the views of interest groups; and a consideration of the forces supporting and opposing devolution.

The system prior to change includes an analysis of its history, values, goals, structure, processes, leadership, readiness for change, and effectiveness-efficiency. The change process includes a consideration of the source, goals, magnitude, and speed of change; the resources provided; and the processes of planning, communicating, legitimizing, managing conflict, and evaluating.

At the system level, direct effects include changes in goals, priorities, structures, staffing, roles, and actual personnel as well as revised processes of policy making, planning, communication, physical and human resource management, information management, external relations, accountability, and leadership. At the school level, direct effects include changes in the degree of control the school obtains over inputs,

FIGURE 17.1
Research on Devolution — A Paradigm

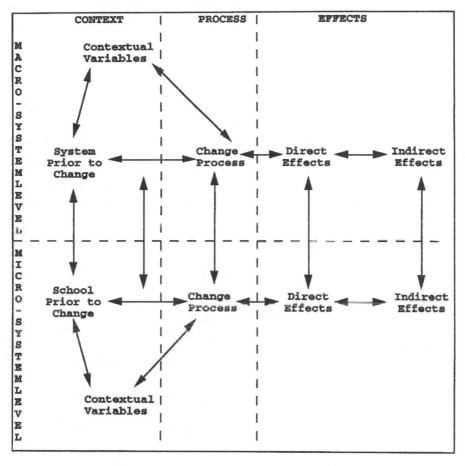

structures, processes, and the environment as well as the changes to the role of the principals.

At the system level, indirect effects include changes in the leadership-management styles of school principals, changes in staff values and attitudes, perceptions and levels of satisfaction and morale, community perceptions, and corporate effectiveness and efficiency. At the school level, indirect effects include changes in staff attitudes and values, perceptions, involvement in decision making, career paths, and need for professional development; the changing role of parents and local community, their levels of involvement, understanding, satisfaction, and sense of ownership; effects on matters related to teaching and learning, such as curriculum relevance, challenge and choice, and the quality and effectiveness of teaching; effects on the school's cohesiveness, culture, effectiveness, and efficiency; implications for student involvement, satisfaction, commitment, expectations, and learning outcomes; and the impact of devolution on social justice and equity.

AN IMPORTANT QUESTION: DEVOLUTION AND STUDENT OUTCOMES

Probably the most significant yet perplexing area of the framework for researchers at present is that which relates to the nature of the relationships at the school level that lie between devolution and the quality and equity of student outcomes. (See Sackney & Dibski [1994] for a "critical perspective" on these issues.)

It seems clear that student outcomes, which are labeled as indirect effects in the framework, are not affected directly by the act of devolution. If there are any changes to student outcomes as a result of devolution (which is at present by no means clear) they are mediated through a range of direct effects (such as leadership style and the principal's role, increased or decreased teacher involvement in decision making, changed levels of community involvement, changes to school culture, and so on). A critical task for researchers then is to establish the nature of the relationships between devolution and its direct effects on the school's inputs, structures, processes, culture, and environmental relations and the role of the school principal and then to link these direct effects in a logical way with important indirect effects, such as the quality and equality of student outcomes.

The research task is to determine whether conceptually there can be and, in actuality, is a relationship between devolution and improved student outcomes, and, if so, what are the necessary mediating conditions that constitute the missing link(s) in the causal chain. This view is in line with the argument of Bossert (1986) who stated: "If the primary function of school management is to foster an effective instructional programme, research must address how the formal organizational milieu of the school affects schooling outcomes. This will happen only when studies explicitly examine the linkages among management activities, the use of resources by teacher and students in the classroom context, and institutional practices" (p. 164).

Interesting work has been done by Wildy (1991) and Dimmock (1991) at the University of Western Australia "to unravel the links between management processes and what is done to improve school outcomes" (Wildy, 1991: 168), by examining the relationship in several western Australian schools between degrees of self-management and school effectiveness as measured by academic achievement. While the findings at this stage remain somewhat equivocal, important steps have been taken toward developing a conceptual framework and methodology to conduct further empirical studies on the subject. Dimmock's present work is focused on the relationships between devolution as the independent variable, instructional goal setting and the provision of feedback as linking variables, and student outcomes as the dependent variable.

Wohlstetter and Odden (1992: 542) call this the "one step removed approach" in which researchers "assess the degree to which SMB has helped implement new curriculum standards, new forms of instruction, staff development programs to train teachers in the requisite new knowledge and skills, and a new collegial, professional culture." They further point out that the curriculum is a major determinant of student learning, that school culture has an important influence on learning, and that the principal's role in school-based management can have a powerful impact on these variables that influence learning.

Ongoing research at the University of New South Wales on self-managing schools in Australia and Hong Kong is currently examining the relationships between devolution and the quality of teaching and learning through an examination of such mediating variables as systematic school-level planning focused on student outcomes, principals' values and leadership styles, levels of teacher and parent participation in decision making, processes and outcomes of school-based financial management, and the introduction of performance appraisal for teachers. For most, if not all, intermediary variables there is not one simple link but a complex chain of links lying between devolution and improvements in the quality and equity of student outcomes. For example, if school-level planning is the intermediary variable being examined, the issue is far more complex than simply being able to demonstrate that self-managing schools are more likely to engage in systematic school planning than other schools. We will also want to examine the role of the principal in planning; the nature of the planning processes typically used; the nature and level of involvement of various participants (particularly teachers) in the planning process; the degree to which the plans are focused on teaching and learning issues; levels of understanding of and commitment to the plans; the degree to which the plans actually affect events and behaviors in the school; their responsiveness and flexibility in light of changing circumstances; how they are evaluated, modified, and, ultimately, affect the use of resources and methodologies by teachers in the teaching process; and how the learning of students is influenced by these changes.

A similar complex array of interrelated factors will be associated with the examination of any of the key intermediary variables. For example, in the principal's role as a link between devolution and student learning there are a number of key questions that need to be explored. These include:

1. What external variables influence principal behavior?
2. What internal variables influence principal behavior?
3. What are the links between principal behavior and improved student outcomes?
4. What leadership practices lead to improved student outcomes?
5. Does greater principal involvement in management tasks lead to improved student outcomes?

These questions suggest a complex set of relationships that need to be identified if one is to explore the impact of devolution upon the principal's role and the influence of principal behavior directly and indirectly upon student learning. Some links have already been established. For example, Fullan and Hargreaves (1991) have demonstrated a link between types of school cultures, improvements in the quality of teaching, and, hence, improved student outcomes.

CONCLUDING STATEMENT

Devolution that decreases the management role of central authorities and increases responsibility and decision making at the school level is still taking place in the Australian school scene. The limited research literature on devolution so far provides a mixed picture of its impact upon system administrators, school principals, teachers, students, and parents. This chapter has focused upon the role of the school principal and has suggested that, in NSW, in the context of devolution, school principals have increasingly faced a range of dilemmas associated with their management and leadership roles in schools. It is further suggested that extensive research needs to be undertaken on the impact of devolution on the principal's role and how the principal's behavior may directly or indirectly influence student learning outcomes.

18

Knowledge-in-use: Reconceptualizing the Use of Knowledge in School Decision Making

Robert B. Stevenson

During the past decade systemic educational reforms in many Western countries have focused on the decentralization from the state to individual schools of decision-making authority in relation to many core areas of schooling (for example, budget, staffing and programs). State policies have also emphasized that this vertical devolution of authority should be accompanied by a horizontal devolution of decision making within the school, such that teachers, other staff, students (at least in secondary schools), parents, and community members are active participants in school-based management. Thus, there is intended to be a shift from the individual or principal as the decision-making authority to a shared or collective notion of decision making where authority is redistributed among the members of, or stakeholders in, the school community.

A direct consequence of these devolution policies is that school planning and decision making become more public activities. Not only are more decisions expected to be made at the school site but also more people are involved in those decisions and decisions are supposed to be made collectively rather than individually. To reach a meaningful consensus on decisions, the knowledge and values that inform how individuals view a particular issue and what constitutes an appropriate decision on that issue need to be articulated and debated. Yet, despite the widespread implementation of and extensive literature on devolution or school-based decision making, the epistemological question of how knowledge informs school leaders' educational decision making has not been addressed.

By school leaders, in the context of current school reforms, I refer to building administrators (such as principals); teachers (in formal leadership positions); and other teachers, school staff, parents, or community representatives who are members of school-based management or shared decision-making committees or groups. Because such committees are now playing a larger role in school planning and decision making, it is important to examine how knowledge might inform their work.

In this chapter I examine conceptualizations of the way in which knowledge is used to inform and shape school leaders' educational decisions. I begin by analyzing traditional approaches to the study of knowledge utilization by educational practitioners, focusing on the assumptions about the production, purpose, implementation, and conception of knowledge that underlie this approach. Then the changing educational context (at least in North America, Great Britain, and Australasia) is further analyzed in terms of, first, the increasing recognition and acceptance of the importance of practitioners' contextualized knowledge of practice, and, second, reform efforts to increase school-based management and shared decision making, which are purportedly creating more opportunities for teachers and administrators to make decisions about issues affecting their school. Finally, an alternative conceptualization is offered of the role of knowledge and ways of knowing in understanding and informing school leaders' decisions and actions. This conceptualization views practitioners' knowledge use as part of an informal process of reflective inquiry in which thoughtful school leaders engage in making decisions about appropriate educational actions.

TRADITIONAL APPROACHES TO THE STUDY OF KNOWLEDGE UTILIZATION

As Michael Huberman (1983) points out, "we know a great deal more about knowledge use in situations of planned institutional change than we do about the ways in which teachers and administrators customarily generate or use information or expertise" (p. 479). Furthermore, the conceptualization of knowledge utilization in planned change studies may not be helpful in guiding research on the knowledge and theories that inform typical everyday decision making by school leaders. The limitations of this conceptualization are revealed by examining the underlying assumptions about the production and use of knowledge. Traditional studies of knowledge use assume that knowledge of practice is externally produced (usually by "authorities" in universities) and that school personnel should directly apply such knowledge in their classrooms and offices. In other words, teachers and administrators are seen as the consumers or implementers of a product or commodity that is generated outside schools by experts or specialist researchers.

This view of knowledge production is reflected in a current comparative study of the use of knowledge by school principals in Australia and the United States. Although not restricted to the context of planned innovations, this study is examining principals' recall and reported use of research knowledge generated by university scholars (Biddle, 1994). While acknowledging the existence of other forms of knowledge, the interest of the researchers in this project lies in investigating the extent to which published research knowledge is considered by principals when making policy decisions in their schools.

Clearly, knowledge is seen in both this study and planned change studies as serving an instrumental purpose. There is assumed to be a direct, linear relationship between a proposition or theory generated by external researchers and its application to the improvement of practice. Stated another way, use constitutes the making of a decision and knowledge is assumed to be directly informative in that decision (Kennedy, 1984). Three further assumptions are important to note. First, embedded in this linearity is an assumption of compatibility between the purposes and perspectives of the knowledge generator and the knowledge implementer. In other words, the notion that a researcher and a practitioner may have a different set of questions about practice and a different need or purpose for investigating or informing practice does not receive primary attention (Green & Chandler, 1990). Second, these studies focus on a particular kind of knowledge, namely knowledge claims that have been derived from empirical propositions and have been validated by the scientific method. This type of knowledge is variously referred to as propositional, formal, scientific, theoretical, research, or empirical knowledge. Finally, generalized propositions are assumed to be applicable in any school context and to take precedence over other kinds of information that might be available to school personnel, such as students' interests and needs, institutional norms of the school, and the specific conditions and organizational structures in which teachers and administrators work.

Paradoxically, in contrast to these assumptions, our understanding of the acquisition and use of knowledge by teachers and administrators to inform their decision making provides a quite different picture. For example, "the kind of information communicated between teachers appears predominantly to involve exchanges of craft wisdom or 'recipe knowledge'" (Huberman, 1983: 481). Rather than being received from external authorities who have empirically tested the knowledge claims, practitioners are reported to acquire knowledge of practice either experientially through a process of trial and error or from internal "authorities" in the shape of experienced colleagues. In the latter case, ideas, techniques, materials, and explanations are traded among practitioners but then apparently undergo verification or validation through an intuitive test against the accumulation of personal experience to determine if the information or product seems to fit one's situation. As Huberman states, "one practitioner cannot tell another something; they can only exchange experiences" (p. 482). Thus, in contrast to propositional knowledge, which provides an abstract representation of some aspect of an event, practitioners rely on personal knowledge, which is acquired from direct sensory experience of an event (Biddle, 1994). It is worth noting that educators are not unique in relying on craft-validated sources because studies of a diverse range of administrators and other professionals, including scientists, have revealed the same tendency (Huberman, 1983).

Besides seeking knowledge that resides in craft wisdom, practitioners have been characterized as concerned with practical information. Practical refers to the use of algorithms rather than propositions to guide action. Practical theories are concerned with action and can be usefully distinguished from explanatory theories, which are concerned with understanding (Strike, 1979) and attempt to explain empirical propositions (Biddle, 1994). Described in the literature as practical, personal, experiential, craft, or recipe knowledge, its purpose is still viewed as instrumental. This craft model of knowledge utilization differs, however, from the scientific model in its type, source, and method of validation of knowledge claims. Formal or propositional knowledge and explanatory theories generated by scientific inquiry are more often used by practitioners, especially administrators, for political reasons, that is, as "ammunition" to support a particular argument or position, rather than for guiding practice (Huberman, 1983).

To summarize, the image emerging from "studies of knowledge use by teachers is that of practically oriented professionals drawing chiefly on their own and their peers' experience to resolve problems or otherwise modify their instructional practices" (Huberman, 1983: 483). There seems no reason to expect that school administrators or any other members of a school community use knowledge any differently. The few studies that have included administrators suggest that they also rely on collecting and exchanging recipe knowledge in order to expand their managerial and leadership repertoire. However, Huberman also has suggested that: "the absolute amount of extraindividual knowledge-seeking, -exchanging and -using may not be very great. Both teachers and administrators may be caught up in the immediacy and diversity of daily classroom and building-level demands while being isolated from other classrooms and buildings, such that problem-solving becomes an essentially private process of trial and error, recourse to personal experience and, when appropriate, retrieval of fragments of preservice training" (p. 484).

THE CHANGING CONTEXT OF KNOWLEDGE
UTILIZATION AND DECISION MAKING

The traditional focus of knowledge utilization studies is not surprising because practitioners' knowledge of practice historically has been "discounted as too subjective, too nonscientific" (Wasley, 1991: 161). Recently, however, educational policy and research have begun to recognize the voice of practitioners and to respect the importance of their personal, practical, and contextual knowledge. Central to this newfound respect for the knowledge of school professionals are a recognition that educators must constantly make professional judgments about both the means and ends of practice and an emerging appreciation of the importance of context (Petrie, 1990) and the need to be responsive to local circumstances by making decisions about school practices at the point of service delivery (Wise, 1991). In fact, one of the goals of the current restructuring reform movement in the United States is to locate the authority for educational decisions in teachers' and principals' professional judgments.

Recent educational reform and policy initiatives in the United States, and elsewhere (for example, Australia, England) also have emphasized the devolution of decision making to the school site. In site-based management, decisions on administrative issues, such as budgets and the allocation and organization of resources, as well as on educational issues concerning curriculum, teaching, and professional development, are supposed to be made at the school level. By reducing the bureaucratic constraints on school-level decision making, the assumption is that administrators and teachers will have more freedom to make decisions and will work collectively, in conjunction with support staff and parents, on professional issues. Paradoxically, however, at the same time that this decentralization is occurring, there is also a push toward centralized reforms, such as national curriculum standards and testing. Nevertheless, in schools where site-based management and shared decision making are practiced, administrators and teachers are likely to have more opportunities to participate in decision making and more need to engage in discourse about those decisions. Little is known to date about the kinds of decisions that school site personnel are involved in making.

Accompanying this decentralization is the creation of new leadership roles for teachers. These roles include grade-level chairs and team leaders, master and mentor teachers, staff development specialists (Wasley, 1991), and chairs of various school committees. A survey of teachers in these leadership positions indicated that a majority of their work focused on staff development, curriculum development, and instructional improvement, although most positions lacked specific job descriptions. Therefore, instead of the previously popular notion of the principal as the instructional leader, restructuring reforms call for a broader based and shared concept of leadership. This sharing of leadership roles demands a collegial relationship among teachers and between teacher leaders and administrators — a relationship that should be grounded in constant and intensive dialogue about curriculum, teaching, and the organizational norms and structures for the improvement of the school's educational practices.

This changed context of decentralized decision making and shared leadership raises questions about the epistemological dimensions of the work of school leaders. Research on epistemology indicates that individuals can hold different positions regarding knowledge and ways of knowing (Belenky, Clinchy, Goldberger, & Tarule, 1986; Perry, 1970) and suggests the need to consider how epistemological perspectives interact in the professional relationships among school leaders (Lyons, 1990). For example, dualistic knowers believe there is one truth or a single right position on any issue, while relativistic knowers hold that truth is context-bound: that is, that situations and circumstances dictate what one ought to believe. In other words, a relativistic thinker is driven by an "it depends" point of view. Such people might honor debate among colleagues if their colleagues share a respect for context rather than seek a resolution that is right or wrong without qualification. Those who are at a transitional stage between dualistic and relativistic thinking might claim that continued dialogue would be unproductive because "everyone has their own opinion and yours is no better than mine." Despite the existence and potential significance of these epistemological differences, the press for school-based and shared decision making has emerged without a conceptualization of the role of knowledge and ways of knowing in informing practitioner decisions and actions. I now turn to such a conceptualization.

AN ALTERNATIVE CONCEPTUALIZATION OF THE STUDY OF KNOWLEDGE USE

In addition to the scientific and craft conceptions of knowledge and knowledge utilization, a third alternative can be offered that has different assumptions about the kind of knowledge that informs or guides educational practice. Instead of knowledge about practice being viewed as externally produced and then applied by practitioners or acquired by an experiential process of trial and error, it is conceived as actively constructed by teachers or administrators (from externally or formally derived as well as internally or practically generated knowledge). This does not preclude the need for externally produced formal knowledge, but such knowledge is treated as only one source for informing professional judgments that are made by interpreting and integrating this knowledge with various other kinds of knowledge (such as knowledge of goals and objectives; personal knowledge of one's leadership style and philosophy; and contextual knowledge of students, school culture, and organizational constraints). Stated another way, research knowledge (as well as these other kinds of knowledge) is interpreted in relation to the particular circumstances and occasion in which it is to be used.

In this "conceptual" model, both types of knowledge that have been discussed are recognized. However, rather than knowledge having an instrumental role, "use" involves "thinking about the evidence" or knowledge, and new evidence "influences the user's working knowledge of the issues at hand (Kennedy, 1984: 207). Furthermore, the process of use, instead of being one way, is bi-directional in that new knowledge or information can influence an individual's point of view and the individual's existing knowledge can influence the interpretation of the new knowledge (Kennedy, 1984). Thus, knowledge is repeatedly and conceptually in use. This conceptualization of practitioners' use of knowledge is, of course, analagous to the "constructivist" model of learning.

However, teachers and administrators must be concerned with more than their own learning or understanding because they are continually required to take practical pedagogical or administrative actions. Therefore, in the case of practitioners, learning — and, hence, constructivism — must be viewed as a part of a larger process for informing one's decisions about such actions. Such a process is encompassed in the concepts of reflection-on-action and reflection-in-action as practiced by reflective practitioners (for example, Schön, 1983, 1987). These concepts, however, emphasize a process of reflecting on either actions already taken or actions immediately to be taken. Furthermore, they focus on practical or professional decision making as an individual, rather than collective, and private, rather than public, process.

In the context of public and collective school decision making about actions to be taken at a later time, the interpretation and integration of knowledge outlined above is more appropriately viewed as a component of a process of inquiry. I have argued elsewhere that outstanding teachers and administrators engage in an informal or professional form of inquiry in making intelligent curriculum, pedagogical, and administrative decisions. "They consider a range of alternative actions for achieving their goals and purposes, make judgments about an appropriate course of action based on available knowledge and relevant values, informally observe the consequences of the action that is taken, and then reflect on and assess the overall effects of the action. This process which professionals use in their everyday activities differs only in function, timeframe and rigor from the systematic inquiry of the scholar" (Stevenson, 1993: 110–111). Therefore, instead of differentiating between the researcher as the inquirer and the consumer as the implementer of the researcher's findings, both are regarded as engaged in inquiry, albeit for somewhat different purposes. In this conceptualization the process of knowledge use is viewed as part of a larger process of inquiry. The function of this informal inquiry is to generate answers or practical knowledge to inform actions that need to be taken, while the function of the more formal scholarly inquiry is to produce reliable knowledge about perplexing questions (Short, 1991). Of course, "the more trustworthy is the state of knowing in which practitioners make decisions about appropriate actions the better informed are their actions likely to be" (Stevenson, 1993: 111).

Acknowledgment that each practitioner, or group of practitioners, has his or her own purpose for exploring and informing practice (Green & Chandler, 1990) creates an important distinction from the scientific and craft conceptions that are essentially concerned with questions of means. Inquiry, consequently, should be addressed toward the ends as well as the means of educational practice because professional judgments about practice need to be based not only on technical knowledge (some of which may have been produced by outside experts) of the most effective means to attain prescribed goals but also on the outcomes of morally deliberating about what those goals or ends ought to be. By inquiring into one's intentions and the means of realizing those intentions, the assumption is that school leaders will make better informed professional judgments and thereby improve school practices.

This conceptualization is consistent with the belief that teachers can further their knowledge about teaching and improve their teaching by critically inquiring into their own classroom practices (Holmes Group, 1990). Action research offers one method by which practitioner inquiry can be more systematic but still be embedded in the "temporal and spatial flow" of practitioners' work (Feldman & Atkin, 1995). The increasing acceptance of and attention paid to action research, even in academic circles, reflects a recognition that practitioners can inform and improve their practice through a form of systematic inquiry. Although there are many different versions of action research, the teacher research work of Lawrence Stenhouse in England or the critical or emancipatory form associated with the work of scholars at Deakin University in Australia (Kemmis & McTaggart, 1988) emphasize the role of practitioners in generating knowledge to inform practical actions.

CONCLUSION

A major problem is that we have no empirical understanding of factors that impinge on the extent to which school leaders engage in this kind of inquiry in making individual or collective decisions on educational issues. At an individual level, it could be argued that the disposition of school leaders to engage in an inquiry approach to knowledge use is dependent on the possession of a sophisticated epistemological perspective. For example, using Perry's (1970) scheme of epistemological development, an individual might need to hold the position that truth seeking is based on a process of rational inquiry into which some knowledge claims have greater validity than others. At an institutional level, cultural norms and structural conditions in schools are likely to affect the ways in which knowledge is used. For example, norms of experimentation and critique where teachers are encouraged to treat external policy documents and research findings as merely offering tentative proposals to be tried and critically assessed in the context of the school's particular interests and needs are likely to support a conceptual knowledge-in-use approach to professional decision making.

A number of important empirical questions needs to be addressed to extend the conceptualization of how knowledge informs decision making by school leaders. Such questions might include: What kinds and sources of knowledge are explicitly considered by school leaders, both individually and collectively, in making school-wide decisions? To what extent is this knowledge made problematic? How are any competing knowledge claims handled? To what extent do decisions emerge from discourse among school leaders?

The alternative conceptualization of knowledge use that has been described has interesting implications for administrative or leadership preparation and professional development programs. In the past, these programs have been founded on the assumptions of the craft or technical-scientific conceptions of practitioners' knowledge acquisition and utilization. The problem-based approach to the professional development of principals discussed by Limerick and Crowther (Chap. 13, this volume) is an example of how such programs might respond to contemporary contexts and emerging understandings of shared decision making in schools. This approach does not assume a top down model of the relationship of theory to practice — that theoretical or scientific knowledge should be applied to practice. Instead, practitioners are provided with the opportunity to integrate theoretical knowledge with their contextualized or local knowledge in order to make sense of the problems and dilemmas they encounter in their daily practice. Such a reconceptualization of the use of theoretical knowledge is needed to improve both our understanding of school decision making and the quality of decisions made.

ACKNOWLEDGMENT

I thank Stephen Brown for his insightful comments and helpful suggestions on an earlier version of this chapter.

References

Ackroyd S., Hughes, J. A., & Soothill, K. (1989). Public sector services and their management. *Journal of Management Studies, 26*(3), 603–619.

Aldrich, H. E. (1979). *Organization and environment.* Englewood Cliffs, NJ: Prentice Hall.

American Association of School Administrators. (1993). *Professional standards for the superintendency.* Arlington, VA: Author.

Antos, J., & Rosen, S. (1975). Discrimination in the market for public school teachers. *Journal of Econometrics, 3,* 123–150.

Appleton, N. (1983). *Cultural pluralism in education.* New York: Longman.

Aram, J. (1976). *Dilemmas of administrative behaviour.* Englewood Cliffs, NJ: Prentice Hall.

Arbon, D. (1994, February). Week by week. *Education, 4.*

Argyris, C., & Schön, D. (1974). *Theory in practice: Increasing professional effectiveness.* San Francisco, CA: Jossey-Bass.

Argyris, C., & Schön, D. (1978). *Organizational learning: A theory of action perspective.* Reading, MA: Addison-Wesley.

Armstrong, G. (1993). *View from the bridge.* London: Institute of Personnel Management.

Ashby D. (1991). On the job mentoring for administrator renewal. *Planning and Changing, 22,* 218–230.

Atchorena, D. (1993). *Educational strategies for small island states.* Paris: United Nations Educational, Scientific, and Cultural Organization, International Institute for Educational Planning.

Bacharach, S. B., & Lawler, E. J. (1982). *Power and politics in organizations.* San Francisco, CA: Jossey-Bass.

Bacharach, S., & Mundell, B. (1993). Organizational politics in schools: Micro, macro and logics of action. *Educational Administration Quarterly, 29*(4), 42–52.

Baden-Fuller, C., & Stopford, J. (1992). *Rejuvenating the mature business: The competitive challenge.* London: Routledge.

Baird J. R. (1993). A personal perspective on mentoring. In B. Caldwell & E. Carter (Eds.), *The return of the mentor.* London: Falmer Press.

Ball, S. (1987). *The micro-politics of the school: Towards a theory of school organization.* New York: Methuen.

Ball, S. (1993a). Education markets, choice and social class: The market as a class strategy in the UK and the USA. *British Journal of the Sociology of Education, 14*(1), 3–19.

Ball, S. (1993b). The education reform act: Market forces and parental choice. In A. Cashdan & J. Harris (Eds.), *Education in the 1990s.* Sheffield: Sheffield Hallam University Pavic Publications.

Banks, J. (1981). *Multi-ethnic education.* New York: Allyn & Bacon.

Barcan, A. (1992). The ambiguities of devolution. *Discourse: The Australian Journal of Educational Studies, 13*(1), 95–111.

Barman, J., Hebert, Y., & McCaskill, D. (Eds.). (1986). *Indian education in Canada,* Vol. 1: *The legacy.* Vancouver: University of British Columbia Press.

Barnett, B. G. (1990a, April). *Mentoring programs for administrator preparation: Mentors' and interns' perceptions of program success.* Paper presented at the annual meeting of the American Educational Research Association, Boston, Massachusetts.

Barnett, B. G. (1990b). The mentor-intern relationship: Making the most of learning from experience. *NASSP Bulletin, 74*(526), 17–24.

Barnett, B. G., & Mueller, F. L. (1989). Long term effects of the peer-assisted leadership program on principals' actions and attitudes. *The Elementary School Journal, 89*(5), 559–574.

Barrett, W. (1986). *Death of the soul: From Descartes to computer.* Garden City, NY: Anchor/Doubleday.

Barrow, R. (1988). Some observations on the concept of imagination. In K. Egan & D. Nadaner (Eds.), *Imagination and education* (pp. 79–90). New York: Teachers College Press.

Barrows, H. S. (1985). *How to design a problem-based curriculum for the preclinical years.* New York: Springer.

Barrows, H. S., & Tamblyn, R. M. (1980). *Problem-based learning: An approach to medical education.* New York: Springer.

Barth, R. S. (1986). *Principal-centred professional development.* Presented at the Annual Meeting of the American Educational Research Association, Chicago, Illinois.

Bassett, G. (1992). The training of educational administrators in Australia. *Unicorn, 18*(4), 4–18.

Bates, R. J. (1989). Leadership and the rationalization of society. In J. Smyth (Ed.), *Critical perspectives on educational leadership* (pp. 131–156). London: Falmer Press.

Beauchamp, T., Childress, J., & West, E. (1984). Morality, ethics, and ethical theories. In P. Sola. (Ed.), *Ethics, education and administrative decisions: A book of readings.* New York: Peter Lang.

Becker, H. (1970). *Sociological work: Method and substance*. Chicago, IL: Aldine.

Becker, L. (1973). *On justifying moral judgments*. London: Routledge and Kegan Paul.

Belenky, M., Clinchy, B., Goldberger, N., & Tarule, J. (1986). *Women's ways of knowing*. New York: Basic Books.

Bell, L. (1993, September). *Devolution and schools in England and Wales*. Paper presented at the Conference of Australian Council for Educational Administration, Adelaide, Australia.

Ben-Peretz, M., & Kremer-Hayon, L. (1990). The content and context of professional dilemmas encountered by novice and senior teachers. *Educational Review*, 42(1), 31–40.

Berg, G. (1990). *Skolledning och professionellt skolledarskap*. Uppsala: Uppsala universitet, Pedagogiska institutionen.

Berg, G. (1993). *Curriculum and state schools as organizations*. Uppsala: University of Uppsala, Department of Education.

Berlak, A., & Berlak, H. (1981). *Dilemmas of schooling: Teaching and social change*. New York: Methuen.

Berman, M. (1981). *The reenchantment of the world*. Ithaca, NY: Cornell University Press.

Bibby, P., & Lunt, I. (1994). Special costs *Managing Schools Today*, 4(1), 7–8.

Biddle, B. (1994). *Research knowledge and its use in education*. Paper presented at the annual meeting of the American Educational Research Association, New Orleans.

Billig, M., Condor, S., Edwards, D., Gane, M., Middleton, D., & Radley, A. (1988). *Ideological dilemmas: A social psychology of everyday thinking*. London: Sage.

Blairs, D. (1992). The primary school principal: Administrative manager or instructional leader? *The Practising Administrator*, 14(21), 30–34.

Blase, J. (1989). The teachers' political orientation vis-à-vis the principal: The micropolitics of the school. In J. Hannaway & R. Crowson (Eds.), *The politics of reforming school administration*. London: Falmer Press.

Blau, P. M. (1964). *Exchange and power in social life*. New York: John Wiley & Sons.

Bloom, A. (1987). *The closing of the American mind: How higher education has failed democracy and impoverished the souls of today's students*. New York: Simon & Schuster.

Blumberg, A. (1985). *The school superintendent: Living with conflict*. New York: Teachers College Press.

Blunden, A. (1991). Problem-based learning and its application to in-house law firm training. *Journal of Professional Legal Education*, 8(2).

Boettinger H. M. (1975). Is management really an art? *Harvard Business Review*, 53(1), 54–64.

Bok, S. (1982). *Secrets: On the ethics of concealment and revelation*. New York: Pantheon Books.

Bolam, R., McMahon, A., Poclington, K., & Weindling, D. (1993). *National evaluation of the headteacher mentoring pilot schemes*, Report for the Department for Education. London: Her Majesty's Stationery Office.

Bolin, F. S., & Panaritis, P. (1992). Searching for a common purpose: A perspective on the history of supervision. In C. D. Glickman (Ed.), *Supervision in transition: 1992 yearbook of the association for supervision and curriculum development* (pp. 30–43). Alexandria, VA: Association for Supervision and Curriculum Development.

Bolman, L. G., & Deal, T. E. (1991). *Nytt perspektiv på organisasjon og ledelse*. Oslo, Norway: Ad Notam.

Booth, W. C. (1988). *The company we keep: An ethics of fiction*. Berkeley: University of California Press.

Bossert, S. (1986). Instructional management book. In E. Hoyle & A. McMahon (Eds.), *The management of schools*. London: Kogan Page.

Bowen, E. (1988, February). Getting tough. *Time Magazine, 131*, 100–106.

Boyer, E. (1983). *High school: A report on secondary education in America*. New York: Harper & Row.

Bradley, A. (1990, December 12). Rapid turnover in urban superintendencies. *Education Week*, 1–2.

Brah, A., & Minhas, R. (1985). Structural racism or cultural difference: Schooling for Asian girls. In G. Weiner (Ed.), *Just a bunch of girls: Feminist approaches to schooling*. Milton Keynes: Open University Press.

Brantford Expositor. (1984, June 15). p. 13.

Bridges, E., & Hallinger, P. (1993). Problem-based learning in medical and managerial education. In P. Hallinger, K. Leithwood, & J. Murphy (Eds.), *Cognitive perspectives in educational leadership* (pp. 253–267). New York: Teachers College Press.

Brown, B., & Saks, D. (1975). The production and distribution of cognitive skills within schools. *Journal of Political Economy, 83*(3), 471–593.

Brown, D. (1990). *Decentralization and school based management*. London: Falmer Press.

Brown, L. (1984, July 2). Separate school move was swift but Davis chewed it over slowly. *The Toronto Star*, p. A1.

Bruner, J. (1986). *Actual minds, possible worlds*. Cambridge, MA: Harvard University Press.

Buber, M. (1966). *The way of response*. New York: Schoken Books.

Bullivant, B. (1986). Towards radical multiculturalism: Resolving tensions in curriculum and education planning. In S. Modgil, G. Verma, K. Mallick, & C. Modgil (Eds.), *Multicultural education: The interminable debate*. London: Falmer Press.

Bullivant, B. (1981). *The pluralist dilemma in education*. Sidney: Allyn & Unwin.

Burke, C., Limerick, B., Cawte, J., & Slee, R. (1986). *Devolution in sight*. Brisbane: Queensland Institute of Technology.

Burroughs, S. (1986). Dilemmas in the role of the support teacher. In R. Winter (Ed.), *Learning from experience: Principles and practice in action-research* (pp. 96–111). New York: Falmer Press.

Bush, T., Coleman, M., & Glover, D. (1993). *Managing autonomous schools: The grant-maintained experience*. London: Open University Press.

Busher, H., & Saran, R. (1994). Towards a model of school leadership. *Educational Management and Administration, 22*(1), 5–13.

Caines, E. (1993). Personnel paradise — How it was lost and how it might be regained in the NHS. In G. Armstrong (Ed.), *View from the Bridge*. London: Institute of Personnel Management.

Calabrese, R. L., & Bartz, D. E. (1990). Preparing school administrators: An action-learning model. *Canadian Administrator, 30*(3), 1–6.

Calabrese, R. L., & Tucker-Ladd, P. R. (1991). The principal and the assistant principal: A mentoring relationship. *NASSP Bulletin, 75*(533), 67–74.

Caldwell, B. (1992). The principal as leader of the self-managing school in Australia. *Journal of Educational Administration, 30*(3), 6–19.

Caldwell, B. (1993). Decentralising the management of Australian schools. Commissioned paper. Melbourne: National Industry Education Forum.

Caldwell, B., & Carter, E. (Eds.). (1993). *The return of the mentor.* London: Falmer Press.

Caldwell, B. J., Lawrence, A., Peck, F., & Thomas, F. J. (1994, January). *Leading Victorian schools of the future: Base-line survey of principals in 1993.* Paper presented at the International Congress for School Effectiveness and Improvement, Melbourne, Australia.

Campbell, E. (1992). *Personal morals and organizational ethics: How teachers and principals cope with conflicting values in the context of school cultures.* Unpublished doctoral dissertation, University of Toronto.

Campbell, E. (1993, June). *Strategic leadership or suspended morality? How principals cope with ethical conflicts in schools.* Paper presented at the twenty-first annual conference of The Canadian Society for the Study of Education, Ottawa, Canada.

Canadian Education Association. (1990, May). *Sentenced to school: The young offenders act and Canadian school boards.* Ottawa, Ontario: Author.

Carlson, R. O. (1975). Environmental constraints and organizational consequences: The public school and its clients. In J. V. Baldridge & T. E. Deal (Eds.), *Managing change in educational environments.* Berkeley, CA: McCutchan.

Carnegie Forum on Education and Economy. (1986). *A nation prepared: Teachers for the 21st century. The report of the task force on teaching as a profession.* New York: Carnegie Corporation.

Carr, W., & Kemmis, S. (1986). *Becoming critical: Education, knowledge and action research.* London: Falmer Press.

Carrick, J. (1989). *Report of the committee of review of New South Wales schools.* Sydney: New South Wales Government.

Carter, E. (1993). Measuring the returns. In B. Caldwell & E. Carter (Eds.), *The return of the mentor.* London: Falmer Press.

Caruso, R. E. (1992). *Mentoring and the business environment.* Aldershot, NH: Dartmouth Publishing.

Cave, E., & Wilkinson, C. (1992). Developing managerial capabilities in education. In N. Bennett, M. Crawford, & R. Riches (Eds.), *Managing change in education: Individual and organizational perspectives.* London: Paul Chapman Publishing/The Open University.

Cazden, C. B., & Leggett, E. L. (1981). Culturally responsive education: Recommendations for achieving Lau remedies II. In H. Trueba, G. Guthrie, & K. Au (Eds.), *The cultural and the bilingual classroom* (pp. 69–86). London: Newbury.

Chadbourne, R., & Clarke, R. (Eds.). (1994). *Devolution: Its impact on W. A. secondary schools.* Draft report. Perth: Western Australian Secondary

Principals Association.

Chambers, J. (1981). The hedonic wage technique as a tool for estimating the costs of school personnel: A theoretical exposition with implications for empirical analysis. *Journal of Education Finance, 6,* 330–354.

Chao, G. T., & Gardner, P. D. (1992). Formal and informal mentorships: A comparison of mentoring functions and contrast with non-mentored counterparts. *Personnel Psychology, 45,* 619–636.

Chapman, D., & Hutcheson, S. (1982). Attrition from teaching careers: A discriminant analysis. *American Educational Research Journal, 19*(1), 93–105.

Chapman, J. D. (1994, March). *Lessons from the OECD Project on the Effectiveness of Schooling and of Educational Resource Management.* Unpublished paper presented at Conference of Western Australian Institute of Educational Administration, Perth, Australia.

Charters, W. (1967). Some "obvious" facts about the teaching career. *Educational Administration Quarterly, 3*(2), 183–193.

Cheng, Y. C. (1993). Theory and characteristics of school-based management. *International Journal of Educational Management 7*(6), 6–17.

Chubb, J. E., & Moe, T. M. (1988). Politics, markets, and the organization of schools. *American Political Science Review, 82*(4), 1065–1087.

Chubb, J. E., & Moe, T. M. (1989). *Give choice a chance.* Washington, DC: Brookings Institution.

Churchill, S., & Kaprielian-Churchill, I. (1991). Ethnicity, language and school retention in Ontario: The unfinished agenda. In D. Allison & J. Paquette (Eds.), *Reform and relevance in schooling: Dropouts, de-streaming and the common curriculum* (pp. 39–60). Toronto: OSIA Press.

Clifton, R. (1975). Self-concept and attitudes: A comparison of Canadian Indian and non-Indian students. *Canadian Review of Sociology and Anthropology, 12*(4), 577–584.

Clifton, R. (1977). Factors which affect the education of Canadian Indian students. In R. Carlton, L. Colley, & N. MacKinnon (Eds.). *Education, change and society: A sociology of Canadian education.* Toronto: Gage.

Codd, J. A. (1993, September). As quoted in K. Rae, *The plucking of the flaxbush.* Unpublished paper presented at the Conference of Australian Council for Educational Administration, Adelaide, Australia.

Codding, J. B. (1993, September). *The need to build a new infrastructure for American public education.* Unpublished paper presented at the Conference of Australian Council for Educational Administration, Adelaide, Australia.

Cohen, M., March, J., & Olsen, J. (1972). A garbage can model of organizational choice. *Administrative Science Quarterly, 17*(3), 1–25.

Cohn, K. C., & Sweeney, R. C. (1992, April). *Principal mentoring programs: Are school districts providing the leadership?* Paper presented at the annual meeting of the American Educational Research Association, San Francisco, California.

Cole, M. (1992). Education in the market-place: A case of contradiction, *Educational Review, 44*(3), 335–343.

Cole, M., & Scribner, S. (1973). Cognitive consequences of formal and informal education. *Science, 182,* 553–559.

Coleman, W. D., & Skogstad, G. (1990). *Policy communities and public policy in Canada: A structural approach.* Mississauga, Canada: Copp Clark Pitman.

Confederation of British Industry. (1989). *Towards a skills revolution.* London: Author.

Connock, S. (1993). The power of vision. In G. Armstrong (Ed.), *View from the bridge* (pp. 141–160). London: Institute of Personnel Management.

Cooper, B. (1991). Parent choice and school involvement: Perspectives and dilemmas in the United States and Great Britain. *International Journal of Educational Research, 15*(3/4), 251–264.

Coopers & Lybrand. (1989). *Paying for performance in the public sector.* London: Income Data Services and Coopers & Lybrand.

Corson, D. (1992). Minority cultural values and discourse norms in majority cultural classrooms. *The Canadian Modern Language Review, 48*(3), 472–496.

Crittenden, B. (1984). The moral context of decision making in education. In P. Sola (Ed.), *Ethics, education and administrative decisions: A book of readings.* New York: Peter Lang.

Crowther, F., & Limerick, B. (1994). *Current views on corporate leadership* (cassette recording). Queensland: University of Southern Queensland, Open Learning Unit.

Crystal, L. (1993, July). *Funding bid to the Department of Employment.* (In the personal collection of the author.)

Cuban, L. (1994). *Reforming the practice of educational administration through managing dilemmas.* Paper presented at the 8th Quadrennial International Intervisitation Program, Toronto, Ontario, and Buffalo, New York.

Cuban, L. (1992). Managing dilemmas while building professional communities. *Educational Researcher, 21*(1), 4–11.

Cuban, L. (1988). *The managerial imperative: The practice of leadership in schools.* Albany: State University of New York Press.

Cuban, L. (1976). *Urban school chiefs under fire.* Chicago, IL: University of Chicago Press.

Daft, R., & Weick, K. (1984). Towards a model of organizations as interpretation systems, *Academy of Management Review, 9*(2), 284–295.

Daresh, J. C. (1988a, April). *An assessment of alternative models for the delivery of principal inservice.* Paper presented at the annual meeting of the American Educational Research Association, New Orleans, Louisiana.

Daresh, J. C. (1988b, April). *The role of mentors in preparing future principals.* Paper presented at the annual meeting of the American Educational Research Association, New Orleans, Louisiana.

Daresh, J. C. (1987, April). *The beginning principalship: Preservice and inservice implications.* Paper presented at the annual meeting of the American Educational Research Association, Washington, DC.

Daresh, J. C., & LaPlant, J. (1983, April). In-service for school principals? A status report. *Executive Review, 3*(7): 1–5.

Daresh, J. C., & Playko, M. (1992a, April). *What do beginning leaders need? Aspiring and practicing principals' perceptions of critical skills for novice administrators.* Paper presented at the annual meeting of the American Educational Research Association, San Francisco, California.

Daresh, J. C., & Playko, M. (1992b). *The professional development of school administrators: Preservice, induction, and inservice applications.* Boston, MA: Allyn & Bacon.

Daresh, J. C., & Playko, M. (1992c). Mentoring for headteachers: A review of major issues. *School Organisation, 12*(2), 145–152.

Daresh, J. C., & Playko, M. (1990a). Mentoring for effective school administration. *Urban Education, 25*(1), 43–54.

Daresh, J. C., & Playko, M. (1990b). Mentor programs: Focus on the beginning principal. *NASSP Bulletin, 74*(527), 73–77.

Daresh, J. C., & Playko, M. (1989a). *Administrative mentoring: A training manual.* Westerville, OH: Ohio LEAD Center.

Daresh, J. C., & Playko, M. (1989b). *The administrative entry-year program in Ohio: A resource guide.* Westerville, OH: Ohio LEAD Center.

Daresh, J. C., & Playko, M. (1988, November). *Mentorship for beginning school administrators: Prelude to professional growth.* Paper presented at the annual meeting of the National Council of States for Inservice Education, New Orleans, Louisiana.

Das, J., Kirby, J., & Jarman, R. (1979). *Simultaneous and successive cognitive processes.* New York: Academic Press.

David, J. L. (1989). Synthesis of research on school-based management. *Educational Leadership, 46*(8), 45–53.

David, J. (1990). Restructuring in progress: Lessons from pioneering districts. In R. Elmore (Ed.), *Restructuring schools* (pp. 209–250). San Francisco, CA: Jossey-Bass.

Davies, B., & Hentschke, G. C. (1994). School autonomy: Myth or reality — developing an Australian taxonomy. *Education Management and Administration, 22*(2), 96–103.

Davis has done the right thing. (1984, June 13). *The Toronto Star,* p. A18.

Deem, R., Brehony, K., & New, S. (1993). Education for all? Three schools go to market. In G. Wallace (Ed.), *Local management, central control: Schools in the market place.* Bournemouth: Hyde Publications/British Educational Research Association.

Department for Education. (1994). *Education (special educational needs) regulations 1994.* Brisbane: Queensland Government Printer.

Department for Education. (1992). *Choice and diversity: A new framework for schools* (Cm 2021). London: Her Majesty's Stationery Office.

Department of Education. (1994). *Performance, planning and review: Operational guidelines.* Brisbane: Queensland Government Printer.

Department of Education (1993). *Professional development framework for principalship.* Brisbane: Queensland Government Printer.

Department of Education and Science. (1990). *Standards in education, 1988–89.* London: Her Majesty's Inspectorate.

Department of Education and Science. (1988). *Circular 7/88: Education Reform Act: Local management of schools.* London: Author.

Department of Employment, Education and Training. (1993). *Leaders and their learning: A project of national significance on leadership and management training for principals.* Canberra: Australia Government Publishing Service.

Deyhle, D. (1986). Success and failure: A micro-ethnographic comparison of Navajo and Anglo students' perceptions of testing. *Curriculum Inquiry, 16*(4), 365–389.

Deyhle, D. (1983). Between games and failure: A micro-ethnographic study of Navajo and testing. *Curriculum Inquiry, 13*(4), 347–376.

Dimmock, C. (1991). School-based management and school effectiveness: Developing the concept of linkage. In I. McKay & B. J. Caldwell (Eds.), *Researching educational administration: Theory and practice* (pp. 153–166). Melbourne: Australia Council for Educational Administration.

Divoky, D. (1988). The model minority goes to school. *Phi Delta Kappan, 70*(3), 219–222.

Doern, G. B., & Phidd, R. W. (1983). *Canadian public policy.* Toronto: Methuen.

Douglas-Hamilton, Lord J. (1993). Scottish office headteachers' programme. *Management in Education, 7*(3), 3–4.

Egri, C. P., & Stanbury, W. T. (1989). How pay equity legislation came to Ontario. *Canadian Public Administration, 32*(2), 274–303.

Ehrenberg, R., Ehrenberg, R., Rees, D., & Ehrenberg, E. (1989). *School district leave policies, teacher absenteeism, and student achievement* (Working Paper 2874). Cambridge, MA: National Bureau of Economic Research.

Eisler, R. (1987). *The chalice and the blade.* New York: Harper & Row, Perennial Library Edition.

Elbow, P. (1983). Embracing contraries in the teaching process. *College English, 45*(4), 327–339.

Elliott, J. (1991). *Action research for educational change.* Milton Keynes: Open University Press.

Erickson, F. & Mohatt, G. (1982). Cultural organization of participant structures in two classrooms of Indian students. In G. Spindler (Ed.), *Doing the ethnography of schooling.* Toronto: Holt, Rinehart & Winston.

Erickson, F. (1987). Transformation and school success: The politics of culture of educational achievement. *Anthropology and Education Quarterly, 18*(1), 335–356.

Esp, D. (1993). *Competencies for school managers.* London: Kogan Page.

Etzioni, A. (1968). *The active society.* New York: Free Press.

Etzioni, A. (1964). *Modern organizations.* Englewood Cliffs, NJ: Prentice Hall.

Evans, J., & Lunt, I. (1993). Special educational provision under LMS. *British Journal of Special Education, 20*(2), 59–62.

Evetts, J. (1994). The new headteacher: The changing work culture of secondary headship. *School Organization, 14*(1), 37–47.

Farrar, E. (1990). Reflections on the first wave of reform: Reordering America's educational priorities. In S. Jacobson & J. Conway, (Eds.), *Educational leadership in an age of reform* (pp. 3–13). New York: Longman.

Farrugia, C., & Attard, P. (1989). *The Multi-functional administrator — Educational development in the small states of the commonwealth.* London: Commonwealth Secretariat.

Feilders, J. (1981). *Profile: The role of the chief superintendent of schools.* Belmont, CA: Pitman Learning.

Feiman-Nemser, S., & Parker, M. B. (1993, November). Mentoring in context: A comparison of two U.S. programs for beginning teachers. *International Journal of Educational Research, 17,* 699–718.

Feldman, A., & Atkin, J. M. (1995). Embedding action research in professional practice. In S. Noffke & R. Stevenson (Eds.) *Educational action research:*

Becoming practically critical (pp. 127–137). New York: Teachers College Press.

Fenstermacher, G., & Amarel, M. (1983). The interests of the student, the state, and humanity in education. In L. Shulman & G. Sykes (Eds.), *The handbook of teaching and policy* (pp. 392–407). New York: Longman.

Ferguson, K. E. (1984). *The feminist case against bureaucracy*. Philadelphia, PA: Temple University Press.

Ferguson, M. (1980). *The aquarian conspiracy: Personal and social transformation in the 1980's*. Los Angeles, CA: J. P. Tarcher.

Ferri, J. (1986, February 20). Metro board, teachers to fight funding. *The Toronto Star*, p. A4.

Finn, C. E. (1986, Summer). Decentralise, deregulate, empower. *Policy Review, 37*, 58–61.

Firestone, W. (1990). The commitments of teachers: Implications for policy, administration, and research. In S. B. Bacharach (Ed.), *Advances in research and theories of school management and educational policy*. Greenwich, CT: JAI Press.

Firestone, W. (1994). Redesigning teacher salary systems for educational reform. *American Educational Research Journal 31*(3), 549–574.

Fischer, F. (1980). *Politics, values, and public policy: The problem of methodology*. Boulder, CO: Westview Press.

Foster, W. (1989). Toward a critical practice of leadership. In J. Smyth (Ed.), *Critical perspectives on educational leadership*. London: Falmer Press.

Foucault, M. (1977). *Discipline and punish: The birth of the prison*. New York: Vintage Books.

Foucault, M. (1973). *Madness and civilization*. New York: Random House.

French, O. (1984, June 13). A switch from basic beliefs *The Globe and Mail* (Toronto), p. 7.

Fullan, M. (1991). *The new meaning of educational change*. London: Cassell Educational.

Fullan, M. (1982). *The meaning of educational change*. New York: Teachers College Press.

Fullan, M., & Hargreaves, A. (1991). *What's worth fighting for? Working together for your school*. Toronto: Ontario Public School Teachers' Federation.

Gardner, J. W. (1965). *Self renewal: The individual and the innovative society*. New York: Harper & Row, Harper Colophon Edition.

Gay, J., & Cole, M. (1967). *The new mathematics and an old culture: A study of learning among the Kpelle of Libena*. New York: Holt, Rinehart & Winston.

Geiger, A. H. (1992, February). Measures for mentors. *Training and Development*, 65–67.

Getzels, J. (1982). The problem of the problem. In R. Hogarth (Ed.), *New directions for methodology of social and behavioral sciences: Question framing and response consistency* (pp. 37–49). San Francisco, CA: Jossey-Bass.

Gibble, J. L., & Lawrence, J. C. (1987). Peer coaching for principals. *Educational Leadership, 45*(3), 72–73.

Gibson, M. (1987). The school performance of immigrant minorities: A comparative view. *Anthropology and Education Quarterly, 18*(1), 262–275.

Gibson, M. (1976). Approaches to multicultural education in the United States: Some concepts and assumptions. *Anthropology and Education Quarterly, 7*(4), 7–18.

Giddens, A. (1984): *The constitution of society*. Berkeley: University of California Press.

Gitlin, A., & Price, K. (1992). Teacher empowerment and the development of voice. In C. D. Glickman (Ed.), *Supervision in transition: 1992 yearbook of the association for supervision and curriculum development* (pp. 61–74). Alexandria, VA: Association for Supervision and Curriculum Development.

Glaser, B., & Strauss, A. (1971). *Status passages*. Chicago, IL: Aldine-Atherton.

Glatter, R. (1993a). Looking back and forwards. Module 2, Unit 6, Part 2 of Open University course E326 *Managing Schools: Challenge and Response*. Milton Keynes: The Open University.

Glatter, R. (1993b, September). *Partnership in the market model: Is it dying?* Paper presented to the Annual Conference of the British Educational Management and Administration Society, Edinburgh, Scotland.

Glatter, R. (1991). Developing educational leaders: An international perspective. In P. Ribbins, R. Glatter, T. Simkins, & L. Watson (Eds.), *Developing educational leaders: International Intervisitation Programme 1990* (pp. 222–232). Harlow: Longman/British Educational Management and Administration Society.

Glatter, R. (1972). *Management development for the education profession*. London: Harrap/University of London Institute of Education.

Glatter, R., Johnson, D., & Woods, R. (1993). Marketing, choice and responses in education. In M Smith & H. Busher (Eds.), *Managing schools in an uncertain environment: Resources, marketing and power*. (Sheffield Papers in Education Management No. 94.) Sheffield: Sheffield Hallam University.

Glatter, R., & Woods, P. (1993). *Competitive arenas in education: Studying the impact of enhanced competition and choice on parents and schools*. Paper presented at the conference "Quasi-markets in public sector service delivery: the emerging findings." Bristol: University of Bristol, School for Advanced Urban Studies.

Goffman, E. (1961a). *Asylums: Essays on the social situation of mental patients and other inmates*. Garden City, NY: Doubleday.

Goffman, E. (1961b). *Encounters*. Indianapolis: Bobbs-Merrill.

Goffman, E. (1959). *The presentation of self in everyday life*. Garden City, NY: Doubleday Anchor Books.

Goldman, S., & McDermott, R. (1987). The culture of competition in American schools. In G. Spindler (Ed.), *Education and cultural process: Anthropological approaches* (2d Ed.). Prospect Heights, IL: Waveland Press.

Goldring, E. B. (1992). System-wide diversity in Israel: Principals as transformational and environmental leaders. *Journal of Educational Administration, 30*(3), 49–62.

Goodlad, J. (1983). *A place called school: Prospects for the future*. New York: McGraw-Hill.

Graham-Brown, S. (1991). *Education in the developing world — conflict and crisis*. London: Longman.

Green, J. & Chandler, S. (1990). Toward a dialog about implementation in a conceptual cycle of inquiry. In E. Guba (Ed.), *The paradigm dialog* (pp. 202–215). Newbury Park, CA: Sage.

Greenfield, T. B. (1993). The man who comes back through the door in the wall: Discovering truth, discovering self, discovering organizations. In T. B. Greenfield, & P. Robbins (Eds.), *Greenfield on educational administration*, *towards a human science*. New York: Routlege.

Greenfield, T. B., & Ribbins, P. (Eds.). (1993). *Greenfield on educational administration, towards a human science*. New York: Routledge.

Gregware, P., & Kelly, R. M. (1990). Relativity and quantum logic: A relational view of policy inquiry. In S. S. Nagel (Ed.), *Policy theory and policy evaluation* (pp. 29–42). New York: Greenwood Press.

Grier, T. B. (1988). 15 ways to keep staff members happy and productive. *Executive Educator, 10*, 26–27.

Griffiths, D., Goldman, S., & Mcfarland, W. (1965). Teacher mobility in New York City. *Educational Administration Quarterly, 1*(1): 15–31.

Griffiths, W. (1993). Facing the future — supporting change at Kent County Council. In G. Armstrong (Ed.), *View from the bridge* (pp 36–54). London: Institute of Personnel Management.

Grimmett, P. P., Rostad, O. P., & Ford, B. (1992). The transformation of supervision. In C. D. Glickman (Ed.), *Supervision in transition: 1992 yearbook of the association for supervision and curriculum development*. Alexandria, VA: Association for Supervision and Curriculum Development.

Groundwater-Smith, S. (1993, February). *Introducing dilemmas into the practicum curriculum*. Paper presented to the 5th National Practicum Conference, Macquari University, Sydney, Australia.

Grygier, T. (1977). The bottom of a titled mosaic: The Italian community in urban Canada. In R. Carlton, L. Colley, & N. MacKinnon (Eds.), *Education, change and society: A sociology of Canadian education*. Toronto: Gage.

Gue, L. (1975). Patterns in native education. *CSSE Yearbook, 1*, 7–20.

Guthrie, J., Cibulka, J., & Cooper, B. (1989, September). *Possible paradoxes of international educational reform: Increased regulation and choice*. Symposium prospectus for the Annual Conference of the British Educational Management and Administration Society, Leicester, UK.

Hall, G. (1992). Hank: A 1990s principal. In F. W. Parkay & G. E. Hall (Eds.), *Becoming a principal* (pp. 224–262). Needham Heights, MA: Allyn and Bacon.

Hall, G., & Mani, M. (1992). Entry strategies: Where do I begin? In F. W. Parkay & G. E. Hall (Eds.), *Becoming a principal* (pp. 48–69). Needham Heights, MA: Allyn and Bacon.

Hall, P., Land, H., Parker, R., & Webb, A. (1975). *Change, choice and conflict in social policy*. London: Heinemann.

Hallinger, P., & Bridges, E. M. (1994, Summer). Problem-based learning in educational administration: Defining its major features for application, *Studies in Educational Administration, 59*, 15–23.

Hallinger, P., & McCary, C. E. (1990). Developing the strategic thinking of instructional leaders. *The Elementary School Journal, 91*(2), 89–107.

Hamilton, S. F., & Hamilton, M. A. (1992). Mentoring programs: Promise and paradox. *Phi Delta Kappan, 73*(7), 546–550.

Handal, G. (1989). Lærerne og "den andre profesjonaliteten". i:Jordell, K. & Aamodt, P. O. (Eds.), *Læreren — fra kall til lønnskamp*. Oslo, Norway: Tano.

Handscombe, J. (1989). Mainstreaming: Who needs it? In J. Esling (Ed.), *Multicultural education and policy: ESL in the 1990s*. Toronto: OISE Press.

Handy, C. (1994). *The empty raincoat: Making sense of the future*. London: Hutchinson.

Hannaway, J., & Crowson, R. (1989). *The politics of reforming school administration.* London: Falmer Press.

Hargreaves, A. (1994). *Changing teacher, changing times.* London: Falmer Press.

Hargreaves, A. (1991, April). *Restructuring restructuring: Postmodernity and the prospect for educational change.* Paper presented at the Annual Meeting of the American Educational Research Association, Chicago, Illinois.

Hargreaves, D., & Hopkins, D. (1991). *The empowered school.* London: Cassell Educational.

Hart, A. (1993). A design studio for reflective practice. In P. Hallinger, K. Leithwood, & J. Murphy (Eds.), *Cognitive perspectives in educational leadership* (pp. 213–230). New York: Teachers College Press.

Hatch, E. (1983). *Culture and morality: The relativity of values in anthropology.* New York: Columbia University Press.

Healy, C. C., & Welchert, A. J. (1990). Mentoring relations: A definition to advance research and practice. *Educational Leadership, 19*(9), 17–21.

Heclo, H. (1978). Issue networks and the executive establishment. In A. King (Ed.), *The new American political system* (pp. 87–124). Washington, DC: American Enterprise Institute for Public Policy Research.

Herman, J. J. (1991). Introduction. In P. George & E. C. Potter (Eds.), *School-based management: Theory and practice* (pp. 6–9). Reston, VA: National Association of Secondary School Principals.

Hickcox, E. S., & Li, M. J. (1992). *Education and religious war in Ontario: An updating.* Paper presented at the Annual Meeting of the Canadian Society for Studies in Education. Charlottetown, PEI.

Hill, L. A. (1992). *Becoming a manager.* New York: Penguin.

Hirschorn, L. (1988). *The workplace within.* Cambridge, MA.: MIT Press.

Hiss, T. (1993, April 12). The end of the rainbow. *New Yorker,* pp. 43–54.

HM Government (1991). *The citizen's charter: Raising the standard.* London: Her Majesty's Stationery Office.

Hodgkinson, C. (1978). *Towards a philosophy of administration.* Oxford: Basil Blackwell.

Holderness, S. T. (1992). *Application of the Kingdon model to state educational policy-making.* Paper presented at the Annual Meeting of the American Educational Research Association, San Francisco, California.

Holmes, G. (1993). *Essential school leadership: Developing vision and purpose in management.* London: Kogan Page.

Holmes Group (1990). *Tomorrow's schools: Principles for the design of professional development schools.* East Lansing, MI: Author.

Holmes Group. (1986). *Tomorrow's teachers: A report of the Holmes Group.* East Lansing, MI: Author.

Holmes, M. (1991). *Alasdair MacIntyre and school administration: After the collapse of the common school.* Paper presented at the annual conference of the Canadian Society for the Study of Education, Kingston, Ontario, Canada.

Holmes, M. (1988). *The principal's leadership and school effectiveness: Implications of the New Jersey demonstration schools project.* Paper presented at the annual conference of the American Educational Research Association, New Orleans, Louisiana.

Holmes, M. (1987). *Collective bargaining: Its relationship to traditional and non-tradi-*

tional school models. Paper prepared for the Ministry of the Attorney General, British Columbia, Canada.

Holmes, M. (1986). Traditionalism and educational administration. *Journal of Educational Administration and Foundations, 1*(2) 40–51.

Holmes, M. (1984). The victory and the failure of educational modernism. *Issues in Education, 2*(1) 23–35.

Hoyle, E. (1986). *The politics of school management*. London: Hodder and Stoughton.

Hoyle, E. (1975). Leadership and decision-making in education. In M. Hughes (Ed.), *Administering education: International challenge*. London: Athlone Press.

Hrebiniak, L., & Joyce, W. (1985). Organizational adaptation: Strategic choice and environmental determinism. *Administrative Science Quarterly, 30*, 33–49.

Huberman, M. (1989). The professional life cycle of teachers. *Teachers College Record, 91*(1), 31–57.

Huberman, M. (1983). Recipes for busy kitchens: A situational analysis of routine knowledge use in schools. *Knowledge: Creation, Diffusion, Utilization, 4*(4), 478–510.

Huberman, M., & Miles, M. (1984). *Innovation up close*. New York: Plenum.

Hughes, M. (1985). Leadership in professionally staffed organizations. In Hughes, M., Ribbins, P., & Thomas, H. (Eds.), *Managing education: The system and the institution*. London: Holt, Rinehart & Winston.

Hughes, R. (1986). *The fatal shore*. New York: Knopf.

Ignatieff, M. (1984). *The needs of strangers*. London: Chatto & Windus.

Ignatieff, M. (1978). *A just measure of pain: The penitentiary in the industrial revolution 1750–1850*. London: Penguin Books.

Imich, A. J. (1994). Exclusions from school: current trends and issues. *Educational Research, 36*(1), 3–11.

Inkson, K., & Coe, T. (1993). *Are career ladders disappearing?* London: Institute of Management.

Interim Advisory Committee. (1991). *Fourth report of the Interim Advisory Committee on school teachers' pay and conditions*. London: Her Majesty's Stationery Office.

Irvine, J. J. (1985). The master teacher as mentor: Role perceptions of beginning and master teachers. *Education, 106*(2), 123–130.

Jackson, M. W. (1993). How can ethics be taught? In R. A. Chapman (Ed.), *Ethics in Public Service* (pp. 31–42). Ottawa: Carleton University Press.

Jacobson, S. (1993). The effects of monetary incentives on the labor market behaviors of teachers in the U.S. *East/West Education, 14*, 91–112.

Jacobson, S. (1991a). Attendance incentives and teacher absenteeism. *Planning & Changing, 21*(2), 78–93.

Jacobson, S. (1991b). Performance related pay for teachers: The American experience. In H. Tomlinson (Ed.), *Performance related pay in education* (pp. 34–54). London: Routledge.

Jacobson, S. (1990). Change in entry-level salary and the recruitment of novice teachers. *Journal of Education Finance, 15*(3), 408–413.

Jacobson, S. (1989a). The effects of pay incentives on teacher absenteeism. *Journal of Human Resources, 24*(2), 280–286.

Jacobson, S. (1989b). Pay incentives and teacher absence: One district's experience. *Urban Education, 23*(4), 377–391.

Jacobson, S. (1989c). Change in entry-level salary and its effect on teacher recruitment. *Journal of Education Finance, 14*(4), 449–465.

Jacobson, S. (1989d). Merit pay incentives in teaching. In L. Weis, P. Altbach, G. Kelly, H. Petrie, & S. Slaughter (Eds.), *Crisis in teaching* (pp. 111–127). Albany: State University of New York Press.

Jacobson, S. (1988a). The distribution of salary increments and its effect on teacher retention. *Educational Administration Quarterly, 24*(2), 178–199.

Jacobson, S. (1988b). Alternative practices of internal salary distribution and their effects on teacher recruitment and retention. *Journal of Education Finance, 14*(2), 274–284.

Jacobson, S. (1988c). Merit pay and teaching as a career. In K. Alexander & D. Monk (Eds.), *Attracting and compensating America's teachers* (pp. 161–177). Cambridge, MA: Ballinger Press.

Jacobson, S., & Berne, R. (1993). *Reforming education: The emerging systemic approach.* Newbury Park, CA: Corwin.

Jacobson, S., & Conway, J. (1990). *Educational leadership in an age of reform.* New York: Longman.

Jacobson, S., & Kennedy, S. (1991). Deferred salary leaves for teachers. *The Canadian Administrator, 31*(3), 1–11.

Jacobson, S., & Kennedy, S. (1992). Deferred salary leaves in education: A Canadian alternative to reductions in the teaching workforce. *Educational Evaluation and Policy Analysis, 14*(1), 83–87.

Jenkins, D. (1978). An adversary's account of SAFARI's ethics of case-study. In C. Richards (Ed.), *Power and the curriculum: Issues in curriculum studies.* Nafferton Books. Studies in Education.

Johnson, M. (1993). *Moral imagination: Implications of cognitive science for ethics.* Chicago, IL: University of Chicago Press.

Johnson, S. M. (1984). Merit pay for teachers: A poor prescription for reform. *Harvard Educational Review, 54*(2), 175–185.

Jonathan, R. (1990). State education service or prisoner's dilemma: The "hidden hand" as a source of education policy. *British Journal of Educational Studies, 38*(2), 116–132.

Jonathan, R. (1989). Choice and control in education: Parental rights, individual liberties and social justice. *British Journal of Educational Studies, 37*(4), 321–338.

Josephson Institute. (1989, September–October). The false necessity trap. *Ethics in Action.*

Josephson, M., & the Josephson Institute for the Advancement of Ethics. (1991, January). *Ethics: Easier said than done.* Issue 11.

Josephson, M., & the Josephson Institute for the Advancement of Ethics. (1990, February). *Ethics: Easier said than done.* Issues 7 and 8.

Kalleberg, R. (1990, April). *A constructive turn in sociology.* (Working paper). Oslow: University of Oslo, Institute for Social Research.

Kanter, R. M. (1977). *Men and women of the corporation.* New York: Basic Books.

Karlsen, G. (1993). *Desentralisering — løsning eller oppløsning?* Oslo: Ad Notam Gyldendal.

Katz, L., & Raths, J. (1992). Six dilemmas in teacher education. *Journal of Teacher Education, 43*(5), 376–385.

Kellogg, J. B. (1988). Forces of change. *Phi Delta Kappan, 70*(3) 199–204.

Kelsey, J. (1993). Learning from teaching. In P. Hallinger, K. Leithwood, & J. Murphy (Eds.), *Cognitive perspectives in educational leadership* (pp. 231–252). New York: Teachers College Press.

Kemmis, S., & Mctaggart, R. (Eds.). (1988). *The action research planner* (3rd ed.). Geelong: Deakin University Press.

Kennedy, M. (1984). How evidence alters understanding and decisions. *Educational Evaluation and Policy Analysis, 6*(3), 207–226.

Kiggundu, M., Jorgensen, J., & Hatsi, T. (1983). Administrative theory and practice in developing countries: A synthesis. *Administrative Science Quarterly, 28,* 66–84.

Kingdon, J. (1984). *Agendas, alternatives, and public policies.* Boston, MA: Little, Brown.

Kirst, M. W., Meister, G., & Rowley, S. R. (1984). *Policy issue networks: Their influence on state policymaking* (No. 84–87). Washington, DC: National Institute of Education.

Kitchener-Waterloo Record. (1985, July 24). p. 1.

Kluckhohn, C. (1962). Values and value-orientations in the theory of action: An exploration in definition and classification. In T. Parsons & E. Shils (Eds.), *Toward a general theory of action* (pp. 398–433). Cambridge, MA. : Harvard University Press.

Knippen, J., & Green, T. (1991). Developing a mentoring relationship. *Management Decision, 29*(2), 40–43.

Kotler, P., & Fox, K. (1985). *Strategic marketing for educational institutions.* Englewood Cliffs, NJ: Prentice-Hall.

Kotter, J. (1990). *A force for change: How leadership differs from management.* New York: Free Press.

Kouzes, J. M., & Posner, B. Z. (1993). *Credibility: How leaders gain and lose it, why people demand it.* San Francisco, CA: Jossey-Bass.

Kram, K. E. (1988). *Mentoring at work.* Boston, MA: University Press of America.

Kram, K. E. (1985). Mentoring alternatives: The role of peer relationships in career development. *Academy of Management Journal, 28*(1), 110–132.

Kram, K. E., & Hall, D. T. (1991). Mentoring as an antidote to stress during corporate trauma. *Human Resource Management, 28*(4), 493–510.

Lam, Y. L. J. (1995). Coping with environmental constraints: A comparison of strategies adopted by superintendents and principals. In P. Bredeson & J. Scribner (Eds.), *1995 National Council of Professors of Educational Administration (NCPEA) yearbook.* Lancaster, PA. : Technomic Publishing Co.

Lam, Y. L. J. (1994). Coping with external environmental constraints: Some managerial strategies of chief education officers. *Journal of Educational Administration and Foundation, 9*(2), 22–35.

Lam, Y. L. J. (1993). A typology of negotiated order. *National Forum of Educational Administration and Supervision Journal, 10*(3), 16–27.

Lam, Y. L. J. (1991a). Reaction to "Canada's schools: Report card for the 1990s". *Canadian School Executive, 3,* 27–29.

Lam, Y. L. J. (1991b). A role-specific analysis of the impact of external environment on school systems. In S. C. Holmberg & K. Samuelson (Eds.), *Proceedings of the 35th annual meeting of the international society for systems science.* Ostersund, Sweden: Universal Press.

Lam, Y. L. J. (1984). The changing roles of North American teachers in the eighties. *Education and Society, 2,* 91–96.

Lather, P. (1986). Research as praxis. *Harvard Education Review, 56*(3), 257–277.

Lawton, S. B., & Leithwood, K. L. (1991). Language, religion, and educational rights in Ontario, 1980–1990. *Journal of Education Policy, 6*(2), 201–213.

Le Grand, J. (1991). *Equity and choice: An essay in applied social policy.* London: Harper Collins.

Leithwood, K. A. (1990). The principal's role in teacher development. In D. Joyce (Ed.), *Changing school culture through staff development.* Alexandria, VA: Association for Supervision and Curriculum Development.

Leithwood, K., & Jantzi, D. (1990, June). *Transformational leadership: How principals can help reform school cultures.* Paper presented at the Annual Meeting of the Canadian Association for Curriculum Studies, Victoria, British Columbia.

Leithwood, K., & Steinbach, R. (1993a). The consequences for school improvement of differences in principal's problem-solving processes. In C. Dimmock (Ed.), *School-based management and school effectiveness.* London: Routledge.

Leithwood, K., & Steinbach, R. (1993b). *Total quality leadership: Expert thinking plus transformational practice.* Paper presented at the annual conference of the Canadian Society for the Study of Education, Ottawa, Ontario.

Lemberger, D. (1992, April). *The mantle of a mentor: The mentor's perspective.* Paper presented at the annual meeting of the American Educational Research Association, San Francisco, California.

Levacic, R., & Woods, P. (1994). New forms of financial co-operation. In S. Ranson & H. Tomlinson (Eds.), *Autonomy and interdependence in the new governance of schools.* Harlow: Longman.

Levin, B. (1993). School response to a changing environment, *Journal of Educational Administration, 31*(2), 4–21.

Levine, S. L. (1989). *Promoting adult growth in schools. The promise of professional development.* Boston, MA: Allyn & Bacon.

Levinson, D. J. C. N., Darrow, C. N., Klein, E. B., & McKee, B. (1978). *The seasons of a man's life.* New York: Ballantine.

Limerick, B. (1991). *Career opportunities for teachers in the Department of Education, Queensland.* Brisbane: Queensland Government Printer.

Limerick, B., & Heywood, E. (1993). Training for women in management: The Australian context. *Women in Management Review, 8*(3).

Limerick, D., & Cunnington, B. (1993). *Managing the new organization.* Sydney: Business and Professional Publishing.

Lincoln, J., Hanada, P., & Olson, O. (1985). Cultural orientation and individual reactions: A study of Japanese-owned firms. *Administrative Science Quarterly, 26*(2), 81–120.

Lindblom, C., & Cohen, D. (1979). *Usable knowledge.* New Haven: Yale University Press.

Lipsky, D., & Bacharach, S. (1983). The single salary schedule vs. merit pay: An examination of the debate. *NEA Research Memo.* Washington, D. C. : National Education Association.

Little, J. W. (1988). Assessing the prospects for teacher leadership. In A. Lieberman (Ed.), *Building a professional culture in schools* (pp. 78–106). New York: Teacher College Press.

Ljunggren, C. (1991). *Skolledning och mikropolitisk handling*. Uppsala: Pedagogiska Institutionen, Uppsala universitet.

Local Authorities Conditions of Service Advisory Board. (1989). *Performance related pay: An update*. London: Author.

Lortie, D. (1987). Built in tendencies toward stabilizing the principal's role. *Journal of Research and Development in Education*, 22(1), 80–90.

Lortie, D. (1975). *Schoolteacher: A sociological study*. Chicago, IL: University of Chicago Press.

Louis, K., & Miles, M. (1990). *Improving the urban high school*. New York: Teachers College Press.

Lovin, R. (1988). The school and the articulation of values. *American Journal of Education*, 96(2), 143–159.

Lundgren, U. (1986). *Att organisera skolan*. Stockholm: Liber Utbildningsförlaget.

Lyons J. E. (1993). Perceptions of beginning public school principals. *Journal of School Leadership*, 3, 186–202.

Lyons, N. (1990). Dilemmas of knowing: Ethical and epistemological dimensions of teachers' work and development. *Harvard Educational Review*, 60(2), 159–180.

MacIntyre, A. (1984). *After Virtue*. Notre Dame, IN: Notre Dame University Press.

MacIntyre, A. (1981). *After virtue: A study in moral theory*. London: Gerald Duckworth.

Maclagan, P., & Snell, R. (1992). Some implications for management development of research into managers' moral dilemmas. *British Journal of Management*, 3(3), 157–168.

Macmillan, R. B. (1993). *Principal rotation policies: What price experience?* Paper presented at the annual meeting of the American Association of Educational Research, Atlanta, Georgia.

Macmillan, R. B. (1992). *Principal transfer policies: A "fatal remedy" for change*. Paper presented at the annual meeting of the Canadian Association for the Study of Education, Charlottetown, PEI.

Majone, G. (1989). *Evidence, argument and persuasion in the policy process*. New Haven: Yale University Press.

Malen, B., Ogawa, R., & Kranz, J. (1990). What do we know about school-based management? A case study of the literature — a call for research. In W. H. Clune & J. F. Witte (Eds.), *Choice and control in American education* (vol. 2, pp. 289–342). New York: Falmer Press.

March, J. G., & Olsen, J. P. (1989). *Rediscovering institutions: The organization basis of politics*. New York: Free Press.

Margetson, D. (1994). Current educational reform and the significance of problem-based learning. *Studies in Higher Education*, 19(1), 5–19.

Margetson, D. (1991). Why is problem-based learning a challenge? In D. Boud & G. Feletti (Eds.), *The challenge of problem-based learning*. London: Kegan Paul.

Marshall, C. (1991). The chasm between administrator and teacher cultures. In J. Blase (Ed.), *The politics of life in schools: Power, conflict and cooperation* (pp. 139–160). Newbury Park, CA: Sage.

Marshall, C., Mitchell, D., & Wirt, F. (1989). *Culture and education policy in the American states*. New York: Falmer Press.

Marshall, C., & Rossman, G. B. (1989). *Designing qualitative research.* Newbury Park, CA: Sage.

Marshall, D., & Newton, E. (1983). *The professional preparation of school administrators in developing countries: Some issues for decision-making.* (Occasional Paper No. 3). Alberta, Canada: University of Alberta, Department of Educational Foundations, Centre for International Education and Development.

Martin, W. B. W. (1976). *The negotiated order of the school.* Toronto, Ontario: MacMillan of Canada.

Mawhinney, H. B. (1993) *An interpretive framework for understanding the politics of policy change.* Unpublished doctoral dissertation, University of Ottawa.

Mazzoni, T. (1991a). *Legislating state reforms for American schools: An arena model.* Paper presented at the annual meeting of the American Educational Research Association. Chicago, Illinois.

Mazzoni, T. (1991b). Analyzing state school policymaking: An arena model. *Educational Evaluation and Policy Analysis, 13*(2), 115–138.

McCann I. & Radford R. (1993). Mentoring for teachers, the collaborative approach. In B. Caldwell & E. Carter (Eds.), *The return of the mentor.* London: Falmer Press.

McCarty, C. (1993, September). *Devolution, democracy and equity.* Unpublished paper presented at the Conference of Australian Council for Educational Administration, Adelaide, Australia.

McCarthy, C. (1988). Rethinking liberal and radical perspectives on racial inequality in schooling: The case for nonsynchrony. *Harvard Educational Review, 58,* 265–279.

McCullough, R. C. (1987). Professional development. In R. L. Craig (Ed.), *Training and development handbook. A guide to human resources development* (pp. 35–64). New York: McGraw-Hill.

McDonnell, L. (1994). Assessment policy as persuasion and regulation. *American Journal of Education, 102*(4), 394–420.

McDonnell, L. (1991). Ideas and values in implementation analysis: The case of teacher policy. In A. Odden (Ed.), *Education policy implementation* (pp. 241–258). Albany: State University of New York Press.

McHale, J. P. (1987). Professional networking. In R. L. Craig (Ed.), *Training and development handbook. A guide to human resource development* (pp. 849–861). New York: McGraw-Hill.

Merchant, C. (1989). *The death of nature: Women, ecology and the scientific revolution.* San Francisco, CA: Harper & Row.

Mertz, N., Welch, O., & Henderson, J. (1989, March). *Mentoring for administrative advancement: A study of what mentors do and think.* Paper presented at the annual meeting of the American Educational Research Association, San Francisco, California.

Metherell, T. (1989). *Excellence and equity: New South Wales curriculum reform.* A White Paper on curriculum reform in New South Wales. Sydney, Australia: New South Wales Ministry of Education and Youth Affairs.

Meyenn, B., & Parker, J. (1993, September). *Devolution, dezoning, equity and social justice: The unintended consequences.* Unpublished paper presented at the Conference of Australia Council for Educational Administration, Adelaide, Australia.

Miles, M. B., & Huberman, A. M. (1984). *Qualitative data analysis*. Newbury Park, CA: Sage.

Milgram, S. (1974). *Obedience to authority: An experimental view*. New York: Harper & Row.

Mintzberg, H. (1994, January–February). The fall and rise of strategic planning, *Harvard Business Review, 72*, 107–14.

Miskel, C., & Cosgrove, D. (1985). Leadership succession in school settings. *Review of Educational Research, 55*(1), 87–105.

Mitchell, D. E., Ortiv F. I., & Mitchell, T. K. (1987). *Work orientation and job performance*. Albany NY: State University of New York Press.

Mitroff, I. (1983). *Stakeholders of the organizational mind*. San Francisco, CA: Jossey-Bass.

Møller, J. (1994, March). *Dilemmas in action research*. Paper presented at Nordic Society Educational Research meeting, Vasa, Norway.

Monk, D. (1990). *Educational finance: An economic approach*. New York: McGraw-Hill.

Monk, D., & Jacobson, S. (1985a). The distribution of salary increments between veteran and novice teachers: Evidence from New York State. *Journal of Education Finance, 11*(2), 157–175.

Monk, D., & Jacobson, S. (1985b). Reforming teacher compensation. *Education and Urban Society, 17*(2), 223–236.

Morgan, G. (1986). *Images of Organization*. Beverly Hills, CA: Sage.

Mulkeen, T. A., & Tetenbaum, T. J. (1990). Teaching and learning in knowledge organisations: Implications for the preparation of school administrators. *Journal of Educational Administration, 28*(3), 14–22.

Murdoch, R. T., & Paton, R. T. (1993, September). *Devolution and democracy in New Zealand schools: Preparing a new breed of school principals*. Paper presented at the Conference of Australian Council for Educational Administration, Adelaide, Australia.

Murnane, R., & Cohen, D. (1985). *Merit pay and the evaluation problem: Understanding why most merit plans fail and a few survive*. (Project Report No. 85-A14). Stanford, CA: Stanford University, Stanford Education Policy Institute, School of Education.

Murphy, J., & Hallinger, P. (1992). The principalship in an era of transformation. *Journal of Educational Administration, 30*(3), 77–88.

National Center on Educational Statistics. (1994). *Mini-digest of educational statistics 1993*. Washington, DC: U.S. Department of Education.

National Commission on Excellence in Education. (1983). *A nation at risk*. Washington, DC: U.S. Government Printing Office.

National Union of Teachers. (1992a). *Costs of the national curriculum in primary schools*. London: Coopers and Lybrand Deloitte.

National Union of Teachers. (1992b). *Costs of the national curriculum in secondary schools*. London: Coopers and Lybrand Deloitte.

Nelson, J. (1984). Stands in politics. *The Journal of Politics, 46*, 106–131.

New York State Education Department (1994, February). *New York; the state of learning*. Report to the Governor and Legislature on the Educational Status of the State's Schools. Albany, NY: State Education Department.

Newton, C., & Tarrant, T. (1992). *Managing change in schools: A practical handbook.* London: Routledge.

Newton, E. (1985). Critical issues in the preparation of third world educational administrators. *Caribbean Journal of Education, 12*(1&2), 91–102.

Newton, E. H. (1993). The secondary leadership: Perceptions, conceptions performance and reactions of head teachers in Barbados. *Journal of Educational Administration, 31*(2), 22–42.

Noddings, N. (1992). *The challenge to care in schools: An alternative approach to education.* New York: Teachers College Press.

Noddings, N. (1984). *Caring: A feminine approach to ethics and moral education.* Berkeley: University of California Press.

Noe, R. A. (1988). Investigation of determinants of successful assigned mentoring relationships. *Personnel Psychology, 41*(3), 457–479.

Nozick, R. (1993). *The nature of rationality.* Princeton, NJ: Princeton University Press.

Office for Standards in Education. (1993). *Access and achievement in urban education: A report from the Office of Her Majesty's Chief Inspector of Schools: London· Her Majesty's Stationery Office.*

Ogbu, J. (1987). Variable in minority school performance: A problem in search of an explanation. *Anthropology and Education Quarterly, 18*(1), 312–334.

Olneck, M. R. (1990). The recurring dream: Symbolism and ideology in intercultural and multicultural education. *American Journal of Education, 98*(2), 147–174.

Olson, L. (1988). Crossing the schoolhouse border: Immigrant children in California. *Phi Delta Kappan, 70*(3), 211–218.

Ontario Ministry of Education and Training. (1992). *Changing perspectives: A resource guide for antiracist and ethnocultural-equity education.* Toronto: Ontario Ministry of Education and Training.

Ontario Ministry of Education and Training. (1993). *Antiracism and ethnocultural equity in school boards: Guidelines for policy development and implementation.* Toronto: Ontario Ministry of Education and Training.

Orloff, A. S., & Skocpol, T. (1984, December). Why not equal protection? Explaining the politics of public social spending in Britain, 1890–1911, and the United States, 1880s–1920. *American Sociological Review, 49,* 726–750.

Ornstein, N. (1990, November 14). Dimensions: Tenure of superintendents. *Education Week,* 3.

Ortiz, F., & Marshall, C. (1988). Women in educational administration. In N. Boyan (Ed.), *Handbook of research on educational administration* (pp. 123–141). New York: Longman.

Osterman, K., & Kottkamp, R. (1993). *Reflective practice for education: Improving schooling through professional development.* Newbury Park, CA: Corwin Press.

Pal, L. A. (1992). *Public policy analysis: An introduction. Second edition.* Scarborough: Nelson Canada.

Parkay, F. W. (1992). Herb: The anatomy of an embattled principalship. In F. W. Parkay & G. E. Hall (Eds.), *Becoming a principal* (pp. 196–223). Needham Heights, MA: Allyn and Bacon.

Parkay, F. W., & Currie, G. (1992). Support for the Beginning Principal. In F. W. Parkay & G. E. Hall (Eds.), *Becoming a principal* (pp. 70–84). Needham

Heights, MA: Allyn and Bacon.

Pascual R., & Immegart G. (1992). Preparation for Spanish school directors. *International Journal of Education Management, 6*(6), 13–19.

Perry, W. (1970). *Forms of intellectual and ethical development in the college years.* New York: Holt, Rinehart & Winston.

Peter, M. (1994, April 15). A charter for ways not means. *Times Educational Supplement, 3935,* 19.

Peters, R. (1973). *Authority, responsibility and education.* London: George Allen and Unwin.

Peters, R. (1966). *Ethics and education.* London: George Allen and Unwin.

Peterson, P. (1985). *The politics of school reform, 1870–1940.* Chicago, IL: University of Chicago Press.

Petrie, H. (1990). Reflections on the second wave of reform: Restructuring the teaching profession. In S. Jacobson & J. Conway (Eds.), *Educational leadership in an age of reform* (pp. 14–29). New York: Longman.

Phillips, S. U. (1983). *The invisible culture: Communication in the classroom and community on the Warm Springs Reservation.* New York: Teacher's College Press.

Phillips-Jones L. (1982). *Mentors' proteges.* New York: Arbor House.

Plank, D. (1988). Why school reform doesn't change schools: Political and organizational perspectives. In W. L. Boyd & C. T. Kerchner (Eds.), *The politics of excellence and choice in education.* London: Falmer Press.

Playko, M. (1990). What it means to be mentored. *NASSP Bulletin, 74*(526), 29–32.

Porwoll, P. (1979). *Merit pay for teachers.* Arlington, VA: Educational Research Service.

Purkey, S. C. (1991). Commentary — school-based management: More and less than meets the eye. In W. H. Clune & J. F. Witt (Eds.), *Choice and Control in American Education* (vol. 3, pp. 371–380). New York: Falmer Press.

Ramirez, M. (1989). A bicognitive-multicultural model for pluralistic education. *Early Childhood Development and Care, 51,* 129–136.

Ramsey H. A. (1993). North of the border, they do it this way: A national curriculum for headteachers — the Scottish experience. *Management in Education, 7*(2), 11–12.

Reed, M., & Anthony, P. (1992). Professionalizing management and managing professionalization: British management in the 1980s. *Journal of Management Studies, 29*(5), 591–613.

Renihan, P. (1990). The emerging role of the lobbyist in Canadian education. In Y. L. J. Lam (Ed.), *Canadian public education system: Issues and prospects.* Calgary: Detselig Enterprises Ltd.

Restine N. L. (1993). Mentoring: Assisting and developing a new generation of leaders. *People and Education, 1*(1), 42–51.

Reyes, P. (1990). *Teachers and their workplace: Commitment, performance, and productivity.* Newbury Park, CA: Sage.

Ribbins, P. (1993, September). *The new order of things is hell — secondary headship today?* Unpublished paper presented at the Conference of Australian Council for Educational Administration, Adelaide, Australia.

Rich, J. (1984). *Professional ethics in education.* Springfield, IL. : Charles C. Thomas.

Richards, C., Fishbein, D., & Melville, P. (1993). Cooperative performance incentives in education. In S. Jacobson & R. Berne (Eds.), *Reforming education: The emerging systemic approach* (pp. 28–42). Newbury Park, CA: Corwin.

Ritchie N., & Connolly M. (1993). Mentoring in public sector management: Confronting accountability and control. *Management Education and Development*, 24(3) 266–279.

Roberts, J. (1992a). Building the school culture. In F. W. Parkay & G. E. Hall (Eds.), *Becoming a principal* (pp. 85–102). Needham Heights, MA: Allyn and Bacon.

Roberts, J. (1992b). Mary: A self-reliant survivor. In F. W. Parkay & G. E. Hall (Eds.), *Becoming a principal* (pp. 169–182). Needham Heights, MA: Allyn and Bacon.

Roche G. (1979). Much ado about mentors. *Harvard Business Review*, 57(1), 14–28.

Rosenholtz, S. (1989). *Teachers' workplace: The social organization of schools.* White Plains, NY: Longman.

Ross, B. (1991). Towards a framework for problem-based curricula. In D. Boud & G. Feletti (Eds.), *The challenge of problem-based learning.* London: Kegan Paul.

Rost, J. (1991). *Leadership for the twenty-first century.* Westport, CT: Praeger.

Rothman, D. (1980). *Conscience and convenience: The asylum and its alternatives in progressive America.* Toronto: Little, Brown.

Ryan, J. (1992a). Aboriginal learning styles: A critical review. *Language, Culture and Curriculum*, 5(3), 161–183.

Ryan, J. (1992b). Eroding Innu cultural tradition: Individualization and communality. *Journal of Canadian Studies*, 26(4), 94–111

Ryan, J. (1992c). Formal schooling and deculturation: Nursing practice and the erosion of native communication styles. *The Alberta Journal of Educational Research*, 38(2), 91–103.

Ryan, J. (1991). *Finding time: The impact of space and time demands on post-secondary native students.* Paper presented at the annual conference of the Canadian Society for the Study of Education, Kingston, Ontario.

Ryan, W. (1988). Reason, morality, and relativism: The Wilson-Holmes debate. *Ethics in Education*, 8(1), 13–14.

Rycroft, T. (1989). *Performance related pay: A public sector revolution.* London: British Institute of Management.

Ryle, G. (1953). *Dilemmas* (pp. 111–129). New York: Cambridge University Press.

Sabatier, P. A. (1991, June). Toward better theories of the policy process. *Political Science and Politics*, 24, 144–156.

Sabatier, P. A. (1988). An advocacy coalition framework of policy change and the role of policy-oriented learning therein. *Policy Sciences*, 21, 129–168.

Sackney, L. E., & Dibski, D. J. (1994). School-based management: A critical perspective. *Educational Management and Administration*, 29(2), 104–112.

Sarason, S. B. (1972). *The creation of settings and the future societies.* San Francisco, CA: Jossey-Bass.

Sarason, S. (1982) *The culture of the school and the problem of change.* New York: Allyn and Bacon.

Sawataski, M. (1992). School-based management: Fad, fantasy or movement whose time has come? *The Practising Administrator*, 14(1), 4–8.

Schaef, A. W. (1990). *Escape from intimacy.* San Francisco, CA: Harper & Row.

Schaef, A. W., & Fassel, D. (1988). *The addictive organization.* San Francisco, CA: Harper & Row.

Schein, E. H. (1989). *Organizational culture and leadership*. San Francisco, CA: Jossey-Bass.

Schein, E. H. (1978). *Career dynamics: Matching individual and organizational needs*. Reading, PA: Addison-Wesley.

Schön, D. (1987). *Educating the reflective practitioner*. San Francisco, CA: Jossey-Bass.

Schön, D. (1984): Leadership as reflection-in-action. In T. J. Sergiovanni & J. E. Corbally (Eds.), *Leadership and organizational culture: New perspectives on administrative theory and practice*. Champaign-Urbana: University of Illinois Press.

Schön, D. (1983). *The reflective practitioner: How professionals think in action*. New York: Basic Books.

School Teachers Review Body. (1993). *Second report of the school teachers review body on school teachers' pay and conditions*. London: Her Majesty's Stationery Office.

Schutz, A. (1967). *The phenomenology of the social world*. (Trans. G. Walsh & F. Lehnert). Evanston, IL: Northwestern University Press.

Scott, B. (1994). *Renewing schools: The emerging culture*. (Fourth annual report, External Council of Review, Schools Renewal Program). Sydney: External Council of Review, Schools Renewal Program.

Scott, B. (1990). *School-centred education: Building a more responsive state school system*. (Report of the Management Review, New South Wales Educational Portfolio). Milsons Point: The Management Review, New South Wales Educational Portfolio.

Scott, B. (1989). *Schools renewal*. Sydney, Australia: New South Wales Education Portfolio.

Scott, R. W. (1987). *Organizations: Rational, natural and open systems* (2d Ed.). Englewood Cliffs, NJ: Prentice Hall.

Scott. W., & Hart, D. (1979). *Organizational America*. Boston, MA: Houghton Mifflin Company.

Selznick, P. (1957). *Leadership in administration*. Evanston, IL: Row, Peterson.

Sergiovanni, T. J. (1991). *The principalship: A reflective practice perspective*. Boston, MA: Allyn & Bacon.

Shapira, R., & Haymann, S. (1991). Solving educational dilemmas by parental choice: The case of Israel, *International Journal of Educational Research, 15*(3/4), 277–292.

Shapiro, E. F., Haseltine, F. P., & Rowe, M. P. (1978). Moving up: Role models, mentors and the patron system. *Sloan Management Review, 19*(3), 51–58.

Sharpe, F. G. (1994). Devolution — towards a research framework. *Educational Management and Administration, 22*(2), 85–95.

Sharpe, F. G. (1993, September). *Devolution: Where are we now?* Unpublished paper presented at the Conference of Australian Council for Educational Administration, Adelaide, Australia.

Shaw R. (1992). *Teacher training in secondary schools*. London: Kogan Page.

Shedd, J. B., & Bacharach, S. B. (1991). *Tangled hierarchies: Teachers as professionals and the management of schools*. San Francisco, CA: Jossey-Bass.

Short, E. (1991). Introduction: Understanding curriculum inquiry. In E. Short (Ed.), *Forms of curriculum inquiry* (pp. 1–25). Albany, NY: State University of New York Press.

Sikes, P. J., Measor, L., & Woods, P. (1985). *Teacher careers: Crisis and continuities.* London: Falmer Press.

Silver, P. (1986). Case records: A reflective practice approach to administrative development. *Theory into Practice, 25*(3), 161–167.

Simeon, R. (1976). Studying public policy. *Canadian Journal of Political Science, ix*(4), 548–580.

Simkins, T. (1995) The equity consequences of educational reform in England and Wales. *Educational Management and Administration, 23*(4): 221–232.

Simkins, T. (In press). Education reform in England and Wales. In W. J. Fowler, B. Levin, & H. Walberg (Eds.), *Organizational influences on educational productivity.* Greenwich, CT: JAI Press.

Simkins, T. (1994). Efficiency, effectiveness and the local management of schools. *Journal of Education Policy, 9*(1), 15–33.

Simkins, T. (1993, April). *The consequences of school-based management in England and Wales: A review of some evidence from an economic perspective.* Paper presented at the American Educational Research Association Annual Meeting, Atlanta, Georgia.

Simon, H. (1957). *Models of man.* New York: John Wiley Co.

Simons, H. (1987). *Getting to know schools in a democracy: The politics and process of evaluation.* London: Falmer Press.

Sleeter, C. (1989). Multicultural education as a form of resistance. *Journal of Education, 171*(3), 51–71.

Smith, D., & Tomlinson, S. (1989). *The school effect.* London: Policy Studies Institute.

Smith, M. J. (1989, Summer). Changing agendas and policy communities: Agricultural issues in the 1930s and the 1980s. *Public Administration, 67,* 149–165.

Smyth, J. (1993, September). *Devolution and teachers' work; Human resources implications.* Unpublished paper presented at the Conference of Australian Council for Educational Administration, Adelaide, Australia.

Smyth, J. (Ed.), (1989). *Critical perspectives on educational leadership.* London: Falmer Press.

The Spectator, (1984, June, 14).

Stålhammar, B. (1985). *Skolledning i förändring.* Stockholm: Liber.

Statistics Canada (1990). *Canada year book.* Ottawa: Minister of Supply and Services.

Statistics Canada (1993). *Ethnic Origin: 1991 census of Canada.* Ottawa: Industry, Science and Technology Canada.

Statutes of Ontario. (1986). Bill 30: An Act to amend the Education Act. Chapter 21.

Steiner, R. (1967). *The philosophy of freedom.* (Trans, M. Wilson). Spring Valley, NY: Anthroposophical Press.

Stevenson, L. (1987). *Seven theories of human nature.* New York: Oxford University Press.

Stevenson, R. (1993). Critically reflective inquiry and administrator preparation: Problems and possibilities. *Educational Policy, 7*(1), 96–113.

Stewart, J., & Ranson, S. (1988). Management in the public domain, *Public Money and Management, 8*(2), 13–19.

Stirling, M. (1992). How many pupils are being excluded? *British Journal of Special Education, 19*(4), 128–130.

Strauss, A., & Corbin, J. (1990). *Basics of qualitative research: Grounded theory procedures and techniques.* Newbury Park, CA: Sage.

Strike, K. (1979). An epistemology of practical research. *Educational Researcher, 8*(1), 10–16.

Strike, K. (1988). The ethics of resource allocation in education: questions of democracy and justice. In D. Monk & J. Underwood (Eds.), *Microlevel school finance: Issues and implications for policy* (pp. 143–180). Cambridge, MA: Ballinger.

Strike, K., Haller, E., & Soltis, J. (1988). *The ethics of school administration.* New York: Teachers College Press.

Strike, K., & Soltis, J. (1985). *The ethics of teaching.* New York: Teachers College Press.

Sutherland, N. (1976). *Children in English Canadian society: Framing the twentieth century consensus.* Toronto: University of Toronto Press.

Sutton-Smith, B. (1988). In search of the imagination. In K. Egan & D. Nadaner (Eds.), *Imagination and education.* New York: Teachers College Press.

Sydor, S. (1993). *Redoing time: Cultural performance, transformation and the self. A case study of the exceptional peoples' olympiad, Collins Bay penitentiary. 1993.* Unpublished doctoral dissertation. University of Toronto, Toronto, Ontario, Canada.

Tharp, R. (1989). Psychocultural variables and constants: Effects on teaching and learning in schools. *American Psychologist, 44*(2), 349–359.

Thody, A. M. (1993a). Mentoring for school principals. In B. Caldwell & E. Carter (Eds.), *The return of the mentor.* London: Falmer Press.

Thody, A. M. (1993b). School managed development for educative leadership. In R. Bolam & F. van Wieringen (Eds.), *Educational management across Europe.* The Hague: Academic Books Centre.

Thody, A. M. (1993c). *Developing your career in education management.* Harlow: Longmans.

Thody, A. M. (1991). Strategic planning and school management. *School Organisation, 11*(1), 21–36.

Thody, A. M. (1989). University management observed. *Studies in Higher Education, 14*(3), 279–296.

Thompson, D., Wood, C., & Honeyman, D. (1994). *Fiscal leadership for schools: Concepts and practices.* New York: Longman.

Thurston, P. W., & Lotto, L. S. (1990). *Advances in educational administration, Part A.* Greenwich, CT: JAI Press.

Toulon, S. (1958). *The uses of argument.* Cambridge: Cambridge University Press.

Townsend, R. G. (1991). Policy administration as rhetoric: One leader and his arguments. In K. Musella & D. Musella (Eds.), *Understanding school system administration: Studies of the contemporary chief executive officer* (pp. 42–77). London: Falmer Press.

Troyna, B. (1993). *Racism and education.* Philadelphia, PA: Open University Press.

Trueba, H. (1988). Culturally based explanations of minority students' academic achievement. *Anthropology and Education Quarterly, 19*(2), 270–287.

Tyack, D., & Hansot, E. (1982). *Managers of virtue.* New York: Basic Books.

Tyler, J., & Holsinger, D. (1975). Locus of control differences between rural American Indian and white children. *Journal of Social Psychology, 95,* 149–155.

Urban, W. (1985). Old wine, new bottles? Merit pay and organized teachers. In H. Johnson, Jr. (Ed.), *Merit, money and teachers' careers* (pp. 25–38). Lanham, MD.: University Press of America.

Van der Westhuizen, P. C. (Ed.). (1990). *Effective educational management.* Pretoria, IL: HAUM.

Van der Westhuizen, P. C., & Janson, C. A. (1990). Integration problems of the newly appointed school principal. *South African Journal of Education, 10*(5/6), 495–498.

Vickers, G. S. (1965). *The art of judgment.* New York: Basic Books.

Wadel, C. (1992). Endring av organisasjonskultur. *Tidvise Skrifter* nr. 7. Høgskolesenteret i Rogaland, Stavanger

Walker A. & Stott, K. (1993). Preparing for leadership in schools: The mentoring contribution. In B. Caldwell & E. Carter (Eds.), *The return of the mentor.* London: Falmer Press.

Wallace, M. (1992). Flexible planning: A key to the management of multiple innovations. In N. Bennett, M. Crawford, & R. Riches (Eds.), *Managing change in education: Individual and organizational perspectives.* London: Paul Chapman Publishing/The Open University.

Wallace, R. (1985). Data-driven educational leadership. In *Improving student achievement* (pp. 1–13). Hartford: Connecticut State Department of Education.

Wasley, P. (1991). *Teachers who lead: The rhetoric of reform and the realities of practice.* New York: Teachers College Press.

Watkins, P. (1991). Devolving educational administration in Victoria: Tensions in the role and selection of principals. *Journal of Educational Administration, 29*(1), 22–38.

Watkins, P. (1989). Leadership, power and symbols in educational administration. In J. Smyth (Ed.), *Critical perspectives in educational leadership* (pp. 9–37). London: Falmer Press.

Watt, J. (1989). Devolution of power: The ideological meaning. *Journal of Educational Administration, 27*(1), 19–28.

Weindling, D. (1992). Marathon running on a sand dune: The changing role of the head teacher in England and Wales. *Journal of Educational Administration, 30*(3), 63–76.

Weindling, D., & Earley, P. (1987). *Secondary headship: The first years.* Windsor: NFER-Nelson.

Weindling, R. (1993). Strategic planning in schools. Module 2, Unit 6, Part 1 of Open University course E326 *Managing schools: Challenge and response.* Milton Keynes: The Open University.

White, O. F., Jr., & McSwain, C. J. (1983). Transformational theory and organizational analysis. In G. Morgan (Ed.), *Beyond method* (pp. 292–305). Beverly Hills, CA: Sage.

White, P. A. (1991). An overview of school-based management: What does the research say? In P. George & E. C. Potter (Eds.), *School-based management: Theory and practice* (pp. 3–7). Reston, VA: National Association of Secondary School Principals.

Wignall, R. (1992). *Creating new schools: Recreating self*. Paper presented at the annual meeting of the American Educational Research Association, San Francisco, California.

Wildy, H. (1991). School-based management and its linkage with school effectiveness. In I. McKay & B. J. Caldwell (Eds.), *Researching educational administration: Theory and practice* (pp. 167–182). Melbourne, Australia: Australian Council for Educational Administration.

Wildy, H., & Dimmock, C. (1993). Instructional leadership in primary and secondary schools in Western Australia. *Journal of Educational Administration, 31*(2), 43–62.

Wilkin, M. (Ed.). (1992). *Mentoring in schools*. London: Kogan Page.

Williams, A. (1993). Teacher perceptions of their needs as mentors in the context of developing schoolbased initial teacher education. *British Educational Research Journal, 19*(4), 407–420.

Williams, T. R., & Millinoff, H. (1990). *Canada's schools: Report card for the 1990s*. Ottawa: Canadian Education Association.

Wilson J., & Elman N. (1990). Organisational benefits of mentoring. *Academy of Management Executive, 4*(4), 88–94.

Wintrip, M. (1993, December 8). In school. *New York Times*, p. B8.

Wirt, F., & Kirst, M. (1982). *School in conflict*. Berkeley, CA: McCutchan.

Wise, A. (1967). *Rich schools, poor schools*. Chicago, IL: University of Chicago Press.

Wise, A. E. (1989). Professional teaching: A new paradigm for the management of education. In T. J. Sergiovanni & J. H. Moore (Eds.), *Schooling for tomorrow: Directing reforms to issues that count* (pp. 301–310). Boston, MA: Allyn & Bacon.

Wohlstetter, P., & Odden, A. (1992). Rethinking school-based management policy and research. *Education Administration Quarterly, 28*(4), 529–549.

Wolcott, H. (1973). *The man in the principal's office*. New York: Holt, Rinehart & Winston.

Woods, D. (1985). Problem-based learning and problem solving. In D. Boud (Ed.), *Problem-based learning in education for the professions*. Sydney: Higher Education Research and Development Society of Australasia.

Woods, P. (in press). School responses to the quasi-market. In M. Halstead (Ed.), *Parental choice in education*. London: Kogan Page.

Woods, P. (1994, April). *Parents and choice in local competitive arenas: First findings from the main phase of the PASCI study*. Paper presented at the American Educational Research Association Annual Meeting, New Orleans, Louisiana.

Woods, P. (1992). Empowerment through choice? Towards an understanding of parental choice and school responsiveness. *Educational Management and Administration, 20*(4), 204–211.

Woods, P., Bagley, C., & Glatter, R. (1994). *Dynamics of competition: The effects of local competitive arenas on schools*. Paper presented at CEDAR International Conference on Changing Education Structures: Policy and Practice, University of Warwick, Coventry, England.

Wright R. (1991). Mentors at work. *Journal of Management Development, 10*(3), 25–32.

Yee, G., & Cuban, L. (1994). *When is enough enough? A historical examination of superintendent turnover and tenure in urban school districts.* Unpublished paper. Stanford University.

Zaleznick, A. (1977). Managers and leaders: Are they different? *Harvard Business Review, 15*(3), 67–84.

Zenter, H. (1971). The impending identity crisis among native people. In D. Davis & K. Herman (Eds.), *Social space: Canadian perspectives.* Toronto: New Press.

Zey, M. (1984). *The mentor connection.* Homewood, IL: Dow Jones-Irwin.

Index

About the Contributors

Elizabeth Campbell is Assistant Professor on the Faculty of Education, University of Toronto. She is cross-appointed to the Department of Educational Administration at the Ontario Institute for Studies in Education. Her teaching and research interests focus on ethics in education, moral dimensions of schools, and educational philosophy and policy.

Robert D. Conners is the Coordinator of Educational Administration at the University of New South Wales. His research interests are in the areas of supervision and personnel development, leadership, organizational theory, and program evaluation.

Frank Crowther is Associate Professor and Director of the School Leadership Institute at the University of Southern Queensland. The Institute specializes in action research into problem-solving approaches to educational leadership. He is a former President of the Australian Council for Educational Administration.

Lee Crystal is Head of Professional Development and Training at the University of Luton. She is a chartered psychologist with research interests in training, training support, and work based learning. She is the author of *The Costs & Benefits of Partnership Nurseries* (1995), *Mentoring Between Higher Education and Academe* (1994), and *Staff Placement Programme — Keeping in Touch* (1994).

Larry Cuban is Professor of Education at Stanford University. His major research interests focus on the history of curriculum and instruction, educational leadership, school reform, and school effectiveness. His books include *The Practice of Leadership in Schools* (1988), *Teachers and Machines: The Uses of Classroom Technology Since 1920* (1986), and *How Teachers Taught, 1890–1980* (1984).

Morkel Erasmus is Head of the Department of Educational Management at the College of Education of South Africa. His department's main task is the in-service training and upgrading of underqualified teachers.

Ron Glatter is Director of the Center for Educational Policy and Management in the School of Education, The Open University. He was the founding Secretary of the British Educational Management and Administration Society and later became its national Chair. His major interests and publications are in the fields of educational management development (administrator preparation), school management and governance, and relationships between educational institutions and their environments.

Edward S. Hickcox is Professor of Educational Administration at the Ontario Institute for Studies in Education. He has written extensively in policy areas, such as school board administrative relationships and performance appraisal in education.

Stephen L. Jacobson is Associate Professor of Education and Coordinator of the Educational Administration Program at the State University of New York at Buffalo. His research focuses on teacher compensation and the school workplace and the reform of administrator preparation and practice. His books include *Educational Leadership in an Age of Reform* (1990) and *Reforming Education: The Emerging Systematic Approach* (1993). In 1994 he received UCEA's Jack Culbertson Award for outstanding contributions by a junior faculty member.

Jack Y. L. Lam, currently a Professor and Chair of Graduate Studies, Faculty of Education, Brandon University, is a prolific writer, authoring more than 120 articles, monographs, and chapters and two books. He received the "Merit Award for Leadership in Education" from *Education* (a journal based in California) and the Brandon University Senate Award for Excellence in Research.

Brigid Limerick is Senior Lecturer in the School of Cultural and Policy Studies, Faculty of Education, Queensland University of Technology. She has worked for some years with co-author Frank Crowther in joint university professional development projects for school principals.

Limerick has developed programs and published widely in the area of gender in education and management. In 1995 she authored the *Yearbook of the Australian Council for Educational Administration* on this theme.

Robert B. MacMillan is Assistant Professor at St. Francis Xavier University. He has interests in organizational change, leadership, and the transition people experience during the change process. Currently, he is exploring the impact of site-based management on teachers' and principals' work and the implications of computer technology for teachers and their classrooms.

Hanne B. Mawhinney is Assistant Professor and Director of the Professional Development Program in the Faculty of Education, University of Ottawa. Her current research examines the conceptual, policy, and practice implications of high school — community agency collaborations in nine Canadian provinces. She received the 1994 Canadian Association for Studies in Educational Administration Dissertation Award and the 1995 AERA Politics of Education Association Outstanding Dissertation Award.

Jorunn Møller is Associate Professor of Policy in the Department of Teacher Education and School Development, Faculty of Education at the University of Oslo. Her professional interests are in the areas of educational administration, teacher professionalism, and school evaluation. She has written articles and books about curriculum development in schools, educational administration within the Norwegian context, and action research.

Earle H. Newton is the Dean of the Faculty of Education, The University of the West Indies. His research interests include education in developing nations, continuing education, and supervision in schools.

James Ryan is Associate Professor in the Department of Educational Administration at the Ontario Institute for Studies in Education. His interests include multiethnic and antiracist education and educational administration in a postmodern world.

Fenton G. Sharpe is Professor of Educational Administration at the University of New South Wales. He is a former Director General of the Department of Education in New South Wales. His research interests are in the areas of educational management, curriculum development and implementation, organizational change, policy making, devolution, and the self managing school.

Tim Simkins is Head of Continuing Professional Development at Sheffield Hallam University. His particular interests are strategic and resource management in developing countries. He has written and taught in these areas for many years and undertaken consultancy in Africa, Asia, the Caribbean, and the Middle East.

Robert B. Stevenson is Associate Professor in the Department of Educational Organization, Administration and Policy at the State University of New York at Buffalo where he teaches graduate courses in action research, staff and professional development, and school reform and change. His research interests include the conceptualization, role, and support of critical action research as a means of professional development and school transformation; the assumptions of educational policy makers about how practitioners acquire and develop their knowledge of practice, and the effect of these assumptions on policy development and enactment.

Susan Sydor teaches Education and Law and Professional Practice at the Preservice Department at Brock University. With a background as an elementary school teacher and experience as a School Board Trustee, Dr. Sydor's broad research interest is in the relationship between the individual and society, with a primary focus on the moral and ethical dimensions of Educational Administration.

Angela Thody is Professor of Education Management at the International Centre for Education Management, University of Humberside and Lincolnshire. She is also President of the Commonwealth Council for Educational Administration and editor of *Management in Education*. She has lectured and conducted research nationally and internationally in mentoring for school principals. Her other research areas are in school governance, the roles of strategic leaders in local education authorities, and in the presentation of qualitative research.

Harry Tomlinson is Principal Lecturer in Education Management at Leeds Metropolitan University and Course Leader for the Masters in Business Administration and Chair of the British Educational Management and Administration Society. His edited books include *Performance Related Pay in Education* (1991), *The Search for Standards* (1993), and *Education and Training 14–19* (1993).

Philip C. Van der Westhuizen is Director of the Graduate School of Education at the Potchefstroom University. He has published extensively and is the writer or editor of ten books.

Rouleen Wignall is Executive Head, Field Services and Research, and Assistant Professor in the Department of Educational Administration at The Ontario Institute for Studies in Education. She is involved in a number of research projects that emphasize the social context of organizational life and the complexities of human experience within organizations. Much of this work addresses issues of marginalized groups, including women and ethnocultural minorities as well as illness, health, and well-being.

ISBN 0-275-95247-9

HARDCOVER BAR CODE